Other A to Z Guides from Scarecrow Press

The A to Z of Buddhism by Charles S. Prebish, 2001
The A to Z of Catholicism by William J. Collinge, 2001

The A to Z of Hinduism

Bruce M. Sullivan

The Scarecrow Press, Inc.
Lanham, Maryland, and London
2001

SCARECROW PRESS, INC.

Published in the United States of America
by Scarecrow Press, Inc.
4720 Boston Way, Lanham, Maryland 20706
www.scarecrowpress.com

4 Pleydell Gardens, Folkestone
Kent CT20 2DN, England

Revised and updated text based on Bruce M. Sullivan's *Historical Dictionary of Hinduism* published by Scarecrow Press, 1997. The earlier hardbound edition contains full bibliographical citations.

British Library Cataloguing-in-Publication Information Available

Library of Congress Cataloging-in-Publication Data

Sullivan, Bruce M., 1951–
The A to Z of Hinduism / Bruce M. Sullivan.
p. cm.
"Revised and updated text based on Bruce M. Sullivan's Historical dictionary of Hinduism published by Scarecrow Press, 1997."—T.p. verso.
ISBN 0-8108-4070-7 (pbk. : alk. paper)
1. Hinduism—Dictionaries. I. Sullivan, Bruce M., 1951– Historical dictionary of Hinduism.
BL1105 .S847 2001
294.5'03—dc21 2001031349

∞ ™ The paper used in this publication meets the minimum requirements of American National Standard for Information Sciences—Permanence of Paper for Printed Library Materials, ANSI/NISO Z39.48-1992. Manufactured in the United States of America.

For my wife Patricia, who has had to draw upon her religious faith for patience while this book was compiled, and for Lauren, our joy.

CONTENTS

PREFACE

Hinduism is a religious tradition of remarkable diversity, and no one person, however learned, could profess to know the whole of it. The timespan in which it has flourished, and the large population India has sustained over those many centuries, not to mention the creativity of India's thinkers, has given Hinduism a wonderful array of ideas and practices. Hinduism's linguistic diversity alone is sufficient to provide anyone attempting a work such as this ample frustration. As a Sanskritist, I am comfortable enough with that language, but its modern vernaculars such as Hindi and Bengali are considerably different, and the Dravidian languages such as Tamil are entirely unrelated to Sanskrit except for borrowed terms; yet all these languages, and others, are represented on the pages of this volume. I have provided a pronunciation guide for Indic languages in an effort to aid those who use this volume.

One of the great delights of preparing this work has been the opportunity, in fact, the necessity, of investigating aspects of Hinduism on which I do not lecture or publish research findings. Another has been the willingness of friends who work in the same field to offer their expertise, aiding me in my effort to be clear in what I write about Hinduism. I want particularly to commend Douglas Renfrew Brooks, Andrew O. Fort, and Glen A. Hayes for the information they so graciously provided on short notice. My wife Patricia did proofreading and reference checking, for which I am grateful. It is also my pleasure to thank Charles S. Prebish, who shared with me some of his hard-won ability in computer technology for the representation of the diacritical marks throughout the text. He also encouraged me to persevere with this project, which at times has seemed overwhelming. Whatever errors may be found in this volume are my own, and readers are encouraged to inform me of them for future correction.

Finally, I have the pleasure of thanking Northern Arizona University for providing me with the computer equipment needed for producing this volume. And I especially thank my family for tolerating the long periods in which they saw only the back of my head as I sat at the computer.

Pronunciation Guide

Most of the foreign-language names and terms in this volume are in Sanskrit or a related Indic language. Scholars have established a system of transliteration for Indic languages that is clear and that the nonspecialist can quickly learn. To use the twenty-six letters of the Latin alphabet to represent the forty-nine letters of Sanskrit, some additional markings called diacritical marks are used so that it is possible to distinguish the letters from each other. The following chart will aid readers in pronunciation of words in Indic languages.

1. *Vowels and diphthongs*

a	is pronounced like	a in mica
ā		a in ah
i		i in pit
ī		i in police
u		u in full
ū		u in rule
e		e in grey
o		o in tote
ai		ai in aisle
au		ow in how

2. *Consonants*

(a) Consonants with dots under them (ṭ, ḍ, ṇ, ṣ) are called retroflex or cerebral consonants. Their sounds are made by placing the tip of the tongue on the roof of the mouth at its highest point as the sound is produced. Those not accustomed to Indic languages often find it difficult to hear the distinctive sounds of these consonants. Semi-vowels ṛ, ḷ, ṝ, and ḹ (the latter two very rare) sound like ri and li; so Ṛṣi is pronounced like Rishi. The Tamil underlined l (ḻ) has a similar retroflex sound.

(b) Aspirated consonants (kh, gh, ch, jh, ṭh, ḍh, th, dh, ph, bh) are sounded by expelling breath as the consonant is produced. Thus, th in artha sounds like art-house.

(c) Nasal consonants are of two types. The ñ sounds like the Spanish ñ, so prajñā sounds like prajnyā. The ṅ and ṃ are close in sound quality, and with a following k or g take on a sound like ng, so Sāṃkhya sounds like Sāngkhya.

(d) Indic languages have three sibilants. The Ś in Śiva sounds like Shiva; the ṣ sound is described above in (a). These two sibilants have a similar sound to those who are unaccustomed to Indic languages. The unmarked s sounds like the s in so. C has the sound of ch, so Cakra is pronounced Chakra. Often works in which these diacritical marks are not used will add the h to words, so they appear as Shiva or Chakra; this volume does not, so when looking for entries in the Dictionary, please bear this in mind.

(e) At the beginning of a word or between vowels, the v sounds like a v in English, but combined with other consonants it takes on a sound halfway between v and w.

(f) Doubled consonants are both pronounced.

(g) Other consonants sound like their English equivalents.

Chronology

2500 to 1700 B.C.E.	Indus Valley Civilization flourished.
1500 to 1200 B.C.E.	Āryans occupied the Indus Valley-Punjab area.
1200 to 1000 B.C.E.	*Ṛg Veda* compiled. Āryans occupied the Yamunā and upper Ganges River valleys.
9th century B.C.E.	*Yajur* and *Sāma Veda*s compiled. Brāhmaṇa texts composed.
8th century B.C.E.	Āraṇyaka texts composed.
	Atharva Veda composed.
	Āryans reached southern India.
7th century B.C.E.	*Bṛhadāraṇyaka* and *Chāndogya Upaniṣad*s composed.
6th century B.C.E.	Life of the Buddha (563–483).
	Composition of other Upaniṣads began.
	Persian invasion of western India; establishment of Indian province in Persian Empire (518).
5th century B.C.E.	Composition of Śrauta Sūtras, Gṛhya Sūtras, and Dharma literature began (about 500).
	Ajātaśatru ruled Māgadha (490–458).
4th century B.C.E.	Pāṇini, linguist (400?).
	Alexander the Great invaded western India, and withdrew (327–325).
	Candragupta Maurya ruled north India (323–297). Composition of *Artha Śāstra*.
3rd century B.C.E.	Aśoka Maurya ruled most of South Asia (272–231).
	Mīmāṃsā Sūtra composed (?).
2nd century B.C.E.	Maurya Dynasty overthrown (180); Śuṅga Dynasty founded.
	Yoga Sūtra composed (?).
	Bhagavad Gītā composed (?).

1st century B.C.E.	Vikrama Era, year 1 (58–57), named after King Vikramāditya.
	Brahma Sūtra composed (?).
1st century C.E.	*Mānava Dharma Śāstra* composed (?).
2nd century C.E.	Composition of the *Rāmāyaṇa* completed.
	Composition of *Nāṭya Śāstra* completed.
	Pāśupata sect founded by Lakulīśa.
3rd century C.E.	Hindu immigration to Southeast Asia, and cultural influence there, intensified.
	Pallava Dynasty established in Tamilnadu (3rd through 9th century).
4th century C.E.	Composition of the *Mahābhārata* is completed. Composition of Purāṇas began, compiling ancient material.
	Gupta Dynasty in north India (320–500).
	Cālukya Dynasty in south India (4th through 6th centuries).
5th century C.E.	Kālidāsa flourished (about 400).
6th century C.E.	Nāyanār poets, 6th to 8th centuries.
	Śrīvidyā Tantra sect began.
7th century C.E.	Āḻvār poets, 7th to 9th centuries.
	Māmallapuram temples and carvings of the Pallava Dynasty.
8th century C.E.	Cave shrines of Ellora carved.
	Muslims occupied Sind (Pakistan).
9th century C.E.	*Bhāgavata Purāṇa* composed. Śaṅkara, Advaita Vedānta philosopher.
	Nammāḻvār, Tamil saint.
	Māṇikavācakar, Tamil saint.
10th century C.E.	Abhinavagupta wrote *Tantrāloka* and other works.
	Construction of Cidambaram temple.
	Khajurāho temples built (10th and 11th centuries).
11th century C.E.	Al-Bīrūnī visited India and wrote a description of it.
	Destruction of Somnāth temple.
12th century C.E.	Angkor Wat built in Cambodia.
	Basava began reforms that led to formation of the Liṅgāyat sect.

	Jagannātha temple completed in Purī.
	Nimbārka founded a Vaiṣṇava sect.
	Rāmānuja, Vaiṣṇava theologian.
	Jayadeva composed *Gītagovinda*.
	Muslim dominance of north India began.
13th century C.E.	Sūrya temple at Konārak constructed.
	Madhva, Vaiṣṇava theologian.
14th century C.E.	Caṇḍīdās, Bengali saint.
	Rāmānanda, north Indian saint.
	Vijayanagara founded (1336).
15th century C.E.	Kabīr, north Indian saint.
	Ravidās, north Indian saint.
16th century C.E.	Caitanya (1486–1533), Bengali saint.
	Gosvāmins, Vaiṣṇava theologians.
	Mīrā Bai (1498–1550), female saint.
	Vallabha founded a Vaiṣṇava sect.
	Mughal Dynasty established (1526).
	Vijayanagara sacked (1565).
	Tulsīdās composed *Rām Carit Mānas*.
17th century C.E.	Śivāji, Marāṭha military leader.
	Mughal Emperor Aurangzeb destroyed many Hindu temples.
	British East India Company began trading in India.
18th century C.E.	Bhāskararāya, scholar of Śrīvidyā Tantra.
	Bengal Asiatic Society founded at Calcutta by Sir William Jones (1784).
19th century C.E.	Brahmo Samāj founded by Rām Mohun Roy (1828).
	Mutiny, or War of Independence (1857).
	British East India Company dissolved; British government began to administer India as a Crown Colony (1858).
	Rādhāswāmī Satsang founded (1861).
	Ārya Samāj founded by Dayānand Sarasvatī (1875).
	Theosophical Society founded (1875).
	Rāmakrishna, Bengali saint (1836–86).
	Vedānta Society founded by Vivekānanda (1895).

20th century C.E.	"Mahātmā" Gāndhī, nationalist (1869–1948). Ramana Maharṣi, Tamil saint (1879–1950). Aurobindo, religious leader (1872–1950). Jawaharlal Nehru, India's first Prime Minister (1889–1964). "Veer" Savarkar, nationalist (1883–1966). Ambedkar, Outcaste political leader and convert to Buddhism (1893–1956). S. Radhakrishnan, philosopher and diplomat (1888–1975). Ānandamāyī Mā, female saint (1896–1982). Muktānanda, leader of Siddha Yoga lineage (1908–82). Rabindranāth Tagore won Nobel Prize for Literature (1913). R.S.S. (Rāṣṭrīya Svayamsevak Saṅgh) founded (1925). Self-Realization Fellowship founded by Yogānanda (1935). India regained its independence (1947). Ānanda Mārg founded in India (1955). ISKCON founded in New York (1966) by Bhaktivedānta Swāmī Prabhupāda. The film *Jai Santoshi Mā* is released (1975). Bhāratīya Janatā Party founded (1980). Poonjaji, religious leader (1910–98). Maharishi Mahesh Yogi, founder of Transcendental Meditation (1911–). Satya Sai Baba, religious leader (1926–).

Introduction

BACKGROUND

Hinduism is certainly one of the world's most complex and interesting religions. In Hinduism, we have a religious tradition with no one founder, no one authoritative figure, and no one deity worshipped by all. It is a religious tradition with a history of some forty-five centuries, the longest history of any of the world's major religions. Multiple streams of tradition have merged to create Hinduism.

Some scholars argue that in Hinduism we have not one religion but a group of religions that are distinct from each other. Heinrich von Stietencron is one of the most outspoken in insisting that the term "Hinduism" and the concept that it is one religion are recent phenomena. In his essay "Religious Configurations in Pre-Muslim India and the Modern Concept of Hinduism" (pp. 51–81 in *Representing Hinduism: The Construction of Religious Traditions and National Identity*, edited by H. von Stietencron and V. Dalmia, with references to his earlier articles) he presents the view that Hinduism is not one religion with several sects, but is actually a plurality of religions:

> At least Vaiṣṇavism, Śaivism, the latest form of Śāktism, and some of the other so-called sects of Hinduism must be classed as separate religions. They each have a different theology, rely on different holy scriptures, follow the teaching of a different line of teachers (*guru-paraṃparā*) and worship a different supreme deity reciting different prayers. (p. 51)

Von Stietencron goes on to say that the idea of Hinduism being one religion is to a considerable extent due to Muslim and British misperceptions of India. As he and others have observed, the term "Hindu" derives from Persian and Muslim usage in reference to the people of India; adding "-ism" to the end of that word does not create a unitary religion where, in fact, there are several.

Brian Smith (in "Exorcising the Transcendent," *History of Religions* 27 [1987]: 32–55) has offered the following as a definition of Hinduism:

> Hinduism is the religion of those humans who create, perpetuate, and transform traditions with legitimizing reference to the authority of the Veda. (p. 40)

As Smith observes, this has long been a criterion used within India for determination of whether one is a Hindu or is not. For example, Buddhists, Jains, and Sikhs can be regarded as not Hindu on this basis because each of these traditions holds different literature sacred and authoritative. Most Hindus would affirm that the Vedic revelation (Śruti) is sacred and authoritative, and is the best single criterion for defining Hinduism, but even such a minimal statement as this would be contested in some quarters. The Liṅgāyat or Vīraśaiva tradition of devotion to Śiva generally rejects the authority of the Vedas and the Brahmin class, yet also has a special reverence for the *Śvetāśvatara Upaniṣad*. Most Tantric traditions, and for that matter, many devotional traditions also, largely ignore the Vedic texts in favor of more recently composed works.

Günter Sontheimer in his essay "Hinduism: The Five Components and Their Interaction," (pp. 197–212 in *Hinduism Reconsidered*, edited by G. Sontheimer and G. Kulke), has argued that family resemblances between the various traditions that Hinduism comprises are sufficiently strong to allow us to consider it a single religion with various manifestations. He points to five components constituting a "religious network (that) cannot be refused the label Hinduism," components typically found in Hindu religious traditions: (1) the work and teaching of the Brahmins; (2) renunciation and ascetic practices; (3) tribal religion; (4) folk religion; and (5) Bhakti devotionalism. His first category, the work and teaching of the Brahmins, corresponds to Smith's criterion of transmission of the Vedic heritage, though stated in less specific language. In Sontheimer's view, "Hinduism" is a useful term and refers to a phenomenon that is appropriately regarded as one religion.

For the purposes of this volume, it will not be necessary to settle the question whether Hinduism is one religion with a number of sectarian groups, or several religions that share some historical commonalities and have influenced each other. It is sufficient to indicate to the reader that the scholarly debate exists, and to give some idea why it might matter. One of the points at issue, of course, is the definition of religion. Whether Hinduism is one religion or several is to some extent dependent on how one defines the term "religion." If a religion must, of necessity, have a single theology, the same object of worship for all devotees, and an agreed-upon canon of scripture, it would seem that Hinduism is not one religion, but several. If, on the other hand, one were to define a religion as constituted of groups that may have varying combinations of certain characteristic features, so that a family resemblance is a sufficient criterion for inclusion, then Hinduism may be regarded as one religion consisting of a set of diverse groups. Given the variety inherent in Hindu religious traditions, yet the undeniable resemblances as well, a polythetic approach like Sontheimer's is probably a necessity.

The definition of "Hinduism" is politically and socially significant in India today. As a democracy, India is governed by majority rule. India's census reports that about 83 percent of its citizens are "Hindu" while eleven per cent are Muslim, the remaining 6 percent including Sikhs, Christians, Jains, Buddhists, and a few others. Some Hindu nationalists insist that all who are not Muslim or Christian are Hindu, taking "Hindu" more in a cultural than a religious sense. Some even go so far as to suggest that those who are not in the Hindu category, as they define it, should not be citizens of India. Others argue that Outcastes are not Hindu as they have no Dharma and have been oppressed by the Hindu Caste system of social organization, excluded from full participation in social life. Some south Indians maintain that Brahmanical culture and the Caste system are north Indian traditions, and that southerners should return to Dravidian cultural and social traditions. Such concerns about the nature of what is essential to Hinduism, what the definition of Hinduism should be, have been very much on the minds of the people of India recently. The destruction of the Babri Masjid mosque in Ayodhyā in 1992, the effort to replace it with a Hindu temple, and the ensuing riots in which hundreds died, are indications of the power inherent in the combination of religion and politics. In early 1996, the Bhāratīya Janatā Party, a Hindu nationalist organization that led the Ayodhyā campaign, won control of the national government for a few weeks on the strength of electoral success in north India. The effort to define Hinduism so as to maximize the number of voters in that category and mobilize them against Muslims is a dangerous strategy. If India is to define itself as a nation composed of Hindus versus non-Hindus, the prospect of violent confrontation increases.

This volume itself constitutes a definition of "Hinduism." The choices to exclude a particular group, text, person, or sacred place do not, of course, eliminate them from Hinduism, only from this volume. Needless to say, others would arrange things differently. I trust that this particular construction of Hinduism will be of help to others in defining this complex phenomenon for themselves.

HISTORY OF HINDUISM

Surely one of the most vexing aspects of the study of Hindu civilization and the development of its religious traditions is the wide divergence of views regarding chronology. Dates based on traditional Indian historical accounts are considerably earlier than those of most Western scholars. The nature of transmission of most ancient Indian texts contributes to the dating problem, in that many texts have been reedited repeatedly, sections added or their wording changed in the process. Thus, virtually every text of substantial length has older and younger portions. Dates used in this volume for texts, persons, and events are to some extent conjectural and subject to revision in light of new evidence. In general, the dates used represent the consensus of Western scholarship. Dividing the history of Hinduism into periods, as I have done below and as is typical of the scholarly treatment of Hinduism, is helpful but entirely artificial. The Vedic period and its distinctive cultural pattern do not end at 700 B.C.E., or even at 200 B.C.E. Instead, a new approach begins to appear that becomes characteristic, but the earlier tradition continues to persist and exercise influence. In fact, Vedic sacrifices have been performed and filmed in the twentieth century. The periods described below, then, are only indicative of the appearance of a new pattern based on the previous pattern(s).

One of the greatest discoveries of twentieth-century archaeology is the unearthing of the Indus Valley Civilization in what is now Pakistan and western India. Some eighty sites have been excavated, revealing a civilization spread over some 500,000 square miles, an area much larger than contemporary civilizations in Egypt or Mesopotamia, with both of which the Indus Valley Civilization was in contact. From about 2500 B.C.E. until about 1700 B.C.E. the Indus Valley was the locus of a culture of remarkable uniformity and sophistication. The writing system used by the people of the Indus Valley is as yet undeciphered, so what is known of their society is based on the interpretation of archaeological finds, but not on translation of written documents from the society itself. The two major cities, known now as Mohenjo-Daro and Harappa, are strikingly similar in plan and materials. Elaborate bathing tanks at a number of sites indicate a ritual use of water for purification, similar to later Hindu practices of immersion in water at temples and Ghāṭs. Numerous female figurines, some with carbon deposits on them as if something was burned before them, suggest a widespread tradition of offerings to a female deity. Stone representations of male and female organs suggest a cult of fertility. Most intriguing of all are the hundreds of small, carved-stone seals with writing and scenes depicted on them. Many of the seals have male animals, both fantastic and recognizable species. Scenes include some suggestive of sacrifice of a male animal to a goddess. Several examples have been found of a seal depicting a male figure seated in a cross-legged posture suggestive of the lotus posture of Yoga; he seems to have a buffalo face and horns and an erect phallus, and is surrounded by wild animals, all features reminiscent of the later Hindu deity Śiva. Aspects of the Indus Valley's culture may have survived the demise of the civilization itself and been taken into popular religious practice, later being incorporated into Brahmanical culture and Hindu religious traditions. More certain is the reason for the decline of the Indus Valley Civilization as an organized and centrally directed society: rising levels of salt in the soil due to irrigation led to decreased crop yields and an inability to sustain urban centers on the scale seen previously. This caused some cities and towns to be abandoned or significantly depopulated around 1700 B.C.E., apparently before the appearance in northwestern India of a group of people calling themselves Āryans.

The Vedic Period (about 1500 to 700 B.C.E.)

Early Indologists, familiar with the *Ṛg Veda*'s descriptions of the smashing of fortified places by Indra, the warrior god of the Āryans, concluded that this must refer to combat between the Āryans and the Indus Valley Civilization, and that this was what destroyed that great urban civilization. A century of archaeology, however, has tended to support the view that by 1500 B.C.E. the cities of the Indus Valley were no longer the populous and thriving urban centers they had been 500 years before. The Āryans, speaking a language that would evolve into Sanskrit a millenium later, were nomadic people of Indo-European heritage whose religion and culture are well known to us from the literary collection known as the Veda. The earliest material to be collected into a text is the *Ṛg Veda*, probably compiled about 1100 B.C.E. from poems composed over some centuries. Within a century or so, two more collections were made for the use of different kinds of priests in rituals of sacrifice, the *Sāma Veda* and *Yajur Veda*, most of their material coming from *Ṛg Veda* verses in rearranged order. Our knowledge of the religion of the ancient Āryans is largely based on the Vedic literature.

The Āryans worshipped many gods by offering sacrifices to them, praising them, and praying to them for benefits, both in this life and in the afterlife. Poems of the Vedic collection were chanted to accompany and make effective the ritual procedures. The rituals, correctly performed, gave the sacrificer access to Brahman, the sacred cosmic power embodied in the ritual and in the Vedic verses. The cow and goat were the primary animals sacrificed, but the horse also was offered in certain rituals. The gods were invited to attend the ritual, to share in the food, to hear themselves praised for protecting cosmic order (Ṛta) and the sacrificer, and were asked in return to aid the sacrificer. The rite was conducted in the open without a consecrated building or any images of the deities invoked. Fire was both the means by which the offerings were consumed by the gods and one of the main divine forces invoked, Agni. The gods of cosmic sovereignty, Varuṇa and Mitra, were regarded as overseeing Ṛta and human morality. Indra, the leader of the gods in battle, is represented as a warrior who drinks the hallucinogenic Soma and fights demonic opponents of the gods as well as human opponents of the Āryans. Many other gods were also worshipped, singly and in groups. The chief deities of later Hinduism, Viṣṇu, Śiva, and the Goddess, are not praised in a large number of poems in the Veda, but what is said about them may reveal a prominence and importance greater than the small number of poems would seem to indicate. Viṣṇu makes space for human life, is benevolent in his concern for humanity, and establishes a celestial paradise to which Āryans want to go after death. Rudra (later called Śiva) is fierce and destructive, and presides over wild places, but also has healing medicines. And several goddesses (Vac, Sarasvatī, Uṣas) receive mention in the Veda as powerful presences in this world.

One of the main features of Vedic and later mythology is the opposition between the Devas and Asuras, often translated as Gods and Demons. An Asura in the *Ṛg Veda* is a being of great power, older than the Devas, and eventually dispossessed of the earth by the Devas, their younger relatives. Varuṇa is a complex figure, often called an Asura; he apparently came over to the Deva side in the conflict. Others of the Asuras were defeated by the Devas, who established order and made human life possible. The conflict for sovereignty between the gods and demons comes to be a central feature of Hindu mythology, from the Vedic literature through the Purāṇas.

As the sacrificial ritual became more elaborate, with specialized priests performing separate functions, a fourth Veda was compiled, the *Atharva Veda*, consisting of some material similar to the *Ṛg Veda*, poems in praise of asceticism, and numerous magical spells. At about the same time, perhaps 900 or 800 B.C.E., texts called Brāhmaṇas and Āraṇyakas were composed, the former commenting on the origin and meaning of the sacrificial rituals, the latter focussing less on the sacrifice as such and more on teachings of existential import, the sacrifice having been interiorized for contemplation. These texts were regarded as similar to the collections of Vedic poems, as Śruti, eternal truths glimpsed by sages and seers who transmitted them to later generations. The speculation and philosophical thought of the Brāhmaṇas and Āraṇyakas reached its culmination in texts of a somewhat different perspective called Upaniṣads.

The Upaniṣads (700 to 200 B.C.E.)

Perhaps in the seventh century B.C.E., a new genre of oral literature began to appear, known as Upaniṣads. The term means "sitting down around" and is indicative of the fact that these were teachings transmitted to pupils gathered at the feet of a master. Most of the teachings are set in the forest at hermitages where sages and students lived, but some are set in royal palaces where assemblies of the learned were held. The teachings presented in the earlier Upaniṣads, generally known as the Vedic Upaniṣads, revolve around questions that had first arisen in the Brāhmaṇa and Āraṇyaka literature in regard to the sacrifice and its presiding deity Prajāpati-Puruṣa, whose sacrifice and dismemberment creates the world cyclically. If sacrificial rituals re-create and maintain the cosmos, and if offerings to ancestors must be made to sustain them in a celestial afterlife, might they not die again? And if a person can only perform a finite number of sacrificial rituals in life, how is it possible to attain an infinite reward of an eternal afterlife? Such concerns led to a search for the essence or metaphysical component of a human being that might survive the death of the physical body. The Upaniṣads record an array of teachings on the nature of human life, death, and rebirth according to one's actions (Karma). Passages indicate that one who is without desire is not reborn, and that one who knows the self (Ātman) to be no different than the sacred cosmic power (Brahman) is not reborn; such a person, being Brahman, returns to Brahman after death. Knowledge of Brahman emerged as more important to the sages of the Upaniṣads than performance of the sacrifice itself, though it is evident that they were also intimately familiar with sacrificial procedures as well and refer to them often in their teachings.

Later Upaniṣads were more explicit regarding the method of attaining knowledge of Brahman, namely, the practice of Yoga. Detailed instructions on the techniques of Yoga and on the lifestyle of the renounced ascetic (Saṃnyāsin) appear in Upaniṣads composed as from perhaps the third century B.C.E. until as recently as the fifteenth or sixteenth century C.E. In fact, there are about 250 texts that bear the name Upaniṣad, the most important and longer ones being the thirteen Vedic Upaniṣads.

The Upaniṣads are regarded as the Vedānta, the end of the

Revelation that constitutes Vedic literature. Each Vedic Upaniṣad is appended to the collection of a particular Vedic school as a commentary on the Saṃhitā and its Brāhmaṇa and Āraṇyaka, some forming portions of those texts. Later Upaniṣads are nominally attached to the *Atharva Veda* tradition.

The influence of the Vedic Upaniṣads on later Hindu tradition is enormous. The Vedānta philosophical school is based on the Upaniṣads, and is the most widespread and successful of the six orthodox philosophical schools. Vedānta thinkers have found in the Upaniṣads the basis for both monistic and theistic religious traditions that have ever since dominated Hinduism.

Vedism, Brahmanism, and Hinduism

The period of the composition of Vedic literature, to about 200 B.C.E., is a period for which scholars are often hesitant to use the term "Hinduism," preferring instead the term "Brahmanism" for the religious ideas and practices based on the Vedic sacrifice and the Upaniṣads. Given the prominence of Brahman both in the Vedic sacrificial rituals and in the philosophical pronouncements of the Upaniṣads, the term "Brahmanism" is suitable as a description. Recently scholars have also begun to use the term "Vedism" to refer to the religious system of the Vedic sacrificial cult. The reason for the use of this terminology is the striking difference between the earlier traditions reflected in the Vedic literature and the later traditions of devotion found in the *Mahābhārata*, *Rāmāyaṇa*, and Purāṇas. While there are many continuities, and while there are conscious efforts to link the devotional traditions with the Vedic and Brahmanical heritage from which they emerge, the differences are sufficiently significant that scholars often prefer to use the term "Brahmanism" for the religious ideas and practices prior to about 200 B.C.E., reserving the term "Hinduism" for the later period. Nonetheless, it is also convenient to have a single term for the whole complex of interrelated traditions, and "Hinduism" serves that purpose. There is not absolute uniformity among scholars in this use of terminology, again relating to the definition of "Hinduism" with which this introduction began.

The "Epics" and Dharma Literature (200 B.C.E. to 400 C.E.)

Around the second century B.C.E., evidence begins to point to the development of cults of devotion to one or more gods. Kṛṣṇa, Rāma, and Śiva are the objects of devotion (Bhakti) in the *Mahābhārata*, *Rāmāyaṇa*, and *Śvetāśvatara Upaniṣad*, respectively. Kṛṣṇa and Rāma are royal heroes who are each represented as an earthly manifestation (Avatāra) of Viṣṇu. The *Mahābhārata*, originating in accounts of the heroism of warriors centuries earlier, by about 400 B.C.E. began to take the form we now know as a complex tale that contains profound religious and philosophical teachings, including the *Bhagavad Gītā*, the whole of it attributed to the inspired sage Vyāsa. Kṛṣṇa reveals himself to be Viṣṇu-Nārāyaṇa in human form, on earth to restore Dharma and supervise the defeat of the demonic Kaurava horde. Rāma is depicted in the *Rāmāyaṇa*, attributed to the inspired Brahmin sage Vālmīki, as having a similar purpose. In the *Śvetāśvatara Upaniṣad*, Śiva is presented as the impersonal Absolute Brahman embodied, the model Yogī and a deity to whom one is to offer devotion to attain liberation from rebirth.

The *Mahābhārata* and *Rāmāyaṇa* are narratives that became very popular, existing both in written and oral forms. Though often described in Western scholarship as "epics" since they recount heroic deeds in poetic fashion, in the Indian tradition they are classified in different literary genres: the *Mahābhārata* is seen as a historical work (Itihāsa) and the *Rāmāyaṇa* as poetry (Kāvya). By presenting examples of compliance with Dharma and teachings imparted directly from God, these works showed themselves to be a new revelation. The *Mahābhārata* even proclaims itself the fifth Veda, indicating a desire by its composers that it be seen as part of the Vedic heritage. But both these works are explicitly directed toward a larger audience than the Veda, the whole of society, not just those of Āryan heritage, and women as well as men. Additionally, both works can be seen as having narratives that feature women as central figures. Indeed, to a considerable extent, each of the narratives is motivated by an injustice perpetrated upon the main female character. The prominence accorded the Goddess, in the form of Draupadī and Sītā in these narratives, has added to their appeal.

As these narratives were gaining popular support, the Brahmanical heritage was being codified in the form of Dharma Sūtra and Dharma Śāstra texts. These works specified appropriate behaviors based on one's caste status and stage of life. Rituals to be performed in the home as rites of passage (Saṃskāras), and purification rituals for various circumstances, receive considerable attention. The householder is exalted as the support for all of society, but the ascetic is recognized and accepted. The Dharma literature articulated an ideal of social organization that was probably at no time ever achieved, but remained as a model.

One of the great contributions of this era was the *Bhagavad Gītā*'s advocacy of the Path of Devotion (Bhakti) as a way of being religious that was open to all. As Kṛṣṇa describes it, devotion encompasses both of the earlier ways of being religious, the Path of Action (ritual) and the Path of Knowledge (of Brahman through Yoga). These ways of being religious were subsumed into devotion as subsets. Devotion became the means by which most Hindus have expressed their religious sensibilities in the past 2,000 years. Through offerings (Pūjā) in the home or temple one can express one's devotion and receive blessings.

This period began with the first imperial unification of India, accomplished under the Maurya dynasty (323–180 B.C.E.). The Mauryans were less supportive of Hindu religious traditions than non-Hindu movements (Buddhism, Jainism, Ājīvikas). The replacement of the Mauryas by the Śuṅga dynasty brought support of Brahmanical and Hindu religious traditions, but a decline in imperial power and repeated invasions from the northwest of non-Hindu peoples (Śaka or Scythian, Pāhlava or Parthian, and Kūṣāna) who established kingdoms in northwest India. The Gupta Empire (320 to 500 C.E.) has been described as an era of "Hindu renaissance" after a period of the dominance of Buddhism, Jainism, and the Ājīvikas. More accurate would probably be to say that we begin to see more evidence of Hindu activity in this period, including the beginning of temple construction. Gupta emperors supported the full range of religious groups in their diverse empire, and in a variety of ways. While they personally may have been devotees of Viṣṇu and, in their office as emperor performed the Aśvamedha (Horse Sacrifice), they also donated to the support of the Buddhist and Jain monks and nuns. It might be more appropriate to regard the Gupta period as one of classical Indian civilization's greatest eras.

The Purāṇas, Devotional Poetry, and Tantra (400 to 1700 C.E.)

From the fourth or fifth century C.E., Purāṇas were composed and put in writing. Much of the material in the early Purāṇa texts had existed for centuries as orally preserved traditions. Perhaps with royal support and encouragement, written texts were produced that recorded historical material, cosmological and mythological narratives, devotional teachings, and accounts of sacred places to which one was encouraged to make pilgrimage. The earlier Purāṇas (among them *Viṣṇu*, *Vāyu*, and *Matsya*) tend to accord both Viṣṇu and Śiva respect and veneration. Later Purāṇas (among them *Śiva*, *Bhāgavata*, and *Skanda*) tend to have a more polemical emphasis and to exalt one deity above others as supreme. The Purāṇa literature is vast and Indologists are only recently beginning to produce critical editions of these texts, manuscripts of which show considerable diversity in readings.

In the sixth century a powerful movement of emotional devotion, first to Śiva, then to Viṣṇu as well, began in south India. The Nāyanār poets expressed the devotion in the form of brilliant and moving poems to Śiva. The Āḻvār poets sang of Viṣṇu as a lover whose absence was painful, or whose presence was bliss. That they expressed their devotion in vernacular languages, while all the works mentioned previously were in the elite language of Sanskrit, only increased the appeal their words had to fellow devotees. Their poems remain in the liturgies of south Indian Hindus to the present day, and their influence has extended throughout all of Hinduism. Soon the *Bhāgavata Purāṇa* (ninth or tenth century) and the *Gītagovinda* (twelfth century) expressed similar sentiments in Sanskrit and became revered by Vaiṣṇavas throughout India. North Indian poets such as the Sants expressed in the vernacular Hindi devotion to God, sometimes conceived as Nirguṇa Brahman, the Absolute without limiting attributes. Movements of devotion to Śiva, Viṣṇu, and the Goddess to the present day draw upon these vernacular language collections of poems and songs as well as the Sanskrit Purāṇas for liturgical and theological purposes. The Liṅgāyat or Vīraśaiva movement of reform that began in the twelfth century in south India had and has great appeal due to its emphasis on equality and its criticism of the caste system's discriminatory restrictions and Brahmin privileges.

Tantric Hindu traditions, with techniques different from devotional traditions, began to appear perhaps as early as the sixth century C.E., and in the areas least penetrated by Brahmanical culture: the far northwest, Bengal and Assam in the northeast, and Andhra in the south. Tantra exalts the position of the Goddess, and, while often linking its practices and ideas with the Vedic and Brahmanical heritage, departs from it in many ways. Left-Hand practices make especially evident the intentional inversion of orthodox views regarding purity and pollution. Tantric ideas and practices have influenced devotional and yogic traditions, and continue to attract dedicated practitioners.

The appearance of Muslim cavalry on raids in the heart of the subcontinent of India in the eleventh and twelfth centuries, and the establishment of Muslim-dominated states in north India beginning in the thirteenth century, changed the social setting for the practice of Hinduism decisively. As Muslim political authority was extended to most of south India by the sixteenth century, and the Mughal Empire controlled most of the subcontinent in the seventeenth century, Hindus found themselves in most locations without Hindu sovereigns. Since it was the function of the king to organize the building or repair of a major monument such as a Hindu temple, and to sponsor production and performance of the arts such as literature, sculpture, and theatre, the ability of Hindus to express themselves through these religious arts was substantially curtailed. As the period of Muslim dominance led to the period of British dominance, much the same situation persisted until independence in 1947.

The Modern Era (1700 to the present)

The Mughal Empire was the dominant political power in 1700, but already it was showing signs of weakness. The Marāṭhas proved that the Mughals were not invincible, and rebellions against the Muslim-led Imperial forces grew more frequent in the eighteenth century. But in addition, the presence of the British in the form of the East India Company became much more powerful. By 1800, the Company had taken control of Bengal and most of India's coastline, and the Mughal emperor was virtually irrelevant.

The British generally tried not to interfere in the religious lives of Hindus. Certain Hindu traditions, however, seemed to the British to require elimination: the Thugs, because they were assassins and a threat to public order, and the practice of widow immolation (Satī), because the tradition was regarded as unnecessarily encouraging, even coercing, suicide. Both were outlawed by British authorities. The British sought to govern Hindus and Muslims separately, according to their own legal traditions. For Hindus, the Company determined that the Dharma literature was the main source of law, and even before 1800 Dharma texts were being translated so as to enable judges to administer the law knowledgeably. Christian missionaries, initially kept out of India by the Company due to concerns that they would upset the smooth operation of commerce, were allowed to proselytize freely from the early nineteenth century onward. Many of the missionaries found much to criticize in Hinduism, including the caste system's social class hierarchy and restrictions, polytheism, and the use of images of God in Hindu worship. The transition from Company administration to colonial administration in 1858 changed little and was barely noticed by most Hindus.

Movements for the reform of Hinduism arose with considerable strength in the nineteenth century. Partly in response to British criticisms, and partly as the result of efforts by Hindus to adapt their religious traditions to modernity, reform movements sought to reestablish authentic Hinduism by eliminating certain features deemed invalid. The Brahmo Samāj, founded in Calcutta in 1828 by Rām Mohun Roy, sought to eliminate polytheism and icon worship, and held that the Upaniṣads represented authentic Hinduism. The Ārya Samāj, founded in 1875 by Dayānand Sarasvatī, regarded the Veda as the definitive Hindu text and advocated elimination of icon worship and polytheism, interpreting the Veda as monotheistic. Vivekānanda, a disciple of Rāmakrishna, founded the Vedānta Society in the West and the Rāmakrishna Mission and Rāmakrishna Order of monks in India in the 1890s as organizations to promote social service and the vision of Hinduism as embodying universal truth.

In the twentieth century, the independence movement led by Mahātmā Gāndhī focussed world attention on India and on Gāndhī's use of religious ideas and ideals in mobilizing popular support. He drew on the *Bhagavad Gītā* for inspiration and the example of acting without attachment to the fruits of action. Many Gurus, following the example of Vivekānanda, have come to the

West to establish a following: Paramahaṃsa Yogānanda, Bhaktivedānta Swāmī Prabhupāda, Rajneesh, and Swāmī Muktānanda, to name a few. Also, especially from the 1960s onward, changes in the immigration laws have allowed more immigrants to enter the United States, and a substantial number of Hindus now live in the United States, perhaps 500,000. Canada, a member of the Commonwealth with India, has also seen a significant increase in immigration from India in recent decades. Hindus have built temples and employed priests to serve the needs of these new communities, with the result that Hinduism has become a significant presence in North America.

DOCTRINES OF HINDUISM

Because Hinduism has developed without a single founder whose pronouncements are authoritative, and without a single, powerful authority figure who was recognized as the arbiter of orthodox belief and practice, Hinduism is remarkably diverse in its doctrines. Many Hindus would acknowledge that Ultimate Reality is Brahman, the impersonal Absolute that is the substratum of all reality and all manifest forms. Many others, however, would affirm with equal certainty that the Absolute is a particular God or Goddess such as Kṛṣṇa or Śiva, a being with form and personality who is also the impersonal Brahman. Whether theistic or monistic, there is a strong tendency to see the manifold forms of the world as originating in one divine being or force.

Hindus almost universally accept the ideas of Saṃsāra (the cycle of rebirth) and that rebirth in Saṃsāra is determined by one's Karma (actions). While Madhva's tradition of Vaiṣṇavism is unique in positing the possibility of eternal separation from God due to evil behavior, other Hindu philosophical and religious traditions would affirm that no rebirth situation is permanent unless and until one attains liberation (Mokṣa) from rebirth altogether. Whether conceived in a context that is monistic (merging into Brahman) or theistic (proximity to or equality with God), Mokṣa terminates rebirth and the suffering inherent in human life, or in other life-forms.

The great majority of Hindus would also affirm that the Vedic revelation (Śruti) is sacred and authoritative. It is certainly true, however, that very little of the content of that Vedic revelation is actually known to Hindus in the modern era. Its archaic language prevents even educated Hindus from gaining a direct understanding of a Vedic text without great effort. In fact, texts authored in the post-Vedic era command much more attention from most Hindus than the Vedic literature itself. Yet it is also true that the availability of translations, commentaries, and explications of the Vedic and later literature makes possible a degree of knowledge that was unthinkable until quite recently.

The caste system of social organization, its rationale and myth of origins given in the *Ṛg Veda*, its details specified in the Dharma literature and other works, is also generally accepted by most Hindus to the present day. While it has been subject to criticism and tends to be deemphasized in devotional worship contexts, the caste system continues to be relevant to most Hindus.

Beyond these few commonalities, relatively few ideas could be said to be affirmed by a majority of Hindus.

HINDU COMMUNITY LIFE

Hinduism at the end of the twentieth century is a religion of some 800 million people (including the Outcaste groups, excluding Sikhs, Buddhists, and Jains). The vast majority of the world's Hindus are in India, but there are also Hindu communities elsewhere, including communities with centuries of history in Nepal and Sri Lanka. Significant communities are to be found elsewhere as well, particularly in Europe and North America. As noted above, the United States is home to perhaps 500,000 Hindus. On the verge of entering the twenty-first century, Hinduism is truly a world religion.

Any comments on Hindu community life must take into account the caste system. Its origins surely can be traced to the Āryans, who became dominant socially in India from about 1400 B.C.E. in the northwest, and a few centuries later for northeast and southern India. They were organized as three groups, the two high-status groups of Brahmins and Kṣatriyas having developed specialized skills that separated them from the Vaiśya herders and artisans, who ranked lower in status. As the Āryans settled in India, the indigenous population, which may also have been stratified into social classes of different status, were classified by the Āryans as Śūdra (Serfs). Some groups were almost entirely excluded from social life due to the inability or unwillingness of the society to absorb them. These Outcastes lived on the margin of Indian society, performing the tasks viewed with greatest disdain, and are only recently being integrated more fully. Caste and the subcaste group (jāti) of one's birth, with their social strictures and customs, have exercised a great deal of influence on Hindu life since ancient times. While movements away from caste can be seen, particularly in cities and in Hindu immigrant communities in the West, caste continues to be a major force within Hindu communities. Many Hindus define themselves in terms of their membership in a particular jāti and caste.

Movements in opposition to the caste system of social organization have also existed, and still do. The Bhakti devotional movements that gained great strength from the sixth century onwards, and have come to dominate religious life in India in recent centuries, have tended to criticize caste hierarchy, and to ignore social restrictions based on caste in worship. This has not meant that caste ceased to exist among devotees of particular devotional movements (though Liṅgāyats approach this), but in the context of devotional worship caste tends to be deemphasized and people of various social ranks worship together. The Constitution of the Republic of India, in force since 1950, prohibits all discrimination based on caste status, but such a law is difficult to enforce.

Hindu community life is still to a very considerable extent village life, the majority of Hindus living in agricultural, rural settings. Temples and shrines play an important role in the religious life of any Hindu community, as communal worship is usually organized around the calendar of the temple. Sectarian groups play a large role as well in establishing the calendar of festivals and determining the modes of expression of religious sentiments.

An important distinction exists between those who are following a Dharma based on caste and stage of life versus those who are pursuing Mokṣa by renouncing Dharma. The Saṃnyāsin or ascetic renouncer is a figure of tremendous importance in Hinduism. Many founders of new religious movements have been renouncers, as are religious leaders to the present day. As religious professionals, they are regarded as authorities and are revered, whether members of a specific order such as the Daśanāmi or solitary figures whose specific beliefs and practices are unknown. The Guru is another vitally important figure, around whom movements crystalize. Whether a Brahmin or not, whether a renounced ascetic or not, because of charisma and special knowledge acquired through religious practices or divine grace, the Guru receives devotion and can become the focus of a religious community.

Are Hindus one religious community or many? The question with which this introduction began returns at its end. It is tempting, and somehow appropriate to Hinduism, that we affirm both possibilities.

The Dictionary

— A —

⌘ ABHINAVAGUPTA ⌘

Brahmin scholar and Tantric adept who lived in Kashmir (tenth-eleventh century C.E.). Descended from an eighth-century Brahmin named Atrigupta who had moved to Kashmir from the Ganges River valley, his mother Vimalā died when he was a child and that event was instrumental in his spiritual awakening. He composed an extensive commentary on Bharata's *Nāṭya Śāstra* entitled *Abhinavabhāratī*, and another on Ānandavardhana's *Dhvanyāloka*. In these works he elaborates on the ideas that the aesthetic experience is a distinct mode of consciousness, and that representation onstage of a drama may evoke in a spectator a foretaste of the bliss that one experiences in eternal union with the Absolute, but only temporarily. He also wrote a number of commentaries on philosophical works in which he demonstrated that rival schools such as the Vedānta, Buddhism, and Śaiva Siddhānta are defective but could help prepare one for the ultimate teaching, the monistic tradition he espoused. The best-known of his original works is *Tantrāloka* in which he presents systematically the teachings of the Kaula branch of Kashmir Śaivism, a Tantric tradition. In the *Tantrāloka* (4.77), Abhinavagupta writes as follows: "For knowledge to be fulfilled it must emanate from texts, from investigation with a wise Guru, and directly from oneself." Encyclopedic in his knowledge, taught by several Tantric masters, Abhinavagupta embodied the combination of the orthodox Brahmanical tradition and Tantric spiritual disciplines that at times seem to conflict with orthodox ideals. (*See also* Kashmir Śaivism; Kaula Tantrism; *Nāṭya Śāstra*; Śaivism; Tantra.)

⌘ ĀCĀRYA ⌘

Spiritual preceptor or teacher. The term is often used interchangeably with Guru. (*See also* Guru.)

⌘ ACTION ⌘

See Karma.

⌘ ADHARMA ⌘

The opposite of Dharma: lawlessness, evil, lack of virtue. In the *Bhagavad Gītā* (4.7), Kṛṣṇa states that he takes human form in age after age to support Dharma and to destroy Adharma. (*See also* Dharma.)

⌘ ADHVARYU ⌘

Priest who mutters the *Yajur Veda* during sacrificial rituals and is responsible for butchering and cooking the animal(s) sacrificed. (*See also* Trayī Vidyā; Yajña; *Yajur Veda*.)

⌘ ADITI ⌘

Infinity. Daughter of Dakṣa Prajāpati, married Kaśyapa and gave birth to thirty-three sons, including the twelve Ādityas: Indra, Dhātṛ, Aryaman, Mitra, Varuṇa, Aṃśa, Bhaga, Vivasvat, Pūṣan, Savitṛ, Tvaṣṭṛ, and Viṣṇu. These are the major Vedic deities. Among her other sons are the eight Vasus and eleven Rudras. (*See also* Āditya; Aṃśa; Aryaman; Bhaga; Dhātṛ; Indra; Mitra; Pūṣan; Savitṛ; Tvaṣṭṛ; Varuṇa; Viṣṇu; Vivasvat.)

⌘ ĀDITYA ⌘

Name applied to any of the six to twelve prominent sons of Aditi by Kaśyapa, the main Devas of the Veda. They are celebrated as a group in *Ṛg Veda* 8.18. (*See also* Aditi; Aṃśa; Aryaman; Bhaga; Dhātṛ; Indra; Mitra; Pūṣan; Savitṛ; Tvaṣṭṛ; Varuṇa; Viṣṇu; Vivasvat.)

⌘ ADVAITA VEDĀNTA ⌘

The nondualistic Vedānta tradition. Espoused by the brilliant Śaṅkara through his commentaries on the major Upaniṣads, the

Brahma Sūtra, and the *Bhagavad Gītā*, this monistic tradition views these texts as in harmony with one another. The Advaita position is that the sole reality is Brahman, the impersonal Absolute, about which one cannot posit any qualities (Guṇa); Brahman can thus be described as Nirguṇa, "without qualities" which would limit it. The assumption of limiting qualities such as name and form is due to ignorance and to the operation of illusion (Māyā). For Advaita, the world and individual selves have only an illusory existence; they are not real in an ultimate sense as they are not permanent, and are only temporary manifestations due to ignorant misperception. Even the gods are regarded as temporary manifestations due to ignorance. With the attainment of knowledge of reality, that is, knowledge of Brahman and/or the self, knowledge that Brahman and the self are one, illusion ceases to have power to bind one and one is free of Saṃsāra, the cycle of rebirth and suffering. After death, one who has experienced Brahman is not reborn and instead experiences union with Brahman eternally, described as unlimited being, consciousness, and bliss. Advaita Vedānta has been a very influential tradition of thought and practice, and continues to be today through numerous sects and traditions within Hinduism such as the Smārta Brahmins of south India, and publications of the Advaita Āśrama. (*See also* Brahman; Dvaita Vedānta; Māyā; Nirguṇa Brahman; Philosophical Schools; Śaṅkara; Smārta Brahmins; Vedānta.)

⌘ ĀGAMA ⌘

A type of post-Vedic scripture, composed in Sanskrit and mainly concerned with matters of ritual performance. Most Āgamas present themselves as revealed by one of the main deities, Viṣṇu, Śiva, or the Goddess. Many Vaiṣṇava Āgamas refer to themselves as Saṃhitās, and many in Goddess traditions refer to themselves as Tantras.

⌘ AGNI ⌘

Fire, the Vedic god. Eight of the ten books of the *Ṛg Veda* begin with poems to Agni (the exceptions are Book 8, a miscellaneous collection, and Book 9, dedicated to Soma). Agni was particularly revered by priests as the intermediary between gods and human beings. As in *Ṛg Veda* 1.1, the priests saw Agni as priest-like in his intermediary function, conveying human offerings to the gods. While the other Vedic gods function in one of the three realms (earth, atmosphere, heaven), Agni appears in each (fire, lightning, sun). Hence, the Vedic sacrifice (Yajña) employs three altars symbolically representing earth, atmosphere, and heaven (Gārhapatya, Dakṣiṇa, and Āhavanīya, respectively). Agni is associated frequently with Soma in the *Ṛg Veda*, these two being the principal deities who function on earth. The central role of Agni in the Vedic sacrifice accounts for the prominent place accorded this deity in the Veda, where he is invoked almost as often as Indra. (*See also* Āhavanīya; Dakṣiṇa; Gārhapatya; Yajña.)

⌘ AGNIṢṬOMA ⌘

"Praise of Agni." It is a five-day ritual sacrifice (Yajña) in which offerings of Soma are made to Indra and other gods by a Brahmin householder. It is an adaptation of the Jyotiṣṭoma whereby one would seek heaven as a reward. Sixteen priests would be needed to perform the rite. (*See also* Agni; Soma; Yajña.)

⌘ ĀHAVANĪYA ⌘

One of three fire altars used in the Vedic sacrifice (Yajña). Square in shape, it represents space or heaven with its four directions and is located to the east within the sacrificial compound. (*See also* Yajña.)

⌘ AHIṂSĀ ⌘

Noninjury; nonviolence. Advocated especially in ascetic traditions initially, Ahiṃsā became in time an ideal for most Hindu religious traditions. For example, it is included by Patañjali as one of the restraints the practitioner of Yoga accepts as his lifestyle. Taken to its logical conclusion, vegetarianism is a requirement for one who aspires to live in accord with Ahiṃsā, as is the abandonment of the Vedic animal sacrifice. Mahātmā Gāndhī made it the cornerstone of his program for mobilizing the Indian people to attain independence from Britain. By emphasizing Ahiṃsā as an ethical ideal, Gāndhī was able to appeal to Indians to adopt a moral way of protesting political conditions, one that Britain and other Western nations could admire and respect. (*See also* Cow, Sacred; Gāndhī, Mohandās K.; Satyāgraha.)

⌘ AIHOLE ⌘

Site in northern Karnataka of early Hindu temples. The village of Aihole, forty-three kilometers from Bādāmī, in the fourth through sixth century C.E. was the regional capital of the Cālukya dynasty, which built some seventy structures in the area. They are especially interesting for their stylistic diversity, and show architectural experimentation of considerable scope. Particularly remarkable is the Durgigudi temple, circular in form and with a primitive Gopuram gateway. (*See also* Bādāmī; Cālukya; Paṭṭadakal; Temple.)

⌘ AL-BĪRŪNĪ ⌘

See Bīrūnī, al-.

⌘ ĀḺVĀRS ⌘

"Those who are deeply immersed in God." Twelve saints of south India from all levels of society in the seventh to ninth centuries whose devotional poems to Viṣṇu are still remembered and sung. The collection of their poems is known in Tamil as *Nālāyirap Pirapantam* (*Nālāyira Prabandham* in Sanskrit), and contains some 4,000 poems. Most are attributed to Nammāḻvār and Tirumankai. The lone female Āḻvār, Āṇṭāl, composed some 107 of the poems. Particularly within the Śrīvaiṣṇava community of Tamilnadu, practitioners of devotion (Bhakti) to Viṣṇu, these saints are revered and their poems recited in temples and the homes of devotees. (*See also* Āṇṭāl; Bhakti; Nammāḻvār; Śrīvaiṣṇavism; *Tiruvāymoḻi*; Vaiṣṇavism; Viṣṇu.)

⌘ AMBEDKAR, BHĪMRAO ⌘

An Indian politician (1893–1956) and leader of the Untouchables or Outcastes. Ambedkar was born in a village near Ratnagiri, in Mahārāṣṭra, south of Bombay, the son of an Indian Army school headmaster. With financial support from the Mahārāja of Baroda, he became the first Untouchable to be awarded a B.A. at Elphinstone College in Bombay in 1912; he also earned a Ph.D. at Columbia University in New York, and studied at the London School of Economics, becoming an attorney in England. In the first government of independent India, he was appointed Law

Minister, and was primarily responsible for authorship of the Indian Constitution, which went into effect in 1950. Ambedkar had hoped that provisions of the Consitution making illegal any discrimination based on caste would eliminate the institution of caste quickly. He resigned his post in 1951, in despair at the lack of change effected by the new Constitution, and announced his conversion to Buddhism in a public ceremony at which thousands of his fellow Outcastes also converted. Conversion to Buddhism altered the caste status of the Outcastes, taking them out of the caste system altogether. In India, they are known as Nava Bauddhas (Neo-Buddhists), though many Hindus still refer to them as Dalits (Outcastes). Dr. Ambedkar's leadership gave Outcastes hope, greater recognition both within India and internationally, and an option to passive acceptance of discrimination based on caste status. (*See also* Caste; Outcaste.)

⌘ AMṚTA ⌘

The Elixir of Immortality. The myth of the gods (Devas) and demons (Asuras) churning the Ocean of Milk to produce Amṛta is told often in Indian literature, one extensive version being in the *Mahābhārata* (1.15–17). There the account includes the appearance of the Sun, Moon, the divine horse Uccaiḥśravas, the jewel Kaustubha, and finally Amṛta from the churning effort. The gods and demons fought over possession of the elixir, which the gods gained but the demons stole, only to have Viṣṇu assume the form of a beguiling woman (Mohinī) and recover it for the gods. The gods drank Amṛta and became immortal, and were victorious over the demons. Legend has it that drops of Amṛta fell on earth at four sites (Hardwār, Nāsik, Ujjain, and Prayāga), where a Kumbha Melā festival is held on a rotating basis every three years. The Vedic literature uses the term Amṛta to refer to Soma, and the theme of Soma being the object of contentions between the gods and demonas occurs often. In various systems of Yoga, Amṛta refers to an energy or fluid within the body that one can activate and move to improve health and attain immortality. (*See also* Asura; Deva; Hardwār; Kumbha Melā; Mohinī; Soma; Yoga.)

⌘ AṂŚA ⌘

The name of one of the twelve Ādityas. The word means "portion" and is also used as a term equivalent to Avatāra, the descent to earth of a portion of God in human form as a divine incarnation. (*See also* Āditya; Avatāra).

⌘ ĀNANDA ⌘

"Bliss." In various systems of Yoga it is a term for a heightened state of consciousness, often synonymous with Mokṣa or Mukti (liberation from rebirth). (*See also* Mokṣa; Yoga.)

⌘ ĀNANDA MĀRG ⌘

A new religious movement (The Way of Bliss) founded in 1955 by Ānandamūrti, with its headquarters at Ānand Nagar in West Bengal, India. Ānanda Mārg members have been socially and politically active in India, which has led to some controversy. Indian government authorities imprisoned Ānandamūrti, and some of his followers burned themselves to death in protest. The movement emphasizes a systematic program of meditation and a strict lifestyle, including celibacy for those who are seriously committed to spiritual progress. Marriage is allowed for the purpose of procreation. The movement spread to the West after about 1970.

⌘ ĀNANDAMĀYĪ MĀ ⌘

Religious name of a Bengali holy woman (1896–1982). Born Nirmala Sundarī Devī, she attracted many disciples to centers in Dakka (now in Bangladesh) and Dehradun. She taught a devotional path that culminates in the realization of union with the Absolute, Brahman. She was widely regarded as a saint.

⌘ ANANTA ⌘

Endless. The name of the multiheaded cosmic snake on which Viṣṇu reclines as he dreams worlds into existence. Also known as Śeṣa (Remainder or Remainer), he is left after the universe is absorbed back into Viṣṇu at the end of time. He is a symbolic representation of time. (*See also* Śeṣa; Viṣṇu.)

⌘ ANCESTRAL RITES ⌘

Ritual offerings and recitations in remembrance of one's ancestors is an ancient feature of Hindu traditions. Two different rituals are performed: a funeral ritual (Antyeṣṭi) immediately after death, and commemorative rituals (Śrāddha) that include daily offerings of water and periodic offerings of food. One's deceased ancestors were regarded as worthy of reverence for having continued the family lineage, making one's own life possible. Deceased ancestors required the offering of water and food in the form of balls or cakes of grain (Piṇḍa) to sustain them in the afterlife, without which they would suffer as wandering, hungry ghosts (Preta). Ancestral rites are still performed by many Hindus. (*See also* Death; Funeral; Gayā; Pitṛ; Preta; Śrāddha.)

⌘ ANGKOR WAT ⌘

City Temple, the name of a monumental temple in northern Cambodia (Kampuchea). Built by the Khmer King Sūryavarman II in the twelfth century C.E., it is in the form of a Hindu cosmos, with Mount Meru at the center and representations of Hindu mythological themes such as the churning of the ocean for Amṛta. It is said to be the largest religious building in the world, and is often regarded as the greatest architectural work in all of Southeast Asia. (*See also* Temple.)

⌘ ĀṆṬĀL ⌘

Ninth-century female saint of south India (sometimes spelled Āndāl). She is numbered among the Āḻvārs whose poems of devotion praise Viṣṇu. Her erotic imagery of the bliss of union with God has been popular for a thousand years and her lyrics are still recited and sung. (*See also* Āḻvārs; Bhakti; Vaiṣṇavism; Viṣṇu.)

⌘ *ANUGĪTA* ⌘

The After-Gīta. A section of the *Mahābhārata* (14.16–51) in which, after the war, the revelations of the *Bhagavad Gītā* are recapitulated by Kṛṣṇa for Arjuna. (*See also* Arjuna; *Bhagavad Gītā.*)

⌘ ĀRAṆYAKA ⌘

Of the Forest. A class of Vedic texts composed as commentaries on the Vedic Saṃhitā collections. They are, both in time of composition and in their interests, intermediary between the Brāhmaṇa texts and the Upaniṣads; they seem to have been composed by sages who withdrew into the forest to contemplate the meaning of the Vedic sacrifice. (*See also* Brāhmaṇa; Saṃhitā; Śruti; Upaniṣads; Veda.)

⌘ ARDHANARĪŚVARA ⌘

The Lord who is half female, a representation of Śiva united with the Goddess Śakti, so that the figure's right side is male (Śiva) and the left side female (Śakti). It is a symbolic representation of the union of opposites, the transcending of differences, and of the Absolute as incorporating both male and female qualities. (*See also* Śakti; Śiva.)

⌘ ARJUNA ⌘

The third of the five Pāṇḍava brothers and hero of the *Mahābhārata*, where he is often paired with Kṛṣṇa. The *Mahābhārata* depicts Arjuna as the son of Indra, and an archer so skilled that he is ambidextrous. As the son of Indra, his pairing with Kṛṣṇa is particularly meaningful, in that they continue some of the mythic themes of the *Ṛg Veda*'s pairing of Indra and Viṣṇu. Arjuna wins Draupadī at her Svayaṃvara (Self-Choice) ceremony, and she becomes the wife of all five Pāṇḍavas. He goes on a mission to secure weapons for their use in the future conflict with their cousins, and encounters Śiva in the guise of a hunter, with whom he fights and who grants Arjuna weapons. A warrior with royal and ascetic aspects, his spiritual instruction by Kṛṣṇa constitutes the *Bhagavad Gītā*. (*See also Anugīta; Bhagavad Gītā*; Draupadī; Indra; Kṛṣṇa; *Mahābhārata*; Pāṇḍava.)

⌘ ARTHA ⌘

Profit; prosperity. Artha is one of the Four Goals of Humanity (Puruṣārtha), the pursuits that Hindu civilization has regarded as valid and appropriate for human beings to be engaged in. Artha encompasses one's career and all one does to make a living. For the king, it has a special meaning in that his career is conducted not simply for personal benefit but for the benefit of the entire society he rules. Hence there is a text, the *Artha Śāstra*, that advises rulers on how most effectively to conduct themselves so that they and their realms attain prosperity. As an endeavor, Artha is paired with Kāma (pleasure, or desire) as the two worldly goals that should ideally be subordinate to Dharma (the fulfillment of social and religious obligations). All three of these goals must be abandoned or transcended if one is to pursue Mokṣa, the goal of liberation from rebirth. (*See also Artha Śāstra*; Four Goals of Humanity.)

⌘ ARTHA ŚĀSTRA ⌘

Systematic treatise on prosperity. The Sanskrit text concerns how a king should rule, including all matters of political science and diplomacy, organization of the kingdom and its army, espionage, laws, and the punishments that should be imposed for violations. The text is attributed to Kauṭilya, Brahmin minister of Candragupta Maurya (ruled 323–297 B.C.E.). While he may have been an important contributor to the body of knowledge collected in this work, the text also cites earlier authorities who are otherwise unknown, and probably was also added to by later editors. (*See also* Artha; Dharma.)

⌘ ĀRYA SAMĀJ ⌘

Hindu revivalist movement founded in 1875 by Swāmī Dayānand Sarasvatī. The Ārya Samāj sought to restore Hinduism to what was perceived to be its original purity. It saw in the Vedas the essential teachings of Hinduism, and interpreted the Vedas as presenting a way of being religious that did not involve the use of images or icons in worship, was not polytheistic, and did not emphasize hereditary caste restrictions. The Ārya Samāj enunciated the following principles: that God is one, an eternal and formless presence that cannot be represented in a statue or painting; that the Vedas contain all truth conducive to spiritual progress; and that one should live an ethical life and strive for the welfare of all. God is regarded as transcendent, and liberation from rebirth (Mokṣa) does not constitute union with God, who remains distinct from the human soul, but blissful proximity to God. The Ārya Samāj attitude toward the caste system is complex; while finding Vedic justification for the concept of caste hierarchy in the Veda, notably in the Puruṣa Hymn (*Ṛg Veda* 10.90), the Ārya Samāj rejected the idea that caste status was hereditary, and argued in favor of basing caste status on merit. The Ārya Samāj conducted rites of purification (śuddhi) and reconversion for Hindus who had converted to Islam or Christianity, so as to restore them to the ranks of Hindus, even granting high-caste status to former

Outcastes and Serfs. In 1893 a split occurred between conservative and liberal elements of the movement, conservatives advocating vegetarianism and traditional Hindu educational practices, liberals advocating elimination of dietary restrictions and the establishment of modern educational institutions. The Ārya Samāj became heavily involved in the independence movement in the twentieth century, and certainly instigated much of the violence that accompanied partition of British India into the nations of India and Pakistan in 1947. In independent India, the Ārya Samāj has become a movement of Hindu nationalism and has encouraged the growth of political parties such as the Hindu Mahāsabhā and the Bhāratīya Janatā Party, which have advocated that India become a Hindu state rather than a secular and multireligious state. (*See also* Bhāratīya Janatā Party; Brahmo Samāj; Dayānand Sarasvatī; Hindu Mahāsabhā; Rāj; Rāṣṭrīya Svayamsevak Saṅgh.)

⌘ ARYAMAN ⌘

Name of one of the twelve Ādityas. He is often invoked with another god, especially Mitra, Varuṇa, or Bhaga (as in *Ṛg Veda* 1.90), appropriately for a deity whose name means "companion." No poems of the *Ṛg Veda* are dedicated to Aryaman alone. (*See also* Āditya; Bhaga; Mitra; Varuṇa.)

⌘ ĀRYAN ⌘

Term used in the Veda to refer to those who spoke Sanskrit and were members of the society that composed and preserved the Veda. Most scholars believe that these people were of Indo-European heritage culturally and had slowly immigrated from the northwest into the Indian subcontinent, arriving perhaps about 1500 B.C.E. The word literally means "respected" or "kindly" in the Veda, and came to be used for the upper three social groups in India's Caste system, as distinguished from the non-Āryan groups of Śūdras (Serfs), Outcastes, tribal peoples, etc. (*See also* Caste; Dāsa; Indo-European; Sanskrit; Śūdra.)

⌘ ASCETICISM ⌘

See Brahmacarya; Saṃnyāsa; Tapas; Yoga.

⌘ ĀŚRAMA ⌘

Term for a hermitage, literally, a place for exertion. Here a Guru instructs disciples in spiritual and religious practices. The term is also used to refer to each of the four stages of life in the ideal Hindu social order: student, householder, forest dweller, renouncer. (*See also* Four Stages of Life; Guru.)

⌘ ASURA ⌘

Name of the group of beings who oppose the Vedic gods (Devas). They are comparable to the Titans of Greek mythology, in that they are the older brothers or cousins of the gods whom the gods displace. The victory of the gods over the Asuras is celebrated in the Veda as an event that established order and makes possible human life. Varuṇa is often described in the Veda as an Asura, and seems to have been the chief of the Asuras until he came over to the side of the Devas. Asura is often translated as demon, but the Asuras are not to be confused with Rākṣasas and other classes of beings who disrupt the sacrifices of Brahmins. (*See also* Daitya; Dānava; Deva; Mahiṣa.)

⌘ AŚVAMEDHA ⌘

See Horse Sacrifice.

⌘ AŚVINS ⌘

The Horsemen, name for twin Gods in the Vedic literature, who are also called Nāsatya. The Aśvins are sons of the Āditya Vivasvat (Sun), celestial deities and bringers of light who precede the dawn, preparing the way for her. They also are credited (for example, in *Ṛg Veda* 1.157) with having healing medicines they dispense to humanity. The Aśvins were offered Soma in the Soma sacrifices and poems dedicated to them make frequent mention of such offerings. They are comparable to the Gemini twins of Greek mythology.

⌘ *ATHARVA VEDA* ⌘

A text composed of poems and spells for use both in the Vedic sacrifice and more generally. It was the latest of the four Vedas to be accepted as a Veda, perhaps about 600 B.C.E., as indicated by numerous references in the Upaniṣads to Trayī Vidyā (the "triple knowledge," or three Vedas). Its recitation in the Vedic sacrifice was the special function of the priest known as the Brahmán, who was to sit in the sacrificial compound observing the action and correcting any ritual errors through meditation and silent recitation of the *Atharva Veda*. The *Mahābhārata* credits Vyāsa with dividing what had been one Veda into four texts (*Ṛg*, *Yajur*, *Sāma*, and *Atharva*) and teaching his disciples his edited version; Purāṇas credit each pupil with learning one of the Vedas, Sumantu transmitting the *Atharva Veda*. (*See also* Brahmán; Nambūṭiri Brahmins; Sumantu; Trayī Vidyā; Vyāsa.)

⌘ ĀTMAN ⌘

Self, or soul. The individual self or soul of a person, regarded as eternal and unchanging. This spiritual or metaphysical element of a person is the vehicle for reincarnation, the Ātman leaving the body at death and going to another embryonic body for rebirth. The Upaniṣads generally present the view that the individual Ātman is identical with Brahman, Ultimate Reality or the impersonal and formless Absolute, and that the liberated Ātman merges with Brahman at death. Theistic traditions generally present the view that the Ātman is distinct from God and that liberation from rebirth is not characterized by merging with God but by being in the presence of God. The six philosophical schools regarded as orthodox in Hinduism vary in their articulation of the relationship between Ātman and Brahman. One of the key issues that divides Buddhism from Hinduism is the Buddhist idea that there is no permanent, unchanging entity that takes rebirth; often called the no-self doctrine, it is a Buddhist teaching on the inevitability of change and impermanence, with which Hindus did not agree. (*See also* Brahman; Jīva; Philosophical Schools; Puruṣa; Upaniṣads; Vedānta.)

⌘ AUROBINDO GHOSE ⌘

Also known as Śrī Aurobindo, a famous modern sage (1872–1950). Born to a wealthy and high-caste Hindu family in Calcutta, Bengal, he was educated at Cambridge University in Britain, then was employed by the Mahārāja of Baroda and as a professor in Calcutta. He became a leader of the nationalist movement in India, and was arrested and imprisoned in 1908 by the British for sedition. During his year in prison, Aurobindo experienced a spiritual awakening and renounced the world, settling in the

French colonial holding of Pondicherry, near Madras. He wrote many books describing his philosophy, including *The Life Divine*, *Integral Yoga*, and *The Synthesis of Yoga*. He attracted followers, including Westerners, with whom he formed a community. Aurobindo envisioned the transformation of society through the attainment of "Supermind" or a higher consciousness through the practice of Integral Yoga. A French woman named Mira Richard, known as The Mother to his followers, was regarded by Aurobindo as an embodiment of the divine feminine principle Śakti, and she became the movement's leader after his death. His Āśrama in Pondicherry and the community in nearby Auroville are still functioning. (*See also* Śakti; Yoga.)

⌘ AVATĀRA ⌘

Descent, a term used to describe a god taking human form, or sending a portion of himself to earth to take on a human body. The term is apparently not used until the Purāṇas; related verbal forms appear in the *Mahābhārata*, including the *Bhagavad Gītā*. The Avatāra concept is associated particularly with Viṣṇu. Often, ten incarnations of Viṣṇu are listed, as follows: (1) Matsya (Fish); (2) Kūrma (Turtle); (3) Varāha (Boar); (4) Narasiṃha (Man-Lion); (5) Vāmana (Dwarf); (6) Paraśurāma (Rāma with an Axe); (7) Rāma; (8) Balarāma, elder brother of Kṛṣṇa; (9) Kṛṣṇa; and (10) Kalkin, who is the next incarnation. Some texts and traditions, for example, the *Gītagovinda*, replace the eighth incarnation Balarāma with the Buddha, attributing to the Buddha the purpose of stopping animal sacrifice or leading demonic beings to hell through his teachings. Longer lists of the Avatāras usually include such incarnations as Vyāsa, Garuḍa, and Nārada. As indicated by Kṛṣṇa in the *Bhagavad Gītā* (4.7–9), he comes into being in age after age to support the righteous, to destroy evildoers, and to maintain the Dharma. An Avatāra appears at a time of crisis, with a particular mission to accomplish. Comparable to the Avatāra idea is the Vyūha doctrine of the Pañcarātra sect, in which Vāsudeva (Kṛṣṇa), Saṃkarṣaṇa (Balarāma) and two other manifestations are regarded as complete, not partial, manifestations of Viṣṇu on earth. (*See also* Aṃśa; Balarāma; Buddha; Kalkin; Kṛṣṇa; Kūrma; Matsya; Narasiṃha; Paraśurāma; Rāma; Vaiṣṇavism; Vāmana; Varāha; Viṣṇu; Vyāsa; Vyūha.)

⌘ AYODHYĀ ⌘

Invincible; town in north India near Faizabad in Uttar Pradesh. It is famous as the supposed site of the capital of Rāma, and recently as the site of a dispute between Hindus and Muslims over a piece of land both hold sacred. Some Hindus regard the spot as the birthplace of Rāma, incarnation (Avatāra) of Viṣṇu, on which some four centuries before a Rāma temple was razed to build a mosque for Muslim worship. A mosque known as the Babrī Masjīd (Babur's Mosque) has stood on the site ever since, and been a Muslim place of worship. For decades, Hindus have agitated to replace that mosque with a temple to Rāma, and in 1992 destroyed the mosque. The contested site has been a politically sensitive issue throughout the 1980s and 1990s. In 1990, Hindu nationalists led by the Bhāratīya Janatā Party made a highly publicized journey from Somnāth across north India to Ayodhyā, two of the most well-known sites of Hindu temples destroyed by Muslims, to try to garner support among Hindus for the political campaign of that party. (*See also* Bhāratīya Janatā Party; Rāma; Somnāth.)

⌘ ĀYUR VEDA ⌘

The Knowledge of Life, the indigenous system of medicine in India. Herbs and minerals are used in the treatment of diseases and to maintain health. Some of the medical tradition has been preserved in the *Caraka-Saṃhitā*, though the original composition (if any) has been lost. The Āyur Veda tradition continues in India as a medical system in which specialists known as Vaidikas treat illness.

— B —

⌘ *BACK TO GODHEAD* ⌘

Name of a magazine dedicated to promoting the worship of Kṛṣṇa, the official publication of the Hare Krishna Movement. It was first published in India beginning in 1944 by Abhay Charan De. When he came to America in 1965 as Bhaktivedānta Swāmī Prabhupāda to win converts to Kṛṣṇa and founded the International Society for Krishna Consciousness, he began to publish

Back to Godhead in America. It has been published continuously since 1967. (*See also* Bhaktivedānta Swāmī Prabhupāda; Hare Krishna Movement.)

⌘ BĀDĀMĪ ⌘

Site in northern Karnataka of early Hindu temples. The capital of the Cālukya dynasty during the sixth through eighth centuries C.E., Bādāmī has numerous inscriptions from the Cālukya and other dynasties (for whom it became a fort). Five cave temples have been carved out of the cliffsides, two dedicated to Viṣṇu, one to Śiva, one to the Jains, and one to the Buddhists. The Agastya Tīrtha, a tank cut from the rock, is about 200 by 400 meters, and on its banks stand two temples called the Bhūtanātha (Lord of Beings) temples. (*See also* Aihole; Cālukya; Paṭṭadakal; Temple.)

⌘ BĀDARĀYAṆA ⌘

Name of an author (perhaps about 100 B.C.E.) who composed the *Brahma Sūtra* (also known as the *Vedānta Sūtra*). He is often identified with Vyāsa, who is credited with authorship of the *Mahābhārata* and other works. The *Brahma Sūtra* presents a coherent summary of the teachings of the Upaniṣads, and argues for the importance and benefits of knowledge of Brahman. (*See also* *Brahma Sūtra*; Brahman; Vedānta; Vyāsa.)

⌘ BADRĪNĀTH ⌘

Pilgrimage site in the Himālaya Mountains, in northern Uttar Pradesh, north of Almora. There are many Yoga Āśramas and temples here, including Jyoti Maṭha, one of four monasteries of the Daśanāmi Order founded by Śaṅkara in the ninth century C.E. (*See also* Daśanāmi Order; Śaṅkara.)

⌘ BALARĀMA ⌘

Elder brother of Kṛṣṇa, worshipped by the Pāñcarātra sect as Saṃkarṣaṇa. Later Vaiṣṇava theology makes him an Avatāra of Viṣṇu, or of Śeṣa. He is sometimes replaced in lists of the ten Avatāras by the Buddha. (*See also* Avatāra; Buddha; Pāñcarātra.)

⌘ BANARAS ⌘

See Vārāṇasī.

⌘ BASAVA ⌘

Name of a south Indian saint and religious reformer (twelfth century C.E.). Born in a Brahmin family, he came to regard all people as equal and to reject caste hierarchy. He led a movement that sought to reform Śaivism and became in time the Liṅgāyat or Vīraśaiva sect. (*See also* Liṅgāyat.)

⌘ BĀULS ⌘

A sect of wandering yogīs in Bengal. The name "Bāul" (bāur in Hindi) may be derived either from the Sanskrit word "vyākula" (intent) or "vātula" (mad), both of which can be seen as appropriate due to the God-intoxicated religious fervor and unconventional behavior for which Bāuls are famous. Bāuls are generally Tantric, and can most closely be identified with the Sahajiyā sect. Their songs feature devotional and ascetic themes. (*See also* Caṇḍīdās; Sahajiyā; Tantra; Yoga.)

⌘ BELUR ⌘

Site in southern Karnataka of temples dating to the eleventh and twelfth centuries C.E. Built by the Hoysala dynasty, they are unusual for their star-shaped form and the quality and exuberance of the sculptural decoration. Three temples, one of which is still utilized for daily worship, feature highly decorated pillars. (*See also* Halebid; Temple.)

⌘ BENARES ⌘

See Vārāṇasī.

⌘ BESANT, ANNIE ⌘

Leader of the Theosophical Society (1847–1933). She joined the Theosophical Society in 1889 after reading H. P. Blavatsky's *The Secret Doctrine*, becoming president of the Society in 1907. She established the Central Hindu School in Banaras (Vārāṇasī), which became a university in 1915. Besant was elected Chair of the Indian National Congress in 1917 and was jailed by the British authorities as a threat to the war effort. Besant's effort to prepare Krishnamurti as the next World Teacher under the tutelage of the Society failed, and its influence waned thereafter. Her several books on theosophy borrow much from Hindu philosophical and religious traditions. (*See also* Krishnamurti, Jiddu; Theosophical Society.)

⌘ BHAGA ⌘

One of the twelve Ādityas. He is usually invoked with Aryaman or other Ādityas in the *Ṛg Veda* and praised for his ability to grant prosperity; he also presides over love and marriage. *Ṛg Veda* 7.41 celebrates Bhaga's generosity. (*See also* Āditya.)

⌘ *BHAGAVAD GĪTĀ* ⌘

The Song of the Blessed One. The *Bhagavad Gītā* is the most widely known Hindu religious text. A Sanskrit work of some 700 verses of poetry, it is embedded in the *Mahābhārata* (6.23–40) at a crucial moment in the narrative. In Book Six of the *Mahābhārata*, as the armies of the Pāṇḍavas and Kauravas faced each other at Kurukṣetra, Arjuna had his charioteer Kṛṣṇa drive him out before his army to survey the opposing army, led by his cousins and respected elders. Arjuna raised the question whether he should simply allow himself to be killed rather than kill these family members for the sake of a mere kingdom. Kṛṣṇa's reply was that he should do his duty (Dharma) as a Kṣatriya warrior and fight; to do otherwise would bring disgrace on himself and disorder to society. Arjuna posed another question: if it were his duty as a Kṣatriya to fight and kill, thereby incurring bad Karma, would it not be better to renounce his caste status and its problematic Dharma for the life of an ascetic Saṃnyāsin, thereby performing meritorious rather than demeritorious actions? Kṛṣṇa's response forms the bulk of the *Bhagavad Gītā*. He began by teaching Arjuna to make the distinction between the body and the self (Ātman); the self is immortal, and just as a person takes off worn clothes and replaces them with fresh clothes, the self replaces a worn body with a new one (2.22). Kṛṣṇa went on to say that one cannot avoid action, but that one can act in such a way that one renounces desire for the fruits of one's actions, and thereby avoids accumulating Karma that causes rebirth; in short, that one can act in the world, without renouncing one's Dharma, yet attain liberation from rebirth. Kṛṣṇa praised the Path of Action (Karma-Yoga) in which ritual action and fulfilling one's Dharma are central, and he praised the Path of Knowledge (Jñāna-Yoga), in which attaining the realization of one's identity with Brahman is central, but made both these Paths subordinate to or encompassed by the Path of Devotion (Bhakti-Yoga). The Path of Devotion is a way of being religious that is open to all. Kṛṣṇa revealed his true identity and form to Arjuna, saying that whenever the Dharma languishes and evil flourishes, he creates himself in eon after eon to reestablish Dharma and destroy evil (4.7–9). In the eleventh chapter, Kṛṣṇa revealed his divine form, a dazzling vision that left Arjuna begging him to resume his familiar, human form. The *Bhagavad Gītā* presents itself, then, as a direct revelation from God of the most effective way to be religious. The text has enjoyed wide acceptance since its composition, perhaps about the second century B.C.E. It has a unique status of great authority, but it is not the Vedic revelation (Śruti); unlike the authorless and timeless Śruti, the *Gītā* has an author and is an account of an event that occurred at a specific time. It is most decisively a new revelation, for all its use of Brahmanical and Vedic terminology. Bādarāyaṇa's *Brahma Sūtra* quotes the *Bhagavad Gītā* twice (2.3.45, and 4.1.10), and the Vedānta tradition has enshrined the *Gītā* in an honored place ever since. In teaching the Path of Devotion as the means by which all could express their religious sentiments and attain liberation, the *Bhagavad Gītā* has become the most frequently quoted and most widely known religious text of Hinduism. (*See also* Anugīta; Arjuna; Avatāra; Bhakti; Dharma; Gāndhī, Mohandās K.; Hare Krishna Movement; Kṛṣṇa; *Mahābhārata*; Path of Action; Path of Devotion; Path of Knowledge; Vaiṣṇavism; Viṣṇu.)

⌘ BHAGAVAN (BHAGAVAT) ⌘

Possessing fortune, blessed, divine. The term is used especially as a name of Viṣṇu, Kṛṣṇa, and saints. (*See also Bhagavad Gītā*; *Bhāgavata Purāṇa*; Bhāgavata Sect.)

⌘ *BHĀGAVATA PURĀṆA* ⌘

Known also as the *Śrīmad Bhāgavata*, it is one of the major Purāṇa texts. Composed in Sanskrit, probably in the eighth or ninth century C.E. in south India, it advocates devotional worship of Viṣṇu, particularly in the form of Kṛṣṇa. Its long tenth book is entirely devoted to the life story of Kṛṣṇa, and emphasizes his youth among the cowherders of Vṛndāvana. There Kṛṣṇa is depicted as an endearing and mischievous boy who steals butter, plays tricks on the adults and his fellow cowherds, vanquishes demons, and engages in loveplay with the Gopīs, the milkmaids. The selfless love of the Gopīs for Kṛṣṇa is regarded by Vaiṣṇava theologians as the model for the relationship of the human soul to God. The *Bhāgavata Purāṇa* became a text of central importance to Vaiṣṇava devotional traditions, particularly those of the Bengali lineages inspired by Caitanya and the Vallabha tradition. (*See also* Avatāra; Caitanya; Gopī; Gosvāmins; Kṛṣṇa; Scripture; Smṛti; Vaiṣṇavism; Vallabha; Vṛndāvana.)

⌘ BHĀGAVATA SECT ⌘

One of the earliest devotional traditions in India, becoming part of Vaiṣṇavism. Devotion to Bhagavan (the Blessed One, God), referring to Kṛṣṇa, is advocated in the *Bhagavad Gītā* and the Nārāyaṇīya section of the *Mahābhārata* (12.334–51), apparently the earliest textual sources on this sect. There is also a strong affinity with the Pāñcarātra tradition, though they may not be identical. (*See also* Bhagavan; Kṛṣṇa; Pāñcarātra; Pūjā; Vaiṣṇavism.)

⌘ BHAKTI ⌘

Devotion. The word is derived from the root "bhaj" and means "to participate in." It is first used in the sense of devotion to God in the *Śvetāśvatara Upaniṣad* (4.23), where devotion to one's Guru and to Rudra as God are advocated. Later poets in south India known as the Nāyanārs sang emotional songs of devotion to Śiva. Vaiṣṇava traditions have also emphasized Bhakti, presented in the *Bhagavad Gītā* as a discipline in which one dedicates oneself to a meditative path of remembering God. South Indian poets known as the Āḻvārs sang vernacular songs of love for God that had a profound impact on Vaiṣṇavism. Later texts such as the *Bhāgavata Purāṇa* and *Gītagovinda* present Bhakti as an emotional experience of love for God, and a theology developed around envisioning oneself in one of four possible loving relationships to

God. Bhakti is a major influence also in traditions of worship of the Goddess, where she is revered as the creator and destroyer of the cosmos, and a loving Mother to the world. (*See also* Āḻvārs; *Bhagavad Gītā*; *Bhāgavata Purāṇa*; *Gītagovinda*; Nayanār; Path of Devotion; Śaivism; Sant; Tukārām; Vaiṣṇavism.)

⌘ BHAKTIVEDĀNTA SWĀMĪ PRABHUPĀDA ⌘

Founder (1896–1977) of the International Society for Krishna Consciousness (popularly known as the Hare Krishnas). Born in Bengal as Abhay Charan De, he graduated from the University of Calcutta in 1920 but refused to accept his diploma due to his nationalistic views and adherence to Mahātmā Gāndhī's movement of noncooperation with the British colonial authorities. De married and became the manager of a large chemical company, but religion began to be increasingly important to him. He was a lifelong devotee of the Vaiṣṇava tradition begun by saint and ecstatic Caitanya in the sixteenth century, and was formally initiated in 1933. His Guru instructed him to spread the worship of Kṛṣṇa to the West, a mission he did not undertake for some years. On his retirement in 1954, he began to plan his mission, renouncing his familial and social obligations in 1959 by becoming a Saṃ nyāsin. In 1965 he went to New York City where he opened a small storefront headquarters at 26 Second Avenue on the Lower East Side, at which he lectured and led religious services that included singing and dancing. In 1966, he founded ISKCON, an organization that has published his English translations of many Vaiṣṇava works, and commentaries on them, and which continues to publish *Back to Godhead*, the magazine he founded in India in 1944. Bhaktivedānta's leadership established ISKCON as a prominent new religious movement in the West. He died in India in 1977, and his remains are entombed at a large ISKCON temple in Vṛndāvana, India. (*See also Back to Godhead*; Caitanya; Hare Krishna Movement; Kṛṣṇa; Vaiṣṇavism.)

⌘ BHARADVĀJA ⌘

Brahmin sage descended from Bṛhaspati, and the major seer (Ṛṣi) of Book 6 of the *Ṛg Veda*, where fifty-seven poems are attributed to him and he appears to be the priest of a ruler named Divodāsa. (*See also* Saṃhitā; Veda.)

⌘ BHARATA ⌘

Name of several ancient Āryans, including the reputed author of the *Nāṭya Śāstra*, and of a clan of warriors. The *Mahābhārata* takes its name from the family name of the clan descended from Bharata.

⌘ BHĀRATA ⌘

Of or relating to Bharata. The name Bhārata was used in ancient times as a name for what is now India. The Republic of India has also taken Bhārat(a) as its name, commemorating the ancient name.

⌘ BHĀRATĪYA JANATĀ PARTY ⌘

Indian People's Party, the name of a political party that has considerable strength in north India. Founded in 1980, it is a Hindu nationalist party that seeks to maximize the power of Hindus within India, and takes the position that Hindus need to be awakened to the social and political crisis of their disenfranchisement. It has close ties to the Rāṣṭrīya Svayamsevak Saṅgh and the Vishva Hindu Parishad. In 1990, it led a highly publicized tour, modelled on a procession of a temple's image of God, from Somnāth to Ayodhyā in an effort to mobilize Hindu support for its political campaign and the cause of Hindu nationalism. Under the leadership of A. B. Vajpayee and L. K. Advani, the B.J.P. led a coalition that briefly won control of the central government of India during 1996. (*See also* Rāṣṭrīya Svayamsevak Saṅgh; Vishva Hindu Parishad.)

⌘ BHĀRATĪYA VIDYĀ BHAVAN ⌘

Name of a cultural and educational organization in modern India. Founded in 1938 by Dr. K. M. Munshi, its purpose is to aid in the revival of the Sanskrit language and the ancient culture it transmits. There is a spiritual aspect to the mission of the organization as well as its publishing and educational aims. The headquarters of the organization is Bombay, and it has branches all over India.

⌘ BHĀRGAVA ⌘

Descendant of Bhṛgu. Bhārgava Brahmins apparently had a role in the transmission of the *Mahābhārata*, and included within the text they transmitted numerous myths about Bhārgavas. Many of these myths concern conflict between themselves and Kṣatriya warriors, and involve themes such as the restoration of life. (*See also* Bhṛgu.)

⌘ BHĀSKARARĀYA MAKHIN, or BHĀRATI ⌘

Scholar, author, and interpreter of Śrīvidyā Tantric texts. Originally from Mahārāṣṭra in western India, he travelled widely and settled in Tamilnadu in the mid-eighteenth century, patronized by Seforji, the Marāṭha ruler of Thañjavūr. Bhāskararāya was an initiate of both Vedic and Tantric traditions, and maintained that Śrīvidyā Tantra was both Vedic and Tantric. His work entitled *Setubandha* is the authoritative source book for south Indian Śrīvidyā traditions. Contemporary lineages usually trace their descent from him. (*See also* Śrīvidyā Tantra; Tantra.)

⌘ BHṚGU ⌘

Name of an ancient sage and Ṛṣi celebrated in the *Ṛg Veda* (1.60, and 1.71, for example) for receiving Fire (Agni) from heaven. Though references to Bhṛgu and his descendants appear throughout the *Ṛg Veda*, they are not concentrated in any one book of the text, nor did the Bhṛgu or Bhārgava family preserve and contribute a collection of poems to the Vedic literature, though they were apparently instrumental in transmission of the *Mahābhārata*. There is a temple dedicated to Bhṛgu at Bharuch or Broach, a city on the Narmadā River in Gujarāt with an ancient past. The city's name is a corruption of "Bhṛgukaccha" (Bhṛgu's Shore). (*See also* Bhārgava.)

⌘ BHŪ, BHŪDEVĪ ⌘

See Earth.

⌘ BHUVANEŚVARA (BHUBANESHWAR) ⌘

The capital city of the state of Orissa, and the site of many temples dating from the eighth through thirteenth centuries C.E. The most important is the Liṅgarāja Temple, dedicated to Tribhuvaneśvara (Lord of the Three Worlds), which features a forty-meter-high tower (Śikhara) and dates to about 1100 C.E. Vaital Mandira is dedicated to Kālī in the form of Cāmuṇḍā, and dates to the eighth century C.E. Brahmeśvara Temple is notable for its remarkably detailed sculptures and dates from the ninth century C.E. (*See also* Temple.)

⌘ BĪJA MANTRA ⌘

Seed-Word. A syllable used as a Mantra, or meditation phrase to be recited. Each seed Mantra is regarded, particularly in Tantric traditions, as the essence of a longer Mantra which it represents. Seed Mantras are used to invoke deities in Tantric rituals and Yoga practice. (*See also* Cakra; Mantra; Tantra.)

⌘ BĪRŪNĪ, AL- ⌘

Muslim scholar and traveller who visited India in the eleventh century C.E. and wrote a book (*Kitab al-Hind*) describing the people of India and their religious practices. While in India, al-Bīrūnī learned Sanskrit and translated into Arabic the *Yoga Sūtra* of Patañjali, thereby making available to the Islamic world a greater understanding of Hindu religious thought and practice.

⌘ B.J.P. ⌘

See Bhāratīya Janatā Party.

⌘ BLAVATSKY, HELENA PETROVNA ⌘

Founder (1831–1891) of the Theosophical Society. Born in Russia as Helena Hahn, she was briefly married in her youth to General Blavatsky of the Czarist Russian Army, whose name she kept in later life. She travelled widely, later saying that she had lived in Tibet. She arrived in the United States in 1873 and in New York met Colonel Henry Steele Olcott, with whom in 1875 she founded the Theosophical Society. She moved to India, and established a major center of the Theosophical Society at the Madras suburb of Adyār, which influenced Indian intellectuals for generations. Madame Blavatsky was eclectic in her spiritual interests, and was widely acclaimed for her reputed psychic powers. Her published works include *Isis Unveiled* (1877) and *The Secret Doctrine* (1888), and draw upon both Hindu and Buddhist ideas and meditational practices. Though never a large movement in terms of its number of adherents, members tended to be intellectuals who were prominent and influential, and the Theosophical Society was instrumental both in encouraging Hindus to value and learn about their own traditions, despite the colonized status of India at the time, and in spreading to the West some knowledge of Hindu religious thought and practice. (*See also* Besant, Annie; Krishnamurti, Jiddu; Olcott, Henry Steele; Theosophical Society.)

⌘ BOAR AVATĀRA ⌘

See Avatāra; Varāha.

⌘ BRAHMĀ ⌘

God who personifies and embodies Brahman. He is often depicted as a benevolent deity, credited with creation of the world. He has many qualities in common with the Brahmin class, including an interest in maintenance of the sacred order of Dharma and a this-worldly orientation toward ritual action, rather than the other-worldly values of ascetics and renouncers. Apparently originally distinct from Prajāpati, these two deities became identified with one another. Often called Pitāmaha (Grandfather), he is regarded as the progenitor of the gods and demons in Hindu mythology. Apparently between about 500 B.C.E. and 500 C.E., Brahmā was worshipped widely, but his cult diminished after this time and has been virtually nonexistent for centuries. (*See also* Brahman; Creation; Prajāpati; Puṣkara; World Ages.)

⌘ BRAHMĀ KUMĀRĪ ⌘

A new religious movement founded in 1937. Brahmā Kumārī draws upon Hindu religious ideas and practices, but whether it should be seen as part of Hinduism or not is controversial since members of the movement do not accept the authority or sacredness of the Vedas. Founded by a diamond merchant named Dāda Lekhrāj (who took the religious name Prajāpitar Brahmā) in what is now Pakistan, the organization moved to Mount Abu in Rajasthan, western India, about the time of Partition and independence in 1947. Leadership has since passed into the hands of female followers, with his encouragement. They emphasize the importance of meditation, ethical conduct, celibacy, and abstention from smoking and alcohol. Brahmā Kumārī is a millenarian movement, seeing the end of the world as near at hand, to be followed by a golden age. They maintain the Brahmā Kumārī Spiritual University at Mount Abu, where members from all over the world take courses. There are said to be some 4,000 centers in sixty nations.

⌘ *BRAHMA SŪTRA* ⌘

A text also known as the *Vedānta Sūtra* and attributed to the sage Bādarāyaṇa, often identified with Vyāsa. In some 555 brief verses, the work presents in summary form the essential doctrines of the Upaniṣads, particularly the *Chāndogya*. Its great contribution is that it harmonizes the diverse and sometimes conflicting teachings of the Upaniṣads in a coherent fashion. Its four chapters treat the following topics: (1) the nature of Brahman as the impersonal Absolute; (2) responses to objections from other philosophical positions; (3) the methods of obtaining valid knowledge of Brahman; and (4) the benefits of knowledge of Brahman. It has become the key text of all Vedānta schools, and commentaries on it have been composed by many major thinkers as the foundational documents for their particular systems. The date of the text is difficult to determine, but it may have been composed about 100 B.C.E. It twice (2.3.45, and 4.1.10) quotes the *Bhagavad Gītā*, as all later Vedānta commentators are agreed. (*See also* Bādarāyaṇa; Brahman; Vedānta.)

⌘ BRAHMACARYA ⌘

Conduct in accord with Brahman. Celibacy is the key component of this way of life, and the person living in this way is called a Brahmacārin. *Atharva Veda* 11.5 praises the Brahmacārin as an ascetic whose power fills the three worlds. The practice of classical Yoga requires Brahmacarya, as in *Yoga Sūtra* 2.38, where the practitioner is said to gain energy from this way of life. It is expected that the student, who is in the first of the Four Stages of Life, will adhere to the Brahmacarya mode of life. (*See also* Four Stages of Life; Saṃnyāsa; Tapas.)

⌘ BRAHMAN ⌘

Sacred power. The term is derived from the root bṛh (to grow, to become great). Originally the Veda was regarded as Brahman in verbal form, and the performance of sacrificial ritual (Yajña) was the means of access to this power. In the Upaniṣads, the idea is presented that one can gain access to this sacred power through knowledge and the practice of Yoga meditation, and that Brahman is no different from Ātman, one's self. This presentation of Brahman as a metaphysical principle underlying all of existence has been a very fruitful idea in Hindu thought, and has led to widespread acceptance of the view that Brahman is Ultimate Reality beyond all the multiplicity of forms. Later Hindu traditions make a distinction between Brahman as the impersonal Absolute, transcendent, without attributes or qualities (Nirguṇa Brahman), and Brahman as embodied in a particular divine form, a deity with specific attributes and qualities (Saguṇa Brahman), the two concepts hierarchically arranged depending on whether one's worldview is monistic or theistic. (*See also* Ātman; *Brahma Sūtra*; Brāhmaṇa; Brahmin; God; Nirguṇa Brahman; Philosophical Schools; Saguṇa Brahman; Upaniṣads; Vedānta; Yajña; Yoga.)

⌘ BRAHMÁN ⌘

Priest in the Vedic sacrifice who is to sit near the main fire altar as the overseer of the ritual activities. He is to silently recite verses from the *Atharva Veda* to correct any errors or omissions in the ritual, thus he should be the master of all four Vedas and the ritual procedure as well so as to detect errors. (*See also* Yajña.)

⌘ BRĀHMAṆA ⌘

Literally, having to do with Brahman. The term is used to refer to those people who embody Brahman from having memorized the Veda, that is, the Brahmin social class. It also is applied to a group of texts that are commentaries on the Vedic Saṃhitā texts. (*See also* Brahman; Brahmin; Saṃhitā.)

⌘ BRAHMANISM ⌘

Term used for early Hinduism, including the religious traditions based on the Vedas and Upaniṣads. The adjective "Brahmanical'' is frequently used to refer to these traditions. (*See also* Upaniṣads; Veda.)

⌘ BRAHMIN ⌘

Member of the social class with the highest status in the caste system of social organization. Traditionally, male members of this class became priests capable of reciting the Veda and performing Vedic sacrifices for themselves and others. Such a person would be ''Brāhmaṇa'' meaning ''one who has Brahman,'' descriptive of the fact that the Brahmin embodies Brahman-power in the form of his knowledge of Veda and ritual. The English spelling ''Brahmin'' is a corruption of the Sanskrit word Brāhmaṇa. (*See also* Brahman; Brāhmaṇa; Caste; Dharma; Veda.)

⌘ BRAHMO SAMĀJ ⌘

A reform movement founded in Calcutta in 1828 by Rām Mohun Roy. It became influential among Bengali intellectuals in the nineteenth century, but was never a popular movement. It opposed features of Hinduism that were regarded as later innovations not found in the Upaniṣads, particularly polytheism, the use of images of deities in worship, ritual sacrifice of animals, and pilgrimages. In addition, social practices such as polygamy, the immolation of widows (Satī), child marriage, and caste regulations in general were also opposed by the Brahmo Samāj. Criticism of traditional Hindu practices led to some improvement in the status of women. The leadership of Debendranāth Tagore (1817–1905) and Keshub Chandra Sen (1838–84) were vital to sustaining the program of the movement throughout the nineteenth century. (*See also* Ārya Samāj; Rāj; Roy, Rām Mohun; Satī.)

⌘ BRAJ ⌘

See Vraja.

⌘ *BṚHADĀRAṆYAKA UPANIṢAD* ⌘

The Great Āraṇyaka-Upaniṣad. As its name indicates, the text is both an Āraṇyaka and an Upaniṣad. It is preserved as the concluding section of the *Śatapatha Brāhmaṇa* of the *Śukla Yajur Veda*, and exists in two slightly different recensions, the Kāṇva and the

Mādhyandina. Probably the earliest Upaniṣad, it is datable to perhaps 600 B.C.E. The text has three sections, and it is clear that they must once have circulated as independent texts: each ends with a list of the series of teachers (Guru-Paraṃparā) who transmitted the teachings, and the story of Yājñavalkya and his two wives occurs twice (2.4 and 4.5). The text opens with the often-cited set of correspondences between the sacrificial horse and the cosmos, signalling an interest in moving beyond the performance of the sacrificial rites to an understanding of their meaning. The central section of the text (2.4 to 4.6) is the teachings of the sage Yājñavalkya concerning the self and Brahman. These include some of the earliest statements of Hindu ideas about reincarnation or rebirth (4.4.5–7) in which it is stated that the nature of one's action determines the nature of one's next lifetime, while one who is without desire becomes immortal, merging into Brahman. Chapters five and six of the text are a miscellaneous collection of teachings on Brahman. The *Bṛhadāraṇyaka*, due to its length and the diversity of its teachings, has been one of the most influential Upaniṣads, and one of the main sources of later philosophical and religious traditions of Vedānta. (*See also Chāndogya Upaniṣad*; Rebirth; Upaniṣads; Veda; Vedānta; Yājñavalkya.)

⌘ *BṚHAD-DEVATĀ* ⌘

Great Text on Deities. Name of a Sanskrit text dating perhaps from the fifth century B.C.E. and ascribed to Śaunaka. It presents Vedic mythology and details about the gods in a systematic fashion. (*See also* Deva; Veda.)

⌘ BRITISH EAST INDIA COMPANY ⌘

A commercial organization engaged in trade with India. Chartered by Queen Elizabeth I in 1600, the company was granted a monopoly on trade with Asia, and invested in ships to trade with the Spice Islands (Indonesia). When the Dutch forced the British out of that area, the Company fell back on India as its second choice. Establishing fortified trading posts along the coast led to the foundation of the modern cities of Calcutta, Bombay, and Madras. Controlling large sections of coastal India by 1800 (with British troops and hired Indian mercenaries [Sepoys]), the Company was a major force in Indian political and social life. A rebellion among the Sepoys in 1857, called the Mutiny of 1857 by the British and the War of Independence by Indians, led to a loss of confidence in the Company on the part of the British Government, and the subsequent dissolution of the Company in 1858. All holdings were taken over by the government and Indian territory became a Crown Colony. The Company was instrumental in encouraging or legislating various reforms in Hindu religious practices, such as outlawing the practice of widow immolation (Satī) in 1829. (*See also* Calcutta; Madras; Müller, F. M.; Rāj.)

⌘ BROWN, W. NORMAN ⌘

Indologist (1892–1972) who held the chair in Sanskrit at the University of Pennsylvania, 1926 to 1966. For many years, he was the curator of Indian art at the Philadelphia Museum of Art, and the editor of the *Journal of the American Oriental Society*. (*See also* Indology.)

⌘ BUDDHA ⌘

The Awakened One, the title of Siddhārtha Gautama (about 563–483 B.C.E., or perhaps a century later). The Buddha was born and raised in Kapilavastu, capital of a small republic of the Śākya people, in a region that is now the border between Nepal and India. He became an ascetic renouncer, and after six years of living in the forest and experimenting with various meditational techniques, attained Nirvāṇa at the age of thirty-five. He spent the next forty-five years teaching the means of attaining Nirvāṇa, and organizing the community of renouncers (Saṃgha) who formed up around him. He rejected the authority of the Veda and the efficacy of the Vedic sacrifice (Yajña), as well as the idea that a Brahmin is entitled to any special privileges due to birth in that social class. The movement he founded had a long history in India, some sixteen or seventeen centuries, before it was largely exterminated in India by Muslim invaders in the twelfth and thirteenth centuries C.E. Buddhism had already engaged in missionary activity throughout most of South and East Asia, and some Buddhist monks and nuns migrated to those regions. The Buddha has been viewed with some ambivalence by Hindus, and Hindu literature reflects this. While Buddhism is often seen as one of the main opponents of Hindu philosophical and religious traditions, the Buddha is sometimes viewed quite positively. For example, in the *Gītagovinda* of Jayadeva (twelfth century C.E.), the Buddha is praised as one of the ten Avatāras of Viṣṇu, the one who taught Ahiṃsā (nonviolence) and led people to stop killing animals in the Vedic sacrifice (1.13). In some accounts, he replaces Balarāma, brother of Kṛṣṇa, as the eighth Avatāra. Most Purāṇas, however, present a much more negative view of the Buddha in which his teachings are regarded as appealing to those of demonic nature, leading them to hell (for example, *Agni Purāṇa*, chapter 16; see also *Matsya Purāṇa* 47.247, and *Bhāgavata Purāṇa* 1.3.24, where no value judgment is articulated). This is typical of the Avatāra function, namely, removing demons from the earth, but in addition to this positive aspect there is also the clear implication that Buddhism itself is a defective, demonic doctrine. (*See also* Avatāra; Buddhism; Viṣṇu.)

⌘ BUDDHI ⌘

Wisdom; the higher mind as distinguished from the lower mind (Manas). In *Kaṭha Upaniṣad* 3.3, the famous simile occurs in which the Buddhi is the chariot driver, the body is the chariot, and the self (Ātman) is the rider. "Buddhi" is an important technical term in traditions of Sāṃkhya, Yoga, and Vedānta. It is generally regarded as the first product of Nature (Prakṛti), which then produces all other elements of the psyche, including Manas, the senses, etc. (*See also* Ātman; Citta; Consciousness, States of; Manas; Sāṃkhya.)

⌘ BUDDHISM ⌘

Religious tradition founded by the Buddha. This tradition rejects the authority of the Vedic literature, and has been regarded as an unorthodox philosophical school in conflict with the six orthodox schools of Hindu tradition. (*See also* Buddha; Jainism; Philosophical Schools.)

⌘ BUITENEN, JOHANNES ADRIANUS BERNARDUS VAN ⌘

Sanskrit scholar and Indologist (1928–1979). Born in The Hague, his interest in India began prior to graduation from gymnasium in 1946. He attended the University of Utrecht and studied Sanskrit under Jan Gonda, completing his doctoral dissertation on Rāmānuja's commentary on the *Bhagavad Gītā* in 1953. From then until 1956, at the Deccan College, in Pune, India, he worked on the *Encyclopedic Dictionary of Sanskrit* as assistant editor responsible for Vedānta and Kāvya. In 1957–58, van Buitenen was at Harvard University on a Rockefeller Fellowship to work with Daniel Ingalls, and the following year at the University of Chicago, where he translated *Tales of Ancient India* (1959). Two years in the Netherlands as lecturer in Sanskrit under Gonda were followed by appointment at the University of Chicago, where he founded and chaired the Department of South Asian Languages and Civilizations. His wide-ranging scholarly interests continued to expand, and he published studies entitled *Two Plays of Ancient India* (1964), *The Pravargya, an Ancient Indian Iconic Ritual Described and Annotated* (1968), and, with Eliot Deutsch, *A Source Book of Advaita Vedānta* (1971), among other works. His most remarkable accomplishment, however, is the translation of the first five books of the *Mahābhārata* (1973–1978), representing about forty per cent of the whole work, and the *Bhagavad Gītā*. His contributions to the study of classical Indian civilization have been numerous, and his translations and studies continue to instruct and inspire scholars in a variety of disciplines. (*See also* Indology.)

— C —

⌘ CAITANYA ⌘

Bengali saint (1486–1533 C.E.) also known as Kṛṣṇa Caitanya who led a movement of emotional devotion to Kṛṣṇa in eastern India. Born as a Brahmin in Nadia, Bengal, in eastern India, he was converted to the worship of Kṛṣṇa about 1510, and lived most of the rest of his life in Puri, Orissa, at the large Kṛṣṇa temple of Jagannātha. He is credited with reviving worship of Kṛṣṇa through his example of ecstatic singing and dancing and recitation of the names of God. In so doing, he was probably much influenced by the Bāul singers and by Cāṇḍīdās, whose songs were still being sung in Bengal. Another aspect of his devotion is his adoption of the emotional attitude and even the mannerisms of the Gopīs who loved Kṛṣṇa selflessly; this approach has become an important feature of the Bhakti tradition of devotion to Kṛṣṇa. The devotional tradition he revived (and to some extent created) is largely based on the *Bhāgavata Purāṇa* and *Bhagavad Gītā*. He also was profoundly affected by the *Gītagovinda*, probably from attending performances of it at the Jagannātha temple. He initiated the Gosvāmin theologians and directed them to settle in Vṛndāvana in central India to promulgate the tradition from there, regarded as the site of Kṛṣṇa's birth and early life. During his lifetime he was widely regarded as an Avatāra of Kṛṣṇa or of Kṛṣṇa and his beloved consort Rādhā in a single body. The Hare Krishna movement, officially known as the International Society for Krishna Consciousness, is one of several modern sects that trace their lineage of teachers back to Caitanya. (*See also Bhāgavata Purāṇa*; Bhakti; Cāṇḍīdās; *Gītagovinda*; Gopī; Gosvāmins; Hare Krishna Movement; Jagannātha; Kṛṣṇa; Rādhā; Vṛndāvana.)

⌘ CAKRA ⌘

Wheel. The term is used especially in the context of the practice of Kuṇḍalinī and other forms of Tantric Yoga in reference to centers held to exist within the body. These centers are not regarded as gross physical features of the anatomy, but are features of the subtle body's physiology. From near the base of the spine to the crown of the head, paralleling the spine, there is said to be a channel known as the Suṣumnā Nāḍī (Most Gracious Channel) that serves as a conduit for the life-force (Prāṇa) or energy, along which six, or in some systems seven or more, Cakras are located. The Prāṇa or Kuṇḍalinī can, by correct practice, be caused to rise through the channel, progressing through each Cakra until it reaches the crown of the head, the female energy (equated with the goddess Śakti) there uniting with the male spiritual force (equated with the god Śiva). Such a union brings bliss and liberation from rebirth, Mokṣa. The Cakras are, with various names, sometimes given as having the following locations: (1) at the anus; (2) at the genitals; (3) at the navel; (4) at the heart; (5) in the throat; (6) behind and between the eyes; and (7) in or just above the crown of the head. Cakras are often described and visually depicted as open lotuses, with a variety of presiding deities and Bījā Mantras (Seed-Words), into the meaning of which a practitioner would be initiated by a Guru. (*See also* Bījā Mantra; Kuṇḍalinī; Śakti; Tantra.)

⌘ CALCUTTA ⌘

One of India's largest cities, capital of West Bengal, and site of numerous temples. The British East India Company built a small fort in 1696 at the site, and the rapidly growing city eventually took its name from Kālīghāṭ and the village of Kālīkata. Calcutta became the Indian headquarters of the East India Company and of the colonial administration until 1911. Kālīghāṭ temple in southern Calcutta occupies the site at which a finger of the corpse of Śiva's wife Satī fell to earth; the temple was rebuilt in 1809 on the site of an ancient temple. At the north end of Calcutta stands the Dakṣiṇeśvara Kālī temple at which Rāmakrishna was priest and resident sage. Nearby is Belur Maṭh, headquarters of the Rāmakrishna Mission.

⌘ CĀLUKYA ⌘

Name of a dynasty that ruled in the Deccan during the sixth through eighth centuries C.E. Bādāmī, Paṭṭadakal, and Aihole are major temple complexes they built.

⌘ CĀMUṆḌĀ ⌘

A name of the goddess Durgā or Kālī, in a horrific form. Various Purāṇas relate how Devī plucked her matted hair and threw it down, from which sprung up Cāmuṇḍā (or Cāmuṇḍī) to destroy the demons Caṇḍa and Muṇḍa, ministers of Mahiṣa the Asura. (*See also* Caṇḍī; Devī; Mahiṣa.)

⌘ CAṆḌĀLA ⌘

An Outcaste. The term was used to refer particularly to those Outcastes who handled dead bodies, and were therefore among the most ritually polluted of all Outcastes. (*See also* Caste; Outcaste; Śūdra.)

⌘ CAṆḌĪ (CAṆḌIKĀ) ⌘

A goddess in fierce form, often depicted with either eighteen or twenty hands. Worshipped particularly in Bengal, she is associated with the destruction of Mahiṣa the Asura. (*See also* Cāmuṇḍā; Devī; Mahiṣa.)

⌘ CAṆḌĪDĀS ⌘

Bengali saint of the fourteenth century. He is regarded as belonging to the Sahajiyā movement, and composed numerous poems or songs in which the love of Rādhā and Kṛṣṇa is celebrated. These were well known to Caitanya and were very influential in his formulation of the devotional tradition he founded. (*See also* Caitanya; Sahajiyā.)

⌘ CANDRA ⌘

The Moon. Candra is one of the deities who serve as World Guardians (Lokapāla), Candra protecting the northeast quarter. Candra is often identified with Soma. (*See also* Soma; Sūrya; World Guardians.)

⌘ CĀRVĀKA ⌘

Name of the founder of the materialist tradition of Indian philosophy, a nonorthodox tradition, known by the founder's name, that regarded all of reality as explainable in terms of matter's interaction, without any spiritual component. Hindu and Buddhist teachers frequently castigated the Cārvākas as exponents of the worst of all philosophical doctrines, probably because they saw it as encouraging selfish and aggressive behavior. (*See also* Philosophical Schools.)

⌘ CASTE ⌘

English term, derived from the Portuguese term "casta" (color, race), which was used to describe the various social groups or classes in India several centuries ago. How the caste system originated and functions is the subject of considerable disagreement among scholars. Most scholars accept the theory that the Āryan people who appeared in northwestern India about 1500 B.C.E. were organized into three hierarchically ordered classes, the Brahmin, Kṣatriya, and Vaiśya. Though probably not hereditary in any absolute sense, the Brahmin and Kṣatriya were specialized groups of priests and warriors, respectively, that had developed out of the larger Vaiśya group of artisans and food producers. The Āryans saw themselves as distinct from and superior to the indigenous inhabitants of India, whom they were conquering and upon whom they were imposing much of Āryan culture; the non-Āryan population became the fourth social group, called the Śūdra or Serf class, with a definite barrier between the Āryan and non-Āryan groups, at least in theory. An Āryan view of the system of social organization can be seen in the *Ṛg Veda* (10.90) in the Puruṣa Hymn. There the four groups are depicted as originating from the primordial sacrifice of the Cosmic Man, from whose head originated the Brahmin class, from whose arms originated the Kṣatriya, from whose thighs originated the Vaiśya, and from whose feet originated the Śūdra. This social order is presented as a part of the divinely ordained creation, and, as such, a part of the natural world. That one would perform the duties appropriate to the social group of which one was a member was strongly supported in Brahmanical literature such as the *Bhagavad Gītā* and *Mānava Dharma Śāstra*. The ideal that one marry within one's group so that one's children will clearly fit into society is an important feature of the Dharma Śāstra literature and of Brahmanical culture generally, though it is evident that there were numerous cases in which this did not occur. Each social group or Varṇa was regarded as having a particular set of social and religious obligations (Dharma), fulfillment of which was expected. Moreover, acceptance of the idea of rebirth according to one's Karma reinforced the social class system, in that one would be reborn into the social class appropriate to one's nature and Karma, so one would be suited to perform the Dharma of that Varṇa. Brahmins had the particular Dharma of learning and transmitting the Veda and knowledge of the sacrifice, Kṣatriyas learned weaponry and the methods of ruling, Vaiśyas were to raise food and engage in commerce, while Śūdras were to serve the other groups. In addition to these four groups, there arose a fifth group that was regarded as outside the Caste system, the Outcastes or Untouchables, who performed ritually polluting jobs such as handling dead bodies. While in ancient times a direct connection between one's livelihood and one's Varṇa was the ideal, historical examples show that often this was not the case. In the modern era, the connection is even less likely to be found. The term caste is often used for the Varṇa, but sometimes also for the birth group (Jāti), a group specific to a certain locale and with its own traditions; the term subcaste is also used for Jāti. Today many Hindus continue to identify themselves as members of a particular caste and abide by the rules of the Jāti of their birth. The Constitution of the Republic of India, adopted in 1950, outlaws discrimination based on caste status, but such attitudes persist. (*See also* Ambedkar, Bhīmrao; Āryan; *Bhagavad Gītā*; Brahmin; Caṇḍāla; Dharma; Harijan; Jāti; Kṣatriya; *Mānava Dharma Śāstra*; Outcaste; Puruṣa; Śūdra; Sūta; Twice-Born; Vaiśya.)

⌘ *CHĀNDOGYA UPANIṢAD* ⌘

One of the earliest Upaniṣads, composed perhaps about 600 B.C.E. It is a section of the *Chāndogya Brāhmaṇa*, which belongs to the Tāṇḍya school of the *Sāma Veda*. In this work, Uddālaka presents to his son Śvetaketu teachings on the pervasiveness of Brahman and its identity with one's own soul (Ātman). It also contains speculations on the meaning of the sacred Mantra Oṃ (often called Udgītha or High Chant), regarded as symbolic of Brahman. The text ends with Prajāpati's instruction to the gods and demons on the nature of the self. (*See also* Brahman; *Bṛhadāraṇyaka Upaniṣad*; Mantra; Oṃ; *Sāma Veda*; Upaniṣads; Vedānta.)

⌘ CHATTERJEE, BANKIM CHANDRA ⌘

Bengali author and nationalist (1838–1894). Chatterjee was a very prominent intellectual in Calcutta, and a major influence on Aurobindo Ghosh in his early life. He composed the poem entitled "Bande Mātaram" as a hymn to the goddess Kālī; it has become the national anthem of India.

⌘ CIDAMBARAM ⌘

Site of the famous Nāṭarāja temple dedicated to Śiva. Built during the reign of Vīra Cola Rāja (tenth century C.E.), it is one of the oldest temple complexes in southern India, and one of the largest. The north and south Gopuram gates tower forty-nine meters high, and display 108 different postures of Śiva as Cosmic Dancer. The complex features a large hall with a thousand pillars and the Nṛtta Sabhā, a performing arts hall constructed in the form of a giant chariot. Shrines to Pārvatī, Gaṇeśa, and Subrahmaṇya (Skanda), the members of Śiva's family, grace the complex. (*See also* Nāṭarāja; Temple.)

⌘ CIRCUMAMBULATION ⌘

The tradition of walking around (pradakṣiṇa) a sacred structure such as a temple or a sacred person. One walks clockwise, keeping the object being venerated on one's right as a way of expressing reverence.

⌘ CITTA ⌘

Mind; mentality; character. Citta refers particularly to the conscious mind. Patañjali's definition of Yoga (*Yoga Sūtra* 1.2) is that it is the suppression of mental fluctuations (Citta-vṛtti), the disciplining of the conscious mind. Citta is closely related to Manas, and the terms are often used interchangeably. (*See also* Buddhi; Consciousness, States of; Manas.)

⌘ CIVAVĀKKIYAR ⌘

A Tamil saint of the ninth century. A devotee of Śiva, he composed poems, some 500 of which are still extant, in which he calls people to encounter the divine presence within. He condemned discrimination based on caste, and worship in which images are used. He ridiculed the pretensions of Brahmins and the doctrine of rebirth, rejecting religious orthodoxy in general and the sacredness of the Vedas in particular. (*See also* Nāyanār; Śaivism.)

⌘ COḺA ⌘

Name of a dynasty (ninth through fourteenth century C.E.) that ruled in Tamilnadu and, at times, Sri Lanka also. The great Śiva temple at Tanjore (Thañjavūr) was constructed under Coḻa sponsorship.

⌘ COMMONER ⌘

See Vaiśya.

⌘ CONSCIOUSNESS, STATES OF ⌘

Hindu thought recognizes four distinct states of consciousness: the waking state (Jāgrat), the dream state (Svapna), deep sleep without dreams (Suṣupta or Suṣupti), and, by the time of the *Māṇḍūkya Upaniṣad*, a fourth state (Turīya, meaning "the fourth''), which is equivalent to Brahman. The waking state is regarded as characterized by the greatest degree of superimposition of limitation on reality, or misperception. The dream state is a more subtle state of consciousness in which some limitation is transcended, but duality of thought remains. The deep sleep state is characterized by one's consciousness manifesting itself as Prajñā, awareness. All limitation is removed, bliss (Ānanda) is experienced, but the state is limited to sleep itself and one does not bring awareness back into waking consciousness from deep sleep. While everyone experiences the first three states of consciousness regularly, the fourth state is qualitatively different from the other three; in fact, it is the substratum of the other three states of consciousness, they being mere modifications or aspects of Turīya (or Brahman). Just as the experience of Brahman is synonymous with the attainment of liberation from rebirth (Mokṣa), Turīya as a state of consciousness and Mokṣa as a state of being are identified. One who is liberated while living (Jīvan-mukti) has experienced the Turīya state. The importance of the fourth state of consciousness and its identity with Brahman has been expounded by Śaṅkara and other Advaita Vedānta thinkers especially, but its presence in the Upaniṣads has meant that all Vedānta schools have commented on the idea. (*See also* Advaita Vedānta; Ātman; Brahman; Buddhi; Citta; Jīvan-mukti; Manas; Mokṣa; Samādhi.)

⌘ COOMARASWAMY, ANANDA KENTISH ⌘

Art historian and scholar (1877–1947). Born in Colombo, Ceylon (Śrī Laṅka) of a Ceylonese father and British mother, he was educated at Wycliff College and the University of London, where he earned a Ph.D. in geology. He was appointed director of mineral surveys in 1903, but began to develop an interest in art history. In 1910 he was appointed director of the art museum of the United Provinces Exhibition in Allahabad. In 1917 he accepted the position of research fellow at the Museum of Fine Arts in Boston, where he remained for the last thirty years of his life. He regarded the classical art of South Asia to be an articulation of wisdom that is both specific to its culture and has universally human dimensions. Coomaraswamy saw his role as transmitter of ancient wisdom of South Asian cultures. Among his many contributions to scholarly understanding of Hinduism are his *History of Indian and Indonesian Art,* and numerous articles. (*See also* Indology.)

⌘ COSMOGONY ⌘

See Creation.

⌘ COW, SACRED ⌘

The cow is looked upon by most Hindus with respect and veneration, so that the expression "sacred cow" has come into use in English as a way of describing the attitude common to Hindus, and by extension to refer to anything that is to be treated with great respect. The widespread attitude of veneration for the cow can be traced back to the respect Vedic Āryans had for the animal that provided them with many of their needs: meat, milk, leather, and horn. The cow was the animal most often offered to the gods in sacrificial rituals (Yajña), its meat shared by those present, therefore providing the means by which occurred communication with the gods and the benefits of divine generosity. Thus, it could certainly be said that the Vedic Āryans regarded the cow as sacred; *Atharva Veda* 10.10 is a poem in praise of the cow in which the cow is equated with the universe. Cattle were also a way in which the Āryans measured wealth, and many Vedic poems ask that the gods grant them numerous cattle. Priests who performed Vedic sacrifices often received cattle as their fee. As the Vedic sacrificial tradition came to be criticized by ascetic and non-Brahmanical movements such as Buddhism and Jainism, and the religious significance of the idea of nonviolence (Ahiṃsā) began to be recognized, the killing of a cow, even for sacrificial purposes, came to be questioned. Killing of all kinds came to be seen as bad Karma, while vegetarianism came to be seen as a practice engendering good Karma. With this shift in worldview, Hindus generally turned away from the Vedic sacrifice of animals toward Pūjā offerings in honor of the gods. Cows are venerated for the milk they provide, which can also be made into yoghurt or butter, important components of the diet. In addition, the urine of cows is used as a cleansing agent, and the dried dung is used as fuel for cooking. Because they freely give all these useful products, cows are seen as symbolic of the Mother, both in the sense of the Goddess and the earth. Thus, the cow is still seen as worthy of veneration, now no longer offered to the gods in sacrifice, but protected as symbolic of life itself. (*See also* Ahiṃsā; Pūjā; Yajña.)

⌘ CREATION ⌘

Hindus have numerous myths of creation, in part due to the cyclic worldview that has dominated Hindu thought for over two millenia. Even in the *Ṛg Veda*, however, various myths of the creation and ordering of the world are recounted. Indra's act of killing the demon Vṛtra freed the waters and made human life possible. Viṣṇu's act of taking three strides is regarded as creating space in which humanity could live, as is the act of propping up heaven above earth, attributed to several gods. *Ṛg Veda* 10.129 presents creation as taking place when the One brought order out of the chaos and darkness. *Ṛg Veda* 10.90 attributes creation to the sacrifice and dismemberment of the primordial man Puruṣa. *Ṛg Veda* 10.10 presents the myth of Yama and Yamī, twins who are the first human beings. There seems to be an ancient Indo-European myth of creation in which one twin kills the other to initiate creation; both the Yama and Puruṣa poems may be reflections of this ancient myth. Dakṣa, Dhātṛ, Tvaṣṭṛ, and Viśvakarman are all creator gods in the Veda. Later literature combines these figures into one, the Lord of Creatures, Prajāpati (as in the Brāhmaṇas), for whom the name Brahmā, and the identity as grandfather of the gods and demons, come to be common in the Upaniṣads and later works. *Ṛg Veda* 10.121 is a hymn to Hiraṇyagarbha (Golden Womb, or Embryo) as creator of the world, credited with creating earth and heaven, the waters, and life itself. Purāṇas elaborated on these cosmogonic ideas and images, creating a complex vision of the universe. Hiraṇyagarbha was conceived as an egg (Brahmāṇḍa, the Egg of Brahmā); splitting in two, its halves became heaven and earth, with Mount Meru in the center and rings of continents and seas surrounding it. Six heavenly realms (Loka) where gods reside are arrayed above the earth, seven netherworlds (Tala) are the residences of assorted Nāgas, Daityas, Dānavas, Yakṣas, Pretas, and other beings, while seven hell-realms (Narakas) are the residences of the childless, those awaiting rebirth, those experiencing bad Karma, and others. The cosmos so created exists for a set of four ages of declining quality, which is followed by a destruction and new creation in an infinite cycle. The period of the world being manifest is regarded as a day of Brahmā, its unmanifest state is a night of Brahmā, and Brahmā lives for 100 years until he too is exhausted and must be reabsorbed back into the Absolute (Viṣṇu, Śiva, or Devī, depending on the worldview of the Hindu.) (*See also* Brahmā; Dakṣa; Dhātṛ; Indra; Nāṭarāja; Prajāpati; Puruṣa; Śiva; Tapas; Tvaṣṭṛ; Viṣṇu; World Ages; Yama.)

⌘ CREMATION ⌘

See Funeral.

— D —

⌘ DAITYA ⌘

A class of demons, opposed to the Devas. The name is derived as if from Diti, the opposite of the divine Aditi. (*See also* Aditi; Dānava; Deva; Rākṣasa.)

⌘ DAKṢA ⌘

Vedic creator deity. He is listed as one of the Ādityas, a son of Aditi, and as her father as well. His other daughter was Diti. He is thus the grandfather of gods and demons in some Vedic creation myths. He presided over one of the primordial sacrifices, from which Rudra-Śiva was excluded and then attacked, securing for himself offerings. In later Hinduism, Dakṣa is sometimes regarded as a partial incarnation of Viṣṇu and/or a son of Brahmā.

⌘ DAKṢIṆA ⌘

The fee paid by the patron to the Brahmin priests who perform a sacrifice on his behalf. Also, the name of one of the altars in the Vedic sacrifice, a semicircular altar south of the Vedi in which offerings are made to the ancestors. (*See also* Agni; Yajña.)

⌘ DĀNAVA ⌘

A class of demons, opposed to the Devas. The name means descendant of Danu or Dānu, mentioned as the mother of Vṛtra in *Ṛg Veda* 1.32. (*See also* Daitya; Deva; Rākṣasa.)

⌘ DANDEKAR, R. N. ⌘

Indologist (1909–). Born in Satara, Maharashtra, he was educated at Deccan College and the University of Heidelberg in Germany. He was professor of Sanskrit at Fergusson College in Poona (Pune), India, from 1933 to 1950, then at Pune University until his retirement in 1969. He became the director of the Bhandarkar Oriental Research Institute in Poona, where he is now emeritus. (*See also* Indology.)

⌘ DAṆḌIN ⌘

Author of the seventh century C.E. To him are attributed the work on poetics *Kavyādarśa* and the collection of short stories *Daśakumāracarita*.

⌘ DARBHA ⌘

A variety of grass used in Vedic ritual (Yajña). Darbha is sometimes identified with, sometimes distinguished from, Kuśa grass. One variety known as Darbha is *Saccharum cylindricum*. Darbha grass is said to have originated from the hair and perspiration of Varāha (Boar) Avatāra in *Matsya Purāṇa* 22.89. The term Darbha is also used for a bunch or tuft of grass. (*See also* Kuśa; Vedi; Yajña.)

⌘ DARŚANA ⌘

Sight; viewpoint. The term is used in two significant senses. Every Indian philosophical tradition is referred to as a Darśana, a point of view (see the entry Philosophical Schools for discussion of the six orthodox Darśanas). The term is also used with reference to the idea of auspicious sight, either the sight of a divine image (Mūrti) or oneself being seen by God (in the form of God's image). In the context of devotional worship (Pūjā), the form in which God can be seen is vitally important. Hindu devotional traditions generally take the position that God assumes a form so that human beings can conceive of and come to love God. Those forms are represented in images venerated in temples and homes. To see God's form is an act of devotion that is meritorious, and simultaneously to be seen by God is also meritorious. Hence many temples allow the images of the divine to be taken out of the sanctuary, where a relatively small number of devotees can have Darśana at any one time, and take them on procession through a town or region so that many devotees can have Darśana. The image is regarded as one of the forms God can take to show grace to devotees. (*See also* Mūrti; Philosophical Schools; Pūjā; Temple.)

⌘ DĀSA; DASYU ⌘

Terms used in the *Ṛg Veda* to refer to non-Āryan people encountered in India, described as dark-skinned, snub-nosed, and worshippers of phalluses. In later, post-Vedic Sanskrit the word Dāsa means slave or servant. (*See also* Āryan; Śūdra.)

⌘ DAŚAHRĀ (DUSSEHRA) ⌘

Name of a festival celebrated from the first to tenth days of the bright half of the month Āśvina (September-October). In various locations it celebrates either the victory of Rāma over Rāvaṇa, or the victory of Durgā over Mahiṣa Asura, the Buffalo Demon, where it is often known as Navarātrī Pūjā. (*See also* Durgā; Navarātrī Pūjā; Rāma.)

⌘ DAŚANĀMI ORDER ⌘

Monastic order founded by Śaṅkara in the ninth century C.E. He established four monasteries, one in each of the four corners of India: Śṛṅgerī in Tamilnadu is the headquarters of the order, Puri in the east, Badrīnāth in the Himālayas, and Dvārakā to the west being the other three. (*See also* Badrīnāth; Dvārakā; Puri; Śaṅkara; Śṛṅgerī.)

⌘ DASGUPTA, SURENDRANATH ⌘

Indologist (1885–1952). Born in eastern Bengal, he earned an M.A. in Sanskrit in 1908 and began work for the education department. He was principal of the Sanskrit College in Calcutta, lectured in philosophy at Cambridge University in 1922, and was professor of philosophy at Calcutta University until his retirement in 1945. He authored a five-volume history of Indian philosophy. (*See also* Indology.)

⌘ DAYAL, HAR ⌘

Indian nationalist leader and author (1884–1939). Dayal was born to a Hindu family in the Punjab, he earned a B.A. from Saint Stephen's College in Delhi (1903), and an M.A. from Government College in Lahore (1904), and went to study at Oxford University in England. There he became involved in the revolutionary movement, influenced by "Veer" Savarkar, and resigned his Government of India scholarship in 1907 to return to India to agitate for independence. In 1911 he went to California and served on the faculty of Stanford University. He became a leader of the San Francisco area Indian community and established the Hindu Association of the Pacific Coast in 1913, and its newspaper *Ghadr* (Revolution). He soon changed the name of the association to Ghadr Party and worked for the violent overthrow of the British colonial authorities in India. In 1914 he was arrested by U. S. Immigration officials as an undesirable alien; released on bail, he fled to Germany and spent the years of World War I there (1914–1918), trying to organize resistance to British rule in India. After the war, Dayal returned to India and became a supporter of the India Home Rule movement, and a pacifist. In 1927, he was allowed to return to Britain for the first time, and he completed his Ph.D. at the University of London in 1930. He published many works, including a book entitled *The Bodhisattva Doctrine in Buddhist Sanskrit Literature* (1932). He died in Philadelphia in 1939. (*See also* Ghadr Movement; Rāj; Savarkar, G. D.)

⌘ DAYĀNAND SARASVATĪ ⌘

Founder (1824–1883) of the Ārya Samāj reform movement. He was born to a Śiva-worshipping Brahmin family in Gujarāt, western India, and was raised in a traditional manner. He received a Vedic education and, when marriage was imminent, became a renounced ascetic (saṃnyāsin). He was particularly interested in the Upaniṣads and the practice of Yoga. About 1860, he began to develop his idea that the war described in the *Mahābhārata* was so devastating that India, which had been a nation of great technological and intellectual accomplishments, had not yet recovered from the losses then experienced. Consequently, he classified all literature according to the following categories: (1) the Vedas, which were divinely produced at the creation and are perfectly free of error; (2) ārṣa (of the Ṛṣis) literature, composed by sages in ancient times before the *Mahābhārata* war, and therefore largely reliable to the extent that it does not conflict with the Vedas; and (3) anārṣa (not of the Ṛṣis) literature, produced subsequent to the holocaust and therefore having no validity or authority. Thus, for Dayānand, the Vedic literature through the Upaniṣads is authoritative, while later works such as Purāṇas and Tantras are not. On this basis, he argued against the use of images in worship, stating that in the Vedic literature no such icons were in use. His interpretation of the Vedas was that ancient Āryans were not polytheistic, but that the many names used all referred to a single deity. Moreover, he asserted that the Vedic literature showed caste distinctions to have been less significant and more flexible than they had become more recently. These ideas became the foundation of the Ārya Samāj movement. (*See also* Ārya Samāj; Rāj; Ṛṣi; Veda.)

⌘ DE, ABHAY CHARAN ⌘

See Bhaktivedānta Swāmī Prabhupāda.

⌘ DE, S. K. ⌘

Indologist (1890–1968). Born in Calcutta and educated at Presidency College there, he was lecturer in English and Sanskrit at Calcutta University from 1913 to 1923. He went to Dhaka University as professor of Sanskrit, returning to Calcutta as professor of Sanskrit literature. (*See also* Indology.)

⌘ DEATH ⌘

One of the distinctive features of Hinduism is its attitude toward death. Because of the widespread acceptance of the idea of rebirth according to one's Karma, death is not, for most who die, a passage to an eternal afterlife, but is instead a transition to another life in a long and diverse series of lives. One's actions (Karma) in life are regarded as determining the nature of one's afterlife and rebirth, good actions leading to a good rebirth and bad actions leading to a bad rebirth. Good Karma can be rewarded with a rebirth in a heavenly realm where one enjoys the effects of one's actions in life, while bad Karma can be punished with a rebirth in hell where one suffers. Neither of these states is permanent, lasting only as long as one's Karma dictates. Only one who attains liberation from rebirth (Mokṣa) is spared another lifetime and the suffering that inevitably comes with life in human, or other, form. The dead are typically cremated, the body being burned on a pyre of wood, and the ashes and bone fragments that remain are often scattered in a river or other body of water. To die in Vārāṇasī (Banaras) is regarded as especially auspicious, for it means that one's body will be cremated and the remains immersed in the Ganges River at the most sacred location for Hindus. Consequently, many elderly Hindus who can afford to do so spend the end of their lives in Vārāṇasī. In the Vedic period (1500 to 700 B.C.E.), prior to the acceptance of the idea of rebirth, Āryans performed rituals in honor of their ancestors, offering cakes of grain and the recitation of verses of poetry to commemorate the dead. Performance of such funeral and commemorative (Śrāddha) rituals was necessary to place the deceased among the Pitṛs, or honored ancestors, who enjoyed an afterlife in a celestial realm (Pitṛ Loka). The offerings sustained them in that afterlife. These rituals have persisted despite the acceptance later of the idea of rebirth. (*See also* Ancestral Rituals; Funeral; Karma; Mokṣa; Pitṛ; Preta; Rebirth; Saṃsāra; Satī; Śrāddha; Vārāṇasī.)

⌘ DELHI; NEW DELHI ⌘

India's third-largest city and its capital. There have long been settlements in the Delhi area, apparently including the Pāṇḍava capital of Indraprastha near present-day Purāṇa Qila. There are numerous temples in the Delhi area, the most unusual one being the Lakṣmī-Nārāyaṇa Temple built by the Birla family of industrialists in 1938. Far from traditional, it is a temple at which an attempt has been made to include all the gods, numerous saints, and even the Buddha in a setting with echoes of both Mughal and north Indian temple architectures, more a tourist destination and philanthropic cultural statement than a functional temple.

⌘ DEMON ⌘

The usual English translation for various terms used in Sanskrit, including Asura, Daitya, Dānava, and Rākṣasa. The demons are opposed to the gods (Deva). (*See also* Asura; Daitya; Dānava; Deva; Rākṣasa.)

⌘ DESIRE ⌘

See Kāma.

⌘ DEVA. ⌘

God. The term is used throughout Sanskrit literature to refer to any male deity, and in the plural to refer to all the gods. (*See also* Asura; Demon; God.)

⌘ DEVADĀSĪ ⌘

Female Servant of God. The term is used especially for female temple dancers who received training in dance such as the Bharata Nāṭya tradition and perhaps also in erotic techniques. They were married to the god to whom the temple was dedicated, and the marriage may have been consummated by a priest on behalf of the god. Temple income was derived from payments by pilgrims for sex with Devadāsīs, at least at some temples. By the end of the nineteenth century, under pressure from both British authorities and Hindus who sought reforms, the tradition of employing Devadāsīs as temple servants ended. (*See also* Temple.)

⌘ DEVĪ ⌘

Goddess. The term may be used for any goddess, but is used especially for the Great Goddess, who either is herself the Absolute or in association with Śiva constitutes the Absolute. (*See also* Goddess.)

⌘ DEVOTION ⌘

See Bhakti.

⌘ DHARMA ⌘

Law; social and religious duties. The term is used with a wide array of applications. Used rarely in the *Ṛg Veda,* when Dharma does appear in that text it means proper action (as in 3.17.1, and 3.60.6). In one passage where it appears with the important term Ṛta (5.63.7), Mitra and Varuṇa, who rule the cosmos through Ṛta (cosmic order) are asked to protect the ritual vows (Vrata) with actions that uphold (Dharma) the world. The Vedic poets saw the ritual actions of sacrifice, properly performed, as supporting the cosmic order. Proper action was codified in the Dharma Sūtra and Dharma Śāstra literature, composed about the same time as the domestic ritual texts (Gṛhya Sūtras) and the Vedic ritual texts (Śrauta Sūtras), perhaps 400 B.C.E. to 400 C.E. The Dharma literature concerned primarily the social and religious duties of individuals in regard to their caste status and stage of life (Varṇāśrama Dharma). The Dharma of each social class is different. The Brahmin class is to learn the Vedic texts by memorization and transmit them to the next generation, and perform sacrificial rites for patrons. The Kṣatriya is to learn weaponry and the art of ruling so as to protect those who need protection. The Vaiśya is to raise food and livestock, and engage in trade. All three of these classes of Āryan heritage participate in Vedic rites and are "Twice-Born" through rituals of initiation into society. The fourth social class, the Śūdra, receives no such initiation, cannot participate in Vedic rites, should own no property, and has the Dharma of serving the other classes. Even lower in status is the Outcaste group, entirely lacking in Dharma and excluded from society in many ways. Acceptance of the concept of Karma reinforced the power of Dharma as a normative ideal. Rebirth according to Karma justifies inequity and hierarchy in that one is reborn in a status and with abilities and qualities appropriate to one's past actions. Only fulfilment of one's Dharma in the current life would improve one's social standing in a future life. As the *Bhagavad Gītā* maintains (3.45, and 18.47), it is better to do one's own Dharma poorly than to do another's well. In emergencies or times of social chaos, one is allowed to deviate from one's prescribed Dharma to survive, a loophole frequently cited in justification of members of classes other than Kṣatriya ruling. The *Mānava Dharma Śāstra* is the most widely known of the textual authorities. Dharma texts fall into the category of Smṛti (Remembered Tradition) and are therefore, to a considerable extent, dependent for their authority on the Vedic texts classified as Śruti (Revelation). The *Mahābhārata* contains, in addition to the *Bhagavad Gītā* in which questions of Dharma are considered in depth, a long discussion of issues relating to Dharma, Artha, and Mokṣa in the twelfth (*Śānti Parvan*) and thirteenth (*Anuśāsana Parvan*) books. The term Dharma has become, in modern usage, the Indic equivalent of the Western term religion, especially in the expression Sanātana (Eternal) Dharma as a term for Hinduism. (*See also* Adharma; Brahmin; Caste; Four Goals of Humanity; Kṣatriya; *Mānava Dharma Śāstra*; Outcaste; Ṛta; Saṃskāra; Smṛti; Śruti; Śūdra; Vaiśya.)

⌘ DHĀTṚ ⌘

Name used to refer to the Creator in Vedic literature. As supervisor of the functions of creation, procreation, matrimony, health, and long life, Dhātṛ is credited with having established the ordered world and is asked to give human beings the blessings of a good life, as, for example, in *Ṛg Veda* 10.184, and 10.190. Dhātṛ is associated with, or identified with, other gods in the Vedic literature such as Tvaṣṭṛ, Savitṛ, and Prajāpati. In later literature the name Dhātṛ is used as an epithet of Brahmā. (*See also* Brahmā; Creation; Prajāpati; Savitṛ; Tvaṣṭṛ.)

⌘ DHYĀNA ⌘

Meditation. The term is widely used in all meditation traditions with modifications to its meaning. In Patañjali's *Yoga Sūtra*, Dhyāna is the seventh of the eight stages in the practice. It involves prolonged concentration on the object of meditation, such as a Yantra or Maṇḍala such that the meditator identifies with the object. Dhyāna is preparatory to, and leads into, the eighth stage, Samādhi (Completion), in which a state of nondualistic consciousness is attained and one realizes one's identity with Brahman. Freedom from the effects of Karma and liberation from rebirth are the results of successful practice of Dhyāna that leads to Samādhi. (*See also* Consciousness, States of; Kuṇḍalinī; Mokṣa; Samādhi; Yoga; *Yoga Sūtra*.)

⌘ DĪPĀVALI (DĪWALI) ⌘

The Festival of Lights. A major Hindu festival lasting four to five days, usually in October, the central deity being Śrī-Lakṣmī, consort of Viṣṇu, the goddess of prosperity, who is invited into the home by this celebration. Some regard the festival as a celebration of the marriage of Lakṣmī and Viṣṇu, others as the return of Rāma and Sītā to Ayodhyā after defeating the demon Rāvaṇa, still others as the victory of Kṛṣṇa over the demon Naraka. The house is thoroughly cleaned prior to the festival, perhaps even freshly painted or white-washed. The festival is characterized by the lighting of oil lamps each evening, the drawing of ornate patterns (Raṅgoli), especially lotuses representative of the goddess, giving presents to children, sharing meals with relatives, and in recent decades, fireworks. According to tradition, Lakṣmī resides in oil and Gaṅgā Devī in hot water, so some Hindus take a bath in both and regard themselves as blessed by both goddesses, their bad Karma removed. (*See also* Śrī.)

⌘ DIVINE LIGHT MISSION ⌘

A religious movement founded in the early 1960s by Shri Hans Mahārāj Ji as an offshoot of the Vallabha tradition of Vaiṣṇavism. At his death in 1966, his son Guru Mahārāj Ji, then only nine years old, became the leader of the movement. He moved to the United States in 1971 and became widely publicized. Followers of Guru Mahārāj Ji were known as Premies after the Sanskrit word Prema (love) and after his actual name, Prem Pāl Singh Rawat. Many lived together communally and received instruction from the Guru. Following a rally at the Astrodome in Houston in 1973 that was poorly attended, the Divine Light Mission suffered from debts and its activities were limited. In 1974 the marriage of the Guru to an American woman led to controversy within the family and movement, and a loss of membership. (*See also* Mahārāj Ji, Guru; Vallabha.)

⌘ DOMESTIC RITUALS ⌘

See Gṛhya Sūtras; Pūjā.

⌘ DRAUPADĪ ⌘

Wife of the five Pāṇḍava brothers and the heroine of the *Mahābhārata*. That text recounts that she was born to King Drupada, born from the fire of the sacrifice that also produced her brother Dhṛṣṭadyumna. It also indicates (1.61.95) that she was an incarnation of the goddess Śrī, a goddess associated with kingship and embodying a king's success. Known also as Pāñcālī (Pāñcāla Princess) and as Kṛṣṇā (for her dark color), she was married at a Svayaṃvara (self-choice ceremony), a competition among warriors at which a princess would choose her own mate. Arjuna was the victor in the archery contest and Draupadī chose him as her husband. When the two of them went to where the other Pāṇḍava brothers and their mother were, Arjuna proclaimed, "Look what I have won!" but his mother, without looking, said, "Share equally with your brothers, as always." Because a mother's word is the highest duty, Arjuna and his brothers were all wed to Draupadī, and each had a son by her. At the Rājasūya ceremony, Draupadī saved her husbands by insisting that she could not have been wagered and lost if Yudhiṣṭhira had already lost himself at dice. The shameful way in which the Kauravas treated her in the assembly led Draupadī to vow never to adorn her hair until she could dress it in the blood of her abusers, and Bhīma vowed to kill the chief Kaurava offenders. When they were exiled to the forest, she urged her husbands to reclaim their kingdom by force, but Yudhiṣṭhira prevailed on them to fulfill the terms of the agreement and wait thirteen years. After the battle in which the Kauravas were killed, she sat beside King Yudhiṣṭhira as queen. In many respects, Draupadī incarnates traits of the goddess Śrī. In Tamilnadu, Draupadī is worshipped as the Goddess, her deeds in the *Mahābhārata* celebrated as evidence of her protective abilities. She is regarded as benevolent and Śrī-like in the prewar and postwar periods, and fiercely Kālī-like during the fighting, her unkempt hair suggestive of asceticism and her desire for revenge reminiscent of Kālī's penchant for blood sacrifices. Tamil festivals in her honor feature the enactment of dramas based on Tamil versions of the *Mahābhārata*, and worshippers vow to walk on hot coals if she will grant their requests. (*See also* Goddess; *Mahābhārata*; Pāṇḍavas; Śrī.)

⌘ DRAVIDIAN ⌘

Name of a language family that includes the south Indian languages Tamil, Malayalam, Telugu, and Kannada. By extension, the term is used to refer to the people who speak these languages. Recently the term has been contrasted with "Āryan" to emphasize the indigenous character and culture of the Dravidian people in contrast to the north Indian or even "foreign" culture represented by those of Indo-European language and culture. (*See also* Āryan; Indo-European; Tamil.)

⌘ DREAM ⌘

See Consciousness, States of.

⌘ DUMÉZIL, GEORGES ⌘

French scholar (1898–1986) of Indo-European languages and cultures. Born and educated in Paris, he was steeped in the sociological tradition of Marcel Mauss and Émile Durkheim. As professor of Indo-European civilizations in Paris, and a master of numerous languages, Dumézil did much to revive the comparative study of Indo-European linguistics and cultures. His grand theory of the tripartite nature of the thought and social organization of the inheritors of the Indo-European tradition, while corrected as to certain details, has been widely accepted. He shows how the theology and social organization were parallel, each structured as three groups, and each group around a specific principle. His studies of Sanskrit literature, notably the Vedic collection and *Mahābhārata*, has shed much light on previously ignored or misunderstood aspects of the ritual, religion, and historical traditions of the Greeks, Romans, Celts, and other peoples of Indo-European heritage, and vice versa. His monumental three-volume study of the *Mahābhārata*, entitled *Mythe et épopée*, argued that the poets who created it wove into the story correspondences between the mythic accounts of gods and the heroic accounts of *Mahābhārata* characters, so that the characters are presented as transpositions of gods, Arjuna the son of Indra representing Indra, Aśvatthāman representing Śiva, etc. His theoretical formulations have been very influential. (*See also* Indo-European; Indology, *Mahābhārata*.)

⌘ DURGĀ ⌘

Impassable; unapproachable. Durgā is the name of a goddess whose appearance is often beautiful but whose nature is fierce and ascetic. Created from the combined Tejas or fiery energy of the gods, who had been defeated by Mahiṣa Asura, the Buffalo Demon, she rode forth on her lion to battle the enemy. As with myths of Avatāras, her function is to restore Dharma and the cosmic balance, and to defeat the enemies of the gods. One of the earliest and most influential accounts of her mythology is found in the Devīmāhātmya (Praise of the Goddess), a section of the *Mārkaṇḍeya Purāṇa*. There it is recounted how, in her battles with various demons, she emits the form of Kālī, a fierce goddess; Kālī drinks up the blood of Raktabījā, drops of whose blood falling to the ground cause other demons to arise. In this fashion, the goddess benefits the world and achieves the purpose of the gods. Durgā is usually regarded as a celibate goddess whose asceticism empowers her, but she may also be regarded as the consort and Śakti of Śiva, depending on the tradition. Durgā is prominent in Tantric traditions, and is also one of the five deities worshipped by Smārta Brahmins, for some of whom she is the chosen deity. The annual festival associated with her is the Navarātrī, known in Bengal as Durgā Pūjā. In many regions of India, Durgā's victory over Mahiṣa is celebrated at the end of Daśahrā (Dussehrā), known to her devotees also as Navarātrī and Durgā Pūjā, and in villages she is offered a water buffalo in sacrifice. Such rituals are not Vedic in style, and may well be a very ancient practice comparable to or even derived from rites of the Indus Valley Civilization. Durgā is typically represented iconographically slaying the Buffalo Demon, her calm expression contrasting with her activity of beheading the demon. Many scholars think that Brahmanical culture accepted and endorsed the ancient practices of goddess worship through inclusion of her myth of origins in Purāṇa texts. (*See also* Daśahrā; Goddess; Kālī; Mahiṣa; Navarātrī Pūjā; Śakti.)

⌘ DUSSEHRA ⌘

See Daśahrā.

⌘ DVAITA VEDĀNTA ⌘

Dualistic Vedānta, a theology associated particularly with Madhva. It arose in opposition to Śaṅkara's Advaita (nondualistic) Vedānta, and may be regarded as a variation on Rāmānuja's theology. As in other Vedānta traditions, Brahman is recognized as the Absolute, but is identified with Viṣṇu as Supreme Lord. The souls of individual human beings are regarded as eternal and distinct entities, though each is dependent on God, even in the liberated state. Those who live ethical lives and who receive God's grace attain liberation, the best means of living ethically being seen as the Path of Devotion. One of the unusual aspects of

Dvaita Vedānta is the possibility it offers of eternal separation from God for those who are evil, so that such a person is not simply subject to bad Karma for a time but perhaps for eternity. (*See also* Advaita Vedānta; Madhva; Vedānta; Viśiṣṭha-Advaita Vedānta.)

⌘ DVĀRAKĀ ⌘

Site in Gujarāt of the capital of Kṛṣṇa after he fled Mathurā, and from which he returned to kill Kaṃsa. Dvārakā has a temple complex dedicated to Kṛṣṇa. The temple's main spire is some twenty meters high, supported by sixty columns. Devotees make pilgrimage here to walk where Kṛṣṇa walked. There have been reports of substantial ruins in the ocean offshore. It is also the site of Kālikā Pīṭha, one of the four monasteries of the Daśanāmi Order founded by Śaṅkara in the ninth century. (*See also* Daśanāmi Order; Kṛṣṇa; Śaṅkara; Temple.)

⌘ DWARF AVATĀRA ⌘

See Avatāra; Vāmana.

⌘ DYAUḤ PITṚ ⌘

Heavenly Father, a Deva celebrated in the Veda. The name is cognate with Jupiter, ruler of the Roman gods, and Zeus Pater of the Greeks, and they appear to embody the same concept. Dyauḥ Pitṛ already in the *Ṛg Veda* seems to be a god whose prominence is receding; he is celebrated in relatively few poems, often paired with Earth (Pṛthivī) as a divine couple whose offspring is the Sun. (*See also* Earth.)

— E —

⌘ EARTH ⌘

A goddess in Brahmanism and Hinduism. In the Veda, Pṛthivī is paired with Dyauḥ Pitṛ (Heavenly Father) as a divine couple in certain poems (*Ṛg Veda* 1.159, and 1.160, for example), where they are regarded as parents of the Sun. In later Hindu traditions, the same name is used for the earth, but Bhū or Bhūdevī and other names are also frequently seen.

⌘ EKA ⌘

The One. A term used at times to refer to Ultimate Reality, or the Absolute, as in *Ṛg Veda* 10.82, and 10.129.2. In this famous verse (*Ṛg Veda* 1.164.46) the One is Ultimate Reality behind the manifold appearances: "They call it Indra, Mitra, Varuṇa, Agni, and the celestial bird that flies. The wise speak of the One in many ways; they call it Agni, Yama, Mātarīśvan."

⌘ EKĀDAŚĪ ⌘

The eleventh day after a new moon day or full moon day. Many worshippers of Viṣṇu regard such days as ideal for fasting as a religious observance.

⌘ ELEPHANTA ⌘

An island near Bombay that has an impressive Śiva temple complex carved from the living rock. The most famous sculpture at Elephanta is of Śiva as the Trinity (Trīmurti) in which he takes the roles of Brahmā the Creator and Viṣṇu the Preserver as well as Śiva the Destroyer. The complex probably dates from the fifth through eighth centuries C.E., and may have been carved out under the patronage of the Rāṣṭrakūta dynasty. Named Gharapuri (Fortress City), it was renamed by the Portuguese after the large stone elephant at the landing. (*See also* Trinity.)

⌘ ELIADE, MIRCEA ⌘

Historian of religions (1907–1986). Born in Bucharest, Romania, he studied Indian philosophy and Sanskrit at Calcutta University (1928–31), and was appointed a lecturer in the history of religions and metaphysics at the University of Bucharest (1933–39). During World War II, he was in the Romanian diplomatic service, after which he taught at the Sorbonne in Paris, and at the University of Chicago (1957–85). Eliade was one of the major figures in the comparative study of religion, or the history of religions discipline. His many published works include *Yoga: Immortality and Freedom* (1958), and *Patanjali and Yoga* (1969; French edition 1962), as well as novels and other works. (*See also* Indology.)

⌘ ELLORA (ELŪRĀ) ⌘

A major site of Hindu temples and cave shrines near Aurangabad. In addition to a dozen Buddhist caves and five Jain caves for meditation and worship, there are seventeen Hindu caves and a large Śiva temple called Kailāsa or Kailāsanātha carved from a cliffside. The Kailāsa temple is the finest example of rock-cut temple architecture, covering twice the area of the Parthenon and one-and-a-half times its height. It was produced by carving away a substantial mountain, and it is estimated that some 200,000 tons of rock were removed in the process. One of the most impressive pieces of sculpture adorning the temple depicts Rāvaṇa shaking Kailāsa to demonstrate his strength. Viṣṇu's Avatāras are featured in a number of the caves. The Hindu shrines date from about the eighth century C.E.

⌘ ENLIGHTENMENT ⌘

See Jīvan-mukti; Mokṣa.

⌘ ETAŚA ⌘

Name of a sage whom Indra saved in a battle with a rival, Sūrya (see *Ṛg Veda* 1.61.15, and 1.121.13, and 2.19.5). It is also the name of one of the celestial horses that pulls the chariot of the sun god Sūrya.

— F —

⌘ FISH AVATĀRA ⌘

See Avatāra; Matsya.

⌘ FIVE M's ⌘

Five things that are to play a role in Tantric rituals of the Left-Hand type. Known collectively as the Five M's (Pañca Makāra) because each item begins with the letter M, namely, Māṃsa (meat), Matsya (fish), Mudrā (parched or fermented grain), Mada (alcohol), and Maithuna (sexual intercourse). Meat and fish violate the vegetarian ideal of diet and ritual Pūjā offerings, alcohol is regarded as harmful, and sex with anyone other than one's spouse is a violation of Dharma guidelines. Mudrā is a term the precise meaning of which in this context is disputed; fermented grain would be an alcoholic drink, and parched grain would be unacceptable as a Pūjā offering, hence either meaning may apply. Hindus of non-Tantric traditions avoid ritual use of these, but Tantrics seek to use the power available from these substances and practices to aid in attaining liberation, and intentionally depart from social conventions in ritual settings under the guidance of a Guru in an effort to attain liberation from dualistic thinking. (*See also* Guru; Kāpālika; Kashmir Śaivism; Left-Hand Tantra; Right-Hand Tantra; Tantra.)

⌘ FOUR GOALS OF HUMANITY ⌘

The four Puruṣārtha, or goals of human life: Kāma (desire, especially for sexual fulfillment), Artha (profit, especially in one's career or livelihood), Dharma (fulfillment of social and religious duties), and Mokṣa (liberation from rebirth). From the time of the early Upaniṣads (perhaps 600 B.C.E.) these four pursuits were all regarded as appropriate activities in which people should be engaged. However, the arrangement of the four is hierarchical, ranging from the purely personal to the socially beneficial, and finally to the transcendence of the first three goals in pursuit of the fourth. Kāma includes the range of desires from sexual satisfaction to desire for heavenly rewards from acts of ritual sacrifice. Artha encompasses all aspects of worldly success, and is particularly evident in the actions of rulers, for whom success benefits their entire realm as well as themselves personally. Dharma varies depending on the social class of the individual, but is incumbent on all, and involves fulfilling one's social and religious obligations through abiding by social strictures, performing ritual activity, etc. The fourth goal, liberation from rebirth, is not obligatory; the attainment of Mokṣa is difficult and requires abandonment of the other three pursuits so that one can focus single-mindedly on this transcendent goal. The three mundane goals oriented toward worldly success, as envisioned in the Vedic sacrificial tradition, are rendered secondary to Mokṣa in the world-renouncing ascetic emphasis of the Upaniṣads, where the goal of attaining liberation from rebirth is seen as the only valid purpose of human life. The first three goals each have Sanskrit literature that systematically expounds upon their place in human life: the *Kāma Sūtra, Artha Śāstra*, and numerous Dharma Śāstra and Dharma Sūtra texts. (*See also* Artha; *Artha Śāstra*; Caste; Dharma; Kāma; *Kāma Sūtra*; *Mānava Dharma Śāstra*; Mokṣa.)

⌘ FOUR STAGES OF LIFE ⌘

Hindu legal authorities such as Manu describe the duties and legal status of people as varying in regard to their stage of life (Āśrama) and caste (Varṇa). Four different stages of life are described: (1) Brahmacārin, the celibate student of the Veda who is to live with his Guru; (2) Gṛhastha, the householder who is married and has responsibility for a family and career; (3) Vānaprastha, the forest-dweller who has retired from active engagement with family and career responsibilities, living with his wife in a hut; and (4) Saṃnyāsin, the fully renounced ascetic who has dedicated himself entirely to the pursuit of Mokṣa (liberation from rebirth). These stages of life apply only to Twice-Born (Dvija) males of Āryan heritage, and largely to Brahmins rather than the other castes; non-Āryan Śūdras and Outcastes do not have the opportunity to be educated in the Vedic heritage and to renounce social and religious duties. *Mānava Dharma Śāstra* (6.87–96) makes clear its high regard for the Gṛhastha stage of life, for householders support all those in the other stages, and the text devotes most of its attention to the householder and his duties. Most men did not leave the householder stage of life, but some aspired to achieve spiritual freedom through dedicating themselves to religious pursuits late in life. When one sees one's grandson (*Mānava Dharma Śāstra* 6.2), one may retire to the forest for a contemplative life as a Vānaprastha, and if one aspires to it, renounce one's Dharma, caste status, name, and former identity entirely, becoming a homeless, ascetic wanderer (Saṃnyāsin). Such a person seeks liberation from rebirth through meditation and other religious practices. This system of four stages of life allowed for the practice of renunciation, but only late in life, after the fulfillment of one's responsibilities, including continuing one's lineage. Legal authorities expressed this in terms of a Brahmin having three debts: to the Ṛṣis, satisfied by learning the Veda as a student, to the gods, satisfied by sacrifices, and to the Pitṛs, satisfied by having a son to continue the family line and the offerings to the ancestors. Only after repaying these debts could one abandon the householder stage of life for the forest-dweller or renouncer stages. (*See also* Brahmacarya; Caste; *Mānava Dharma Śāstra*; Marriage; Sacred Thread; Saṃnyāsa; Saṃskāra; Twice-Born; Upanayana.)

⌘ FUNERAL ⌘

After death, a Hindu is typically cremated, the body being burned on a pyre of wood. Traditionally, a funeral ceremony (Antyeṣṭi) is conducted immediately after death, in association with cremation. The Antyeṣṭi is performed once, in contrast to the Śrāddha ceremonies, which include daily offering of water and periodic offerings of food to the deceased to sustain them in the afterlife among the Ancestors (Pitṛ). *Mānava Dharma Śāstra* (5.57–169) presents detailed instructions on how to purify oneself from the ritual pollution associated with the death of a relative. (*See also* Ancestral Rites; Death; Gayā; Pitṛ; Preta; Satī; Śrāddha; Vārāṇasī.)

— G —

⌘ GADAR MOVEMENT ⌘

See Ghadr Movement.

⌘ GĀNDHĪ, MOHANDAS K. ⌘

Indian nationalist and spiritual leader (1869–1948), often called Mahātmā (Great Soul), a title usually given to saints. He was born in Porbandar, Gujarat, in western India to a family of the Vaiśya (Commoner) caste, though his father and grandfather had been prime ministers of local princely states. He went to London at age eighteen to study law, and obtained his law degree. He practiced law in India for two years, then accepted an offer to move to South Africa, then a British colony as was India, to represent people of Indian heritage in legal disputes. He spent the next twenty-one years working to liberalize the discriminatory laws of South Africa, during which time he disciplined himself with prayer, fasting, and ascetic practices similar to those of the traditional Hindu renouncer (Saṃnyāsin). From South Africa he followed with interest the development of the independence movement in India, and returned there in 1914. He began to use civil disobedience as a method of protest against British colonial authorities and practices, but early efforts led to violence and Gāndhī was jailed from 1922 to 1924. In 1925 he was elected president of the Indian National Congress, the main representative body attempting to negotiate with the British on behalf of the people of India. A good example of Gāndhī's method is the Great Salt March of 1930 in which he led a 200-mile march to the sea to manufacture and give away sea salt, thereby breaking the British law requiring payment of a tax on salt and resulting in a public trial and imprisonment that embarrassed British authorities and led to elimination of the tax. Gāndhī often referred to his approach to political activism as Satyāgraha (holding onto truth), and to the importance of the principle of Ahiṃsā (nonviolence). Gāndhī also fasted, both as a personal ascetic discipline and as a method of mobilizing support for a cause. Both his emphasis on Ahiṃsā and on fasting may have been influenced by Jainism, a religious tradition that was strong in his native Gujarat and with which he was familiar. He quoted from many religious texts, Hindu, Muslim, and Christian, but the *Bhagavad Gītā* was his particular favorite. His interpretation of the text was that it called for selfless dedication to action, while being unattached to the possible fruits or outcomes of that action, that such outcomes were in God's hands. For his view, vigorously expressed, that only an independent India could join in a war against Nazi tyranny, Gāndhī was jailed for most of World War II. After the war Gāndhī was one of the main negotiators with the British regarding independence, which was finally granted in 1947, but British India was partitioned into the nations of India and Pakistan, with considerable loss of life among those who moved from one new country to the other. He was assassinated in Delhi on January 30, 1948, by a Hindu nationalist who felt that Gāndhī had allowed the British and Muslims to take away a portion of India, and that Gāndhī was too kindly disposed toward Muslims. Gāndhī's legacy is his emphasis on Ahiṃsā and Satyāgraha, the method of nonviolent civil disobedience as political protest, and that under his leadership India gained independence. For his disciplined, simple lifestyle, for drawing on religion as a source of personal strength and community mobilization, and for his dedication to the betterment of all Indians, he was acclaimed a Mahātmā. Martin Luther King, Jr., drew inspiration from Gāndhī's example in his leadership of the civil rights movement in the United States. (*See also* Ahiṃsā; *Bhagavad Gītā*; Ghadr Movement; Satyāgraha; Tilak, Bal Gangadhar.)

⌘ GAṆEŚA ⌘

A popular god worshipped by many Hindus as the Lord of Obstacles. He is unique for his appearance, with the head of an elephant on a rotund human body. The myth of his origin can be found in Purāṇa texts dating back to about the fifth century C.E., and in iconography of the same era. The goddess Pārvatī, wife of Śiva, missed her husband who was off in the Himālayas doing Yoga, and for companionship and protection she rubbed some sandalwood unguent off her body, forming it into the shape of a man. She marvelled at her powers in creating this "son" and commanded him to guard her door while she bathed, letting in no one at all. Then Śiva came home and wanted to see his wife, but Gaṇeśa blocked his entrance as she had commanded. Śiva's protests about being the Lord of the Universe were to no avail, and a great battle ensued that ended only when Śiva cut off the head of Gaṇeśa. Pārvatī refused to let Śiva in until he brought Gaṇeśa back to life. Desperate to win back his wife's favor, Śiva dispatched his entourage (Gaṇa) to find a head. They returned with the head of an elephant, which was put in place. Gaṇeśa came to life and worshipped Śiva, who adopted him and gave him command over his entourage (hence the name, Lord of the Gaṇa) and stationed him at the doorway, empowering him to facilitate or thwart all undertakings. This myth about the origin of the Lord of Obstacles associates him with Śiva and explains his qualities. Scholars have suggested that he may be an ancient deity of tribal peoples of India, later taken into Brahmanical culture. An annual festival, Gaṇeśa Pūjā or Gaṇeśa Caturthī, is celebrated throughout India in August-September, and with special exuberance in Bombay and Pune. Devotees construct Gaṇeśa Maṇḍalas, large statues of the god, some in very traditional iconographic style, some in surprisingly modern, humorous styles such as a Disco Gaṇeśa or Gaṇeśa in Jurassic Park! At the turn of the century, the nationalist Bal Gangadhar Tilak promoted this festival as a means of instilling Hindu national pride and rallying Indians to oppose British colonial rule of India. Gaṇeśa is worshipped by many Hindus at the beginning of enterprises of many kinds (such as travel or marriage or the opening of a new business) for the removal of obstacles so that success will be attained. Frequently he is also worshipped before a Hindu worships other deities, for the same reason. Gaṇeśa's popularity is due in large measure to the fact that he is seen as accessible and not so transcendent that one cannot bring mundane problems and worldly concerns. Gaṇeśa is not worshipped to attain liberation from rebirth, but for success in this life. (*See also* Pārvatī; Tilak, Bal Gangadhar; Santoshi Mā; Śiva.)

⌘ GAṆEŚAPURI ĀŚRAMA ⌘

A meditation center maintained by the Siddha Yoga tradition of Muktānanda. Located some ninety kilometers northeast of Bombay, it is in a pastoral setting. Founded in 1949 by Bhagwān Nityānanda, it grew particularly under the leadership of his disciple Muktānanda. After the latter's death in 1982, leadership passed to Swāmī Cidvilāsānandā. (*See also* Muktānanda; Siddha Yoga.)

⌘ GAṄGĀ ⌘

See Ganges River.

⌘ GANGES RIVER ⌘

One of the major rivers of South Asia, flowing out of the Himālaya Mountains and across north India from west to east, emptying into the Bay of Bengal near Calcutta. It is seen as sacred by many Hindus, and as the most sacred river in India. It is regarded as the most auspicious funeral if, after cremation, the ashes of a deceased person can be immersed in the waters of the Ganges, particularly at Vārāṇasī (Banaras). Many Hindus make pilgrimage to the Ganges, bathe in it for its reputed power to remove one's bad Karma, and take Ganges water home with them. (*See also* Vārāṇasī; Yamunā River.)

⌘ GARUḌA ⌘

The divine bird, vehicle of Viṣṇu and the mythic enemy of snakes. Temples throughout south India have columns erected as Garuḍa's perches. (*See also* Viṣṇu.)

⌘ GAUḌAPĀDA ⌘

Author of the *Māṇḍūkya Kārikā,* an Advaita Vedānta text (eighth century C.E.). He is reputed to have been the Guru of the Guru of Śaṅkara. (*See also* Advaita Vedānta; Śaṅkara.)

⌘ GAYĀ ⌘

Pilgrimage site sacred to Hindus. Viṣṇu is said to have granted Gayā the power to remove bad Karma, and pilgrims offer funeral cakes (Piṇḍa) here to improve the afterlife of ancestors. The Viṣṇupāda temple, built in 1787, has a forty-centimeter-long footprint of Viṣṇu imprinted into rock and surrounded by a silver basin where devotees make offerings. Nearby is Bodh Gayā, where the Buddha attained Nirvāṇa.

⌘ GĀYATRĪ ⌘

Name of a verse in the *Ṛg Veda* (3.62.10), known also as the Sāvitrī Mantra because it addresses the god Savitṛ, asking that he enlighten our minds. The verse is often regarded as the single most important verse in the Veda, and is taught to every traditionally educated Brahmin. Many recite the verse each morning. Gāyatrī is also the name of a type of Vedic meter having twenty-four syllables, and is sometimes used as the name of a wife of Brahmā. (*See also* Sāvitrī.)

⌘ GHADR MOVEMENT (also GADAR or GHADAR) ⌘

Name of a revolutionary movement that sought the violent overthrow of British colonial authority in India. Under the leadership of Har Dayal, immigrants to North America along the West Coast in 1913 formed the organization known as the Hindu (or Hindustani) Association of the Pacific Coast, and soon thereafter known as the Ghadr Party, headquartered in San Francisco. Its ambitions included fomenting rebellion among Indian troops serving in the British Army, smuggling arms into India to anti-British activists, and gaining support from the United States and other governments for the independence of India. With the outbreak of World War I in 1914, Indian troops were called to fight in Europe on behalf of Britain. In addition, the exclusion of a group of Punjabi immigrants to Canada who were forced to stay aboard their ship, the *Komagata Maru*, angered many in the immigrant community in both Canada and the United States. These events galvanized the Indian community, and hundreds of volunteers began to return to India to work for revolution. British intelligence was well aware of these plans, however, and many of the activists were arrested as they landed in India; forty-two were sentenced to death and 114 to life in prison for their efforts. After World War I, the Ghadr Party became less a factor in the independence movement, and with independence in 1947, suspended its activities altogether. (*See also* Dayal, Har; Gāndhī, Mohandās; Rāj; Tilak, Bal Gangadhar.)

⌘ GHĀṬ ⌘

Name in Hindi (Ghaṭṭa in Sanskrit) for a set of stairs leading down to water in which one can bathe and offer religious devotion.

⌘ *GĪTAGOVINDA* ⌘

Song of the Cowherd (Kṛṣṇa); the title of a Sanskrit poem by Jayadeva. Composed in the twelfth century C.E. in eastern India, the *Gītagovinda* became popular almost immediately. Already in the thirteenth century, it was being quoted in an inscription in Gujarāt, western India. Vaiṣṇavas all over India, but particularly in eastern India, know and love this unique poem. Jayadeva, the author, was a Brahmin whose mastery of Sanskrit is evident in his poetic language, but he also has been innovative in both the language and structure of his work. The *Gītagovinda* is remarkable for its elaborate patterns of alliteration, rhythm, and the use of verses that rhyme at the end of the line, not a feature valued in Sanskrit poetics but typical of folksongs in Bengal. The text is structured as a cycle of twenty-four songs for which melody and rhythm are specified for musical accompaniment. Between the songs are recitative verses in the meters of classical Kāvya poetry. The *Gītagovinda* is conceived as a work to be performed, and the Jagannātha temple of Puri performed it regularly for centuries. The subject of the work is the love between Kṛṣṇa and the Gopī Rādhā, the many moods of their erotic relationship set in the context of their divinity, he as Kṛṣṇa-Viṣṇu whose various incarnations have repeatedly saved the world, she as Śrī-Lakṣmī, his consort and lover. The Bengali saint Caitanya in the sixteenth century lived in Puri and became very enamored of Jayadeva's work, probably from performances at the Jagannātha temple, and the text has been regarded as sacred in the traditions of Vaiṣṇavism that trace their lineage to Caitanya. Vaiṣṇava theologians, such as the Gosvāmins, have seen in their relationship the model for the devotee's relationship to God; just as Rādhā selflessly loved God without regard to social convention or propriety, the devotee should love God without reservation. Jayadeva's text is one of the finest examples of sustained evocation of the Rasa of love (Śṛṅgāra) in the history of Sanskrit literature. (*See also Bhāgavata Purāṇa*; Caitanya; Gosvāmins; *Harivaṃśa*; Jagannātha; Jayadeva; Kṛṣṇa; Puri; Rādhā; Rasa.)

⌘ GOD ⌘

Hindus have many different conceptions of God, both personal and impersonal. Given the diversity of Hindu conceptions and the connotations inherent in the term God, terms such as the Absolute or Ultimate Reality are useful when discussing Hinduism. The term God is the English translation for various Sanskrit terms, including Deva and Devatā, and is a term best used in reference to the Absolute conceived as a being with a particular personality, form, and attributes. Theistic traditions of devotion (Bhakti) tend to be monotheistic, seeing all divine functions and forms to be manifestations of the one God who is the object of worship in that tradition. However, the Vedic tradition was polytheistic, acknowledging the existence of multiple divinities and invoking them together in different combinations in many of the Vedic poems. The Smārta tradition continues the Vedic heritage in certain respects, and invokes five deities in the context of its rituals of worship. Nontheistic traditions of Hinduism conceive the Absolute to be formless and beyond all limitations imposed by attributing names and qualities to Ultimate Reality. The term Brahman is typically used for this impersonal Absolute, as conceived, for example, in the monistic Advaita Vedānta tradition. All Hindu religious and philosophical traditions are concerned with the relationship between the Absolute and human beings, and present means by which the human being can attain union with or proximity to the Absolute. (*See also* Bhakti; Brahman;

Deva; Devī; Gaṇeśa; Goddess; Indra; Īśa; Iṣṭadevatā; Philosophical Schools; Saguṇa Brahman; Śiva; Skanda; Viṣṇu.)

⌘ GODDESS ⌘

One of the striking features of Hinduism is the prominence of the divine feminine principle in the form of goddesses. Although the Vedic and Brahmanical traditions, as represented in the Vedic literature, did not prominently feature goddesses, Aditi was revered as a mother figure who gave birth to the major gods of the Veda, the Ādityas. Sarasvatī and Vāc were praised as goddesses overseeing learning and eloquence, vital qualities in the successful execution of the Vedic sacrifice. Uṣas, the Dawn, is celebrated in a number of Vedic poems of great literary merit as a beautiful goddess. With the emergence of popular devotional movements, worship of the goddess becomes more evident. Many scholars think that the Indus Valley Civilization worshipped a goddess, and that the emergence of goddess worship in Hinduism is at least partially the result of a resurgence of those ideas and practices many centuries later. Hindu goddesses are often associated with a god as his consort, as is Pārvatī or Mīnākṣī with Śiva, or Śrī (Lakṣmī) with Viṣṇu, or Rādhā with Kṛṣṇa; in such cases, the goddesses typically present a benign and motherly aspect. A very different aspect of the divine feminine, however, is presented by other goddesses such as Durgā who was brought into existence to kill the Buffalo Demon (Mahiṣa Asura), or by Kālī who is fierce in appearance and tolerates no evil. These warrior goddesses are often celibate and unmarried, not associated with gods as their consorts, and are sometimes regarded as the Absolute, creator and sustainer of the cosmos. Particularly in association with Śiva, the goddess is called Śakti, and may be regarded as constituting Ultimate Reality with Śiva, or as enlivening Śiva; without her he would be a mere corpse. Tantric traditions particularly emphasize the power and importance of the feminine principle. (*See also* Aditi; Draupadī; Durgā; Earth; God; Kālī; Mīnākṣī; Pārvatī; Prakṛti; Rādhā; Śakti; Santoshi Mā; Sarasvatī; Sāvitrī; Śrī; Śrīvidyā Tantra; Tantra; Vāc.)

⌘ GOLOKA ⌘

The Realm of Cattle, a name for the celestial paradise of Kṛṣṇa, and synonymous with Vṛndāvana. (*See also* Govinda; Kṛṣṇa; Vaikuṇṭha; Vṛndāvana.)

⌘ GONDA, JAN ⌘

Indologist (1905–). Born in Gouda, the Netherlands, he attended the University of Utrecht and earned the Ph.D. in 1929. He was professor of Sanskrit from 1932 to 1970 at Utrecht, and has been a prolific author on many subjects. (*See also* Indology.)

⌘ GOPĪ ⌘

Cowherdess; milkmaid. The term is used especially to refer to the women of the Vraja region who were lovers of Kṛṣṇa. First in the *Harivaṃśa*, later and more explicitly in the *Bhāgavata Purāṇa* and *Gītagovinda*, the love of the Gopīs for Kṛṣṇa is celebrated as the ideal of selfless devotion. They were willing to desert their husbands and risk incurring the disapproval of society to be in the presence of Kṛṣṇa. Their love for him was pure, and untainted by considerations of worldly concerns such as wealth or social conventions. The Gosvāmin theologians wrote that theirs is the most intimate of loving relationships one can have to God, and as such they are the model for devotees to emulate, though relating to Kṛṣṇa as his servant, parent, or friend is also laudable and beneficial. Devotees in Vaiṣṇava traditions have been encouraged to visualize themselves as Gopīs in Vṛndāvana to aid in transforming themselves into perfectly devoted lovers of God. Though she is not mentioned by name in earlier literature, Rādhā emerged as the most important Gopī and most beloved of Kṛṣṇa in the *Gītagovinda*, and is regarded as such in later traditions. (*See also* Caitanya; *Gītagovinda*; Gosvāmins; Kṛṣṇa; Rādhā; Radhakrishnan; Vṛndāvana.)

⌘ GORAKHNĀTH ⌘

Name of the second Guru in the lineage of the Nāth Yogīs (twelfth-thirteenth century C.E.). He is regarded as a Siddha (a perfected saint), and as the inventor of Haṭha Yoga. He is also credited with foundation of the Kāṇphaṭa sect of ascetics. (*See also* Haṭha Yoga; Kāṇphaṭa; Nāth; Siddha.)

⌘ GOSVĀMINS ⌘

Six theologians of the Vaiṣṇava tradition, followers of Caitanya, who lived in Vṛndāvana in the sixteenth century C.E. and formulated the theology of Gauḍīya (Bengali) Vaiṣṇavism. Of the six, Rūpa and Jīva were the most prolific and important authors. The Gosvāmin theologians drew upon the aesthetic theory of Rasa (in which śṛṅgāra, love, is regarded as the most effective primary Rasa for a work of art) to articulate their devotional system. The Gosvāmins utilized the terminology of this aesthetic theory, but in important ways changed its purpose. For them, Kṛṣṇa became the only hero (nāyaka), and his life story the only play; moreover, the spectator was transformed from a passive observer relishing the state of consciousness evoked to an active participant in the drama itself. And while the aesthetic theorist Abhinavagupta had written that the Rasa experience was analogous to the attainment of Mokṣa (liberation from rebirth) but only temporary, lasting as long as the drama that was its catalyst, Rūpa Gosvāmin wrote that the attainment of Rasa through Kṛṣṇa Bhakti (devotion) was equivalent to Mokṣa. Associates of Kṛṣṇa depicted in the scriptures are taken as the models for loving relationships to him, and one is to identify oneself with one of these associates. Four positive relationships with Kṛṣṇa are enumerated: (1) servant (dāsa), (2) parent (vatsālya), (3) friend (sākhya), and (4) lover (madhurya). All four relationships are regarded as varieties of love; indeed, the objective is to develop loving devotion to Kṛṣṇa in one or another of these ways. (*See also* Abhinavagupta; Caitanya; Gopī; Kṛṣṇa; Rasa; Vṛndāvana.)

⌘ GOVARDHANA, MOUNT ⌘

Mountain some twenty-six kilometers west of Mathurā. Vaiṣṇavas hold it sacred for the mythic account of Kṛṣṇa lifting the mountain to shelter residents from Indra's rainstorm. Pilgrims circumambulate the mountain as part of a larger pilgrimage through the region known as the Ban Yātra, a tour of the forests sacred to Kṛṣṇa in the Vraja area associated with his youth. (*See also Bhāgavata Purāṇa*; Kṛṣṇa; Vṛndāvana.)

⌘ GOVINDA ⌘

Cow-finder; herdsman. A name of Kṛṣṇa. (*See also Gītagovinda*; Kṛṣṇa.)

⌘ GṚHYA SŪTRAS ⌘

Domestic ritual texts. These late Vedic texts, composed about the same time as the Dharma Śāstra and Śrauta Sūtra literature (perhaps 400 B.C.E. to 400 C.E.), treat systematically the rituals required for performance in the homes of those of Āryan heritage.

⌘ GUṆA ⌘

String; attribute; quality. The Sāṃkhya philosophical school held that all things in nature (Prakṛti) have varying proportions of the three Guṇas: Sattva (purity), Rajas (energy), and Tamas (inertia). (*See also* Nirguṇa Brahman; Saguṇa Brahman; Sāṃkhya.)

⌘ GUPTA ⌘

Name of a powerful dynasty that ruled most of north India from about 320 to 500 C.E., and the Bengal region until about 550. The dynasty is noteworthy for its patronage of religious institutions and groups, not only Hindu but Buddhist and Jain as well. The large Buddhist monastic university at Nālandā, the finest educational institution of its time in India, was founded and well endowed by Gupta monarchs and their families and ministers, as were other Buddhist sites such as Bodh Gayā and Sāñcī. Gupta rulers performed Vedic horse sacrifices and proclaimed themselves parama-Bhāgavata (preeminent devotees of Viṣṇu-Kṛṣṇa), signalling their support for Hindu-Brahmanical culture as well. Numerous symbols of Vaiṣṇava religious traditions are found on their coins (Viṣṇu as the Archer Śārṅgin, Viṣṇu's consort the goddess Lakṣmī, and Garuḍa, for example) as well as images of the king receiving a gift from Viṣṇu, and making an oblation in a Vedic sacrificial ritual. Under Candra Gupta II, known also as Vikramāditya, cultural life flourished, his court graced by the presence of the great poet and dramatist Kālidāsa, and other brilliant authors and scholars. His son Kumāra Gupta presided over a prosperous realm and issued coins bearing representations of the deity after whom he was named, Skanda or Kārttikeya, known also as Kumāra, the god of war and son of Śiva. The period of Gupta rule, or immediately after it, also saw the construction of the first stone Hindu temples, though it is at present impossible to credit any particular Gupta ruler with sponsoring such a project. Invasions from the northwest by the Hūṇa peoples, thought to be related to the Huns who were so powerful in Europe and Persia in the fifth century, wreaked havoc in the western portion of the Gupta Empire about 500 C.E. and led to its decline. (*See also* Kālidāsa; Vikramāditya.)

⌘ GURU ⌘

Literally meaning heavy, or great, or respected, the word is often used for one's spiritual preceptor or teacher. The Guru typically is an elder male who initiates the young male Āryan and teaches him the scriptural and ritual heritage. Females can also be Gurus, and Tantric traditions especially feature women in this role. (*See also* Sacred Thread; Saṃskāra; Upanayana.)

⌘ GURUVAYŪR ⌘

Site of Śrī Kṛṣṇa temple, where there is an annual performance of eight dramas on his life. Enactment in the Kūṭiyāṭṭam style, with elaborate costume and makeup, includes unique musical performances and constitutes a profound religious experience for devotees. (*See also* Kūṭiyāṭṭam.)

⌘ GWALIOR ⌘

Site in northern Madhya Pradesh of a fort which was an important strategic stronghold from the fifteenth century onward.

— H —

⌘ HALEBID ⌘

Site in southern Karnataka of temples built by the Hoysala dynasty (eleventh to thirteenth centuries C.E.). The Hoysaleśvara temple is particularly noteworthy for its detailed carvings. (*See also* Belur; Paṭṭadakal.)

⌘ HANUMAN, or HANŪMAN ⌘

Large-Jawed. The name of the companion of Rāma and son of Vāyu (god of wind). He has the form of an ape, and is traditionally depicted as golden in color with a reddish face, wearing the sacred thread that is emblematic of Brahmanical status. Tremendous powers are attributed to Hanuman, usually as a result of his celibacy, including great strength, learning, the ability to fly and to change his form. He is regarded as the model devotee, and as such is represented often in temples dedicated to Rāma, where Hanuman is an attendant figure. But he is also more or less divine in his own right (as the son of a Vedic god) and numerous shrines to Hanuman can be found throughout India, independent of any nearby Rāma shrine. In the *Rāmāyaṇa* and its vernacular retellings, Hanuman leaped the ocean to reach Rāvaṇa's realm of Laṅkā, located Sītā, gave her Rāma's signet ring so that she would know that he was Rāma's companion, and promised her that he would return with Rāma soon, then wreaked havoc on Laṅkā until taken to Rāvaṇa himself. There he engaged in banter with the Demon King until, in aggravation, Rāvaṇa had his tail set on fire, with which Hanuman set Laṇkā ablaze. During the final battle, Hanuman was sent to Mount Kailāsa for healing herbs but, unable to distinguish which were the ones needed, he brought the entire mountain back with him. For his devotion and the service he rendered, Rāma granted Hanuman longevity and eternal youth. (*See also Rām Carit Mānas; Rāmāyaṇa.*)

⌘ HARA ⌘

Name of Śiva, meaning "the Destroyer." (*See also* Śiva.)

⌘ HARAPPA ⌘

Major city of the Indus Valley Civilization, sometimes also known as the Harappan Civilization. It flourished from about 2500 B.C.E. until about 1700 B.C.E. It was located toward the northern reaches of the Indus River in the Punjab (Five Rivers) area of what is now Pakistan. The city had a population of some 40,000 to 50,000 people, making it one of the largest cities of the ancient world at the time. (*See also* Indus Valley Civilization; Mohenjo-Daro.)

⌘ HARAPPAN CIVILIZATION ⌘

See Indus Valley Civilization.

⌘ HARDWĀR (HARIDVĀRA) ⌘

Viṣṇu's Gate. Name of a town in north India where the Ganges River leaves the Himālaya Mountains to traverse the plains. It is the site of a Kumbha Melā every twelve years, the next ones scheduled for 1998 and 2010. Hardwār is a major pilgrimage site for many Hindus due to the belief that the Ganges can purify one's Karma; there are many Yoga Āśramas and temples there, though the temples are of relatively recent construction. (*See also* Amṛta; Kumbha Melā.)

⌘ HARE KRISHNA MOVEMENT ⌘

The popularly used name of a devotional tradition, the official name of which is the International Society for Krishna Consciousness (ISKCON). The name is derived from a Mantra frequently chanted by devotees that consists of three common Vaiṣṇava names for God (Hari, Kṛṣṇa, Rāma) in the vocative case. Founded by Bhaktivedānta Swāmī Prabhupāda in 1966 in New York City at the request of his Guru as a means of carrying Kṛṣṇa devotion to the West, the organization has won thousands of converts. Prominent and wealthy converts such as the former Beatle George Harrison and a Ford family heir, as well as businesses operated by devotees, have made the movement fairly secure economically. By 1974, the organization stated that it had some 15,000 members, of whom 9,000 were in the United States, housed in sixty-eight centers worldwide. Once seen regularly in airports, devotees have been much less frequently seen in public since the death of their Swāmī in 1977 and the subsequent passing of leadership to a Governing Board of a dozen longtime devotees. The movement is linked by its Swāmī to a chain of teachers (Guru-Paraṃparā) stretching back to Caitanya, the charismatic reformer and saint of sixteenth-century Bengal. One of the major accomplishments of the movement is the publication of translations and commentaries on Sanskrit texts central to the theology and practice of Kṛṣṇa devotion, including the *Bhagavad Gītā* and *Bhagavāta Purāṇa*. During the 1980s and 1990s, the greatest areas of growth for ISKCON have been in India and among Hindus living in the West. ISKCON is the first organization to have successfully propagated a Hindu devotional (Bhakti) tradition in the Western world. (*See also Back to Godhead*; *Bhagavad Gītā*; *Bhagavāta Purāṇa*; Bhaktivedānta Swāmī Prabhupāda; Kṛṣṇa.)

⌘ HARI ⌘

Name of Kṛṣṇa or Viṣṇu, and of uncertain meaning. (*See also Harivaṃśa*; Kṛṣṇa; Viṣṇu.)

⌘ HARIHARA ⌘

Name of a deity combining the features and attributes of Viṣṇu and Śiva in one form. Sometimes Viṣṇu is depicted in his female form of Mohinī. (*See also* Śiva; Viṣṇu.)

⌘ HARIJAN ⌘

God's Child. A term coined by Mahātmā Gāndhī for the Outcastes or Untouchables to emphasize their humanity and that they were also entitled to be integrated into Indian society. (*See also* Outcaste.)

⌘ *HARIVAṂŚA.* ⌘

The Lineage of Hari, the name of a text that is an appendix (Khila) to the *Mahābhārata*. It relates a detailed story of the life of Kṛṣṇa, for the first time in Indian literature. Composed in Sanskrit, perhaps about 400 C.E., it came to be appended to the *Mahābhārata*, though it must have also circulated independently for some time. The text presents Kṛṣṇa as an Avatāra of Viṣṇu, and celebrates his youth among the cowherding people of the Vṛndāvana area. (*See also* Avatāra; *Mahābhārata*; Viṣṇu; Vṛndāvana.)

⌘ HAṬHA YOGA ⌘

The Yoga of Force. A system of stretching exercises, postures, and breathing exercises designed to perfect the human body to make it the vehicle for the spiritual discipline of Kuṇḍalinī Yoga. It is said to have been invented about the thirteenth century by the Nāth Yogī Gorakṣanāth, or Gorakhnāth. (*See also* Gorakṣanāth; Kuṇḍalinī; Matsyendranāth; Nāth; Yoga.)

⌘ HINDU MAHĀSABHĀ ⌘

Name of an organization founded in 1909 by Pandit Mohan Malaviya and other members of the Ārya Samāj. In the British colonial period until 1947, it was a group seeking independence by any means. Since independence, it has become a political party advocating Hindu nationalism. Their position, largely derived from the writings of "Veer" Ganesh Damodar Savarkar, is that India should be a Hindu state in which all must declare their loyalty to the unity and integrity of Hindusthan (India), and that all of British India, including the areas that are now Pakistan and Bangladesh, should be restored to India. In modern India, the Hindu Mahāsabhā is closely linked with the Bhāratīya Janatā Party (which has eclipsed the electoral appeal of the Hindu Mahāsabhā), the Rāṣṭrīya Svayamsevak Saṅgh, and the Vishva Hindu Parishad. (*See also* Ārya Samāj; Bhāratīya Janatā Party; Rāṣṭrīya Svayamsevak Saṅgh; Savarkar, Ganesh Damodar; Vishva Hindu Parishad.)

⌘ HIRIYANNA, M. ⌘

Indologist (1871–1950). Educated at Christian College in Mysore, where he earned an M.A., he was professor of Sanskrit at Maharaja's College, Mysore, until 1927, and wrote numerous works on Indian philosophy. (*See also* Indology.)

⌘ HOLĪ (HOLIKĀ) ⌘

Name of a popular one-day spring festival (February–March). It is noteworthy for its celebratory mood, the practice of throwing colored (usually red) water on each other, and the widespread indulgence in licentious or otherwise prohibited behavior. Inversion of caste-based hierarchy is a common feature of Holī.

⌘ HOPKINS, E. W. ⌘

Indologist (1857–1932). He earned a B.A. at Columbia University, and a Ph.D. at Leipzig University in Germany. He was professor of Sanskrit at Yale (1895–1926), where he wrote his major works on the *Mahābhārata*. (*See also* Indology.)

⌘ HORSE SACRIFICE ⌘

The Aśvamedha, a ritual performed by rulers in ancient India. Among its purposes are the demonstration of a ruler's sovereignty, atoning for bad Karma, and obtaining offspring. The first Horse Sacrifice was said to have been performed by Brahmā to celebrate his recovery of the Vedas, which had been lost. The *Mahābhārata* has King Yudhiṣṭhira perform a Horse Sacrifice after the internecine war, the stated purpose being to atone for killing his relatives. The Horse Sacrifice as described in ritual texts required a year to complete. A fine young male horse was selected, symbolically identified with the sovereignty of the ruler, and set loose to wander for a year, accompanied by the king's guards. Wherever the horse went, it represented the ruler's sovereignty and therefore compelled rulers of any territory in which it appeared either to submit or fight. If the horse survived the year, it was returned to the capital and the sacrifice was completed with a three-day rite. Ritual activity had been taking place throughout the year at the capital and, with the return of the horse, reached a climax. The horse, identified with Prajāpati, was killed and the queens and priests engaged in dialogue and actions suggestive of sexuality, the event clearly enacting fertility and prosperity. The horse was cut up, cooked, and portions were eaten by the participants and priests, portions also being offered to the gods in the fire. A chariot race and a riddle (Brahmodya) contest also took place. The Horse Sacrifice was performed, more or less grandly, by rulers in ancient India, including the Gupta rulers. Apparently the last performance was in the mid-eighteenth century by the Mahārāja of Jaipur. (*See also* Rājasūya; Vājapeya; Yajña.)

⌘ HOTṚ ⌘

Priest who chants verses from the *Ṛg Veda* during a Vedic sacrifice. (*See also* Brahmin; *Ṛg Veda*; Veda; Yajña.)

— I —

⌘ ICONOGRAPHY ⌘

See Darśana; Mudrā; Mūrti.

⌘ IMAGES IN WORSHIP ⌘

See Darśana; Mudrā; Mūrti.

⌘ IMMORTALITY ⌘

See Ātman; Brahman; Mokṣa; Rebirth.

⌘ INDO-EUROPEAN ⌘

Name of a language family that includes the Indic languages of north India and most languages of modern Europe, as well as certain languages of the Middle East. The Indic languages include Sanskrit, the Prakrit dialects, Pāli, and modern languages descended from Sanskrit such as Hindi, Marathi, Bengali, etc. Ancient and more modern forms of Iranian or Persian are also included, as well as Armenian, Hittite, classical Greek and Latin, Celtic, and Germanic languages. Modern languages descended from these such as the Slavic languages (Russian and Polish), Romance languages (Spanish, French, Portuguese), and the Scandinavian, German, Dutch, and English languages are also related. Close linguistic relationship between these languages has led scholars to hypothesize that they are all descended from a common parent language, no longer spoken and for which no texts have survived, which they call Indo-European. Many scholars also say that the linguistic unity must have been accompanied by geographic and cultural unity at one time, but that the Indo-European peoples split up and went in various directions, accounting for the wide spread of these languages. Comparative study of Indo-European languages, cultures, and mythology has recently been stimulated by the work of French scholar Georges Dumézil, who has brought to light the tripartite ideology and social organization of peoples of Indo-European heritage. (*See also* Dravidian; Dumézil, Georges; Sanskrit.)

⌘ INDOLOGY ⌘

The scholarly study of India. The academic study in the West of India's cultures began in the late eighteenth century as scholars realized that Sanskrit, India's classical language, was closely related to classical Greek and Latin. Sir William Jones, an employee of the British East India Company, was an important pioneer in the study of Sanskrit. He founded the Royal Asiatic Society in Calcutta in 1784 for the exchange of research findings on India's intellectual heritage. Charles Wilkins, who translated the *Bhagavad Gītā* (1785), H. T. Colebrook, and H. H. Wilson continued that tradition. France established its first chair in Indian Studies at the University of Paris in 1814, followed by Germany's at the University of Bonn in 1818, and Britain established the Boden Professorship in Sanskrit in 1832, Wilson being the first to hold the appointment. F. Max Müller (1849–1874) in Britain and Theodore Aufrecht (1861–1863) in Germany produced the first translations of the *Ṛg Veda*. Study of the Purāṇas and Tantras, and popular Hindu religion generally, developed more slowly than the study of the Vedic literature. The dictionaries, grammars, and many of the translations produced by nineteenth- century Indologists are still in use today. In the twentieth century, while classical Indology's concerns with translation continue, new approaches from the social sciences have greatly contributed to our understanding of India and Hinduism. Since about 1950, sociological and anthropological studies of Hindu communities and their religious traditions have been numerous. Among the most important are the work of M. N. Srinivas, who described the rise in social status of a low-caste group occasioned by imitation of the behavior of high-status groups as Sanskritization, and the work of Robert Redfield, who advanced the concept of the interaction between the great tradition and little traditions in India's civilization. University of Chicago anthropologists Milton Singer, McKim Marriott, and Ralph Nicholas developed these themes in brilliant studies of Hindu communities. Louis Dumont's *Homo Hierarchicus* depicted the social organization of the caste system as being based on the opposition of pure and impure. Recent studies of the omitted voices of Indian society by Indian and Western social scientists under the general heading of "subaltern studies" show great promise of correcting an earlier overemphasis on the elite traditions at the expense of the more widespread if less literate traditions. Recent trends in Indology have put more emphasis on the literature of regional languages such as Tamil (both classical and vernacular) and modern vernacular languages such as Hindi, Bengali, Marathi, and Telugu. The last two centuries of Indological research and publication in the West have had a tremendous impact on Hindu self-understanding and the academic study of the Hindu heritage in India. Indian reformers such as Rām Mohun Roy and Vivekānanda, and scholars such as V. S. Sukthankar, R. N. Dandekar, V. Raghavan, and A. K. Ramanujan have greatly contributed to the way both Indian and other scholars understand Hinduism. (*See also* Brown, W. Norman; Buitenen, J. A. B. van; Coomaraswamy, A. K.; Dandekar, R. N.; Dasgupta, Surendranath; De, S. K.; Dravidian; Eliade, Mircea; Gonda, Jan; Hiriyanna, M.; Hopkins, E. W.; Indo-European; Jones, Sir William; Kane, P. V.; Majumdar, R. C.; Müller, Friedrich Max; Radhakrishnan, Sir Sarvepalli; Raghavan, V.; Ramanujan, A. K.; Sanskrit; Sukthankar, V. S.; Wilson, H. H.; Zaehner, R. C.)

⌘ INDRA ⌘

The king of the Vedic gods, a great warrior, the leader of the gods in battle, and one of the dozen Ādityas. He is celebrated in the Vedic literature for his conquest of the demonic Vṛtra (Obstructor, Restrainer), as in *Ṛg Veda* 1.32 and 1.33, where his heroic deed frees the waters and enables life to flourish. Even in the Veda, and more clearly in later literature, Indra stands in need of purification for having killed Vṛtra. Indra is celebrated for having brought Soma from heaven as a falcon, or on a falcon (as in *Ṛg Veda* 4.26–27), and for his consumption of Soma, the psychotropic drink made of crushed mushrooms that gives warriors energy for battle. He is associated with rain and the forces of storm, his weapon being the lightning bolt. Indra is often praised for intervening in human affairs and aiding those who worship him, as in *Ṛg Veda* 7.18. Indra is also unique among the Vedic gods in that the *Ṛg Veda* (4.18) describes his birth; he must kill his father, which is comparable to the actions of Zeus, king of the gods in Greek mythology. Indra figured prominently in the cosmology of the ancient Āryans and was celebrated at a New Year festival annually during which a flagstaff (Indra-Dhvaja) was erected, symbolically representing Indra and his creative act of separating heaven and earth, and defeating the demons, making life possible. In the classical Indian theatre, Indra's flagstaff-weapon is known as the Jarjara and was worshipped onstage prior to performances. Indra's defeat of the demons and creation of order in the world helps to account for the fact that Indra is celebrated in thirty-five per cent of the poems of the *Ṛg Veda*, more than any other god receives, and about twenty-five per cent of its poems are dedicated exclusively to Indra. (*See also* Āditya; Indra-Dhvaja Festival; Jarjara; Namuci; *Ṛg Veda*; Soma; Vṛtra.)

⌘ INDRA-DHVAJA FESTIVAL ⌘

An annual festival of the New Year celebrated throughout India. A large pole would be erected, or a tree shorn of its limbs, symbolically representing the Skambha or pillar supporting heaven above earth. This *Axis Mundi* recalls one of the myths of creation of the Vedic literature, in which a pillar propped heaven above earth, making space for human life.

The festival celebrates the creation of the world, Indra's victory over the demons, and the renewal of life. The pole may also be representative of Indra's weapon, as is the Jarjara flagstaff in theatrical rituals. (*See also* Indra; Jarjara; *Nāṭya Śāstra*.)

⌘ INDRAPRASTHA ⌘

Indra's Place, the name of the capital city of the Pāṇḍavas in the *Mahābhārata*. It is said to be located in Delhi. (*See also* Maya.)

⌘ INDUS VALLEY CIVILIZATION ⌘

Name of one of the great ancient civilizations of the world, though it was not even suspected to exist until archaeological discoveries of the late nineteenth century. This civilization flourished from about 2500 B.C.E. until about 1700 B.C.E. covering some half million square miles of area, mostly in territory of the modern nation of Pakistan along the banks of the Indus River and its tributaries. About eighty sites have been excavated, the two largest found thus far being Harappa and Mohenjo-Daro, named after the villages now at those sites. Each has large walls surrounding a fortified citadel, numerous buildings of baked brick, aqueduct systems that supplied the cities with water, and a pool for ritual bathing. Many samples of the writing system have been found, but there is no agreement on how to translate it. Later Hinduism may preserve certain features of their religious practices; for example, worship of a goddess with sacrificial offerings of water buffaloes, ritual purification by water, and Yoga meditation. The decline of this highly developed civilization, thought by many Indologists of earlier generations to be the result of Āryan invasion, probably was due to increasing salt content in the soil caused by irrigation. It has also been called the Harappan Civilization. (*See also* Harappa; Mohenjo-Daro.)

⌘ INGALLS, DANIEL H. H. ⌘

Indologist (1916–). Educated at Harvard University, he was Wales Professor of Sanskrit from 1956 until his retirement in 1979. He wrote many studies of Indian literature and philosophy. (*See also* Indology.)

⌘ INTERNATIONAL SOCIETY FOR KRISHNA CONSCIOUSNESS (ISKCON) ⌘

See Hare Krishna Movement.

⌘ ĪŚA, ĪŚVARA ⌘

Lord. An epithet associated with many deities from the Vedic literature to the present day. It refers especially to the sovereign power of the deity. The term is associated with Rudra or Śiva especially. In the *Yoga Sūtra* of Patañjali, Īśvara is the model for the Yogī in his practice and the deity to whom the Yogī is to dedicate all his actions. (*See also* Śiva; Yoga.)

⌘ ISKCON ⌘

See Hare Krishna Movement.

⌘ IṢṬADEVATĀ ⌘

Chosen deity. There is a widespread practice in Hindu devotional traditions that one chooses the form of God that one worships. (*See also* Bhakti; Path of Devotion; Smārta.)

⌘ ITIHĀSA ⌘

Thus Indeed It Was, the term used in Sanskrit for writings about history. Itihāsa refers particularly to the *Mahābhārata*, but may also include other works no longer extant (but often is not regarded as including the *Rāmāyaṇa*, which is classed as poetry, Kāvya). The term is often paired with Purāṇa (Ancient Times) to include all writings about historical events. (*See also Mahābhārata*; Purāṇa.)

— J —

⌘ JAGANNĀTHA ⌘

Lord of the World. Name of an image of Kṛṣṇa in the temple of Puri, Orissa. The temple in its current form dates to 1198 C.E. and its tower rises to fifty-eight meters. The temple also houses images of Balarāma and Subhadrā, Kṛṣṇa's siblings. At an annual religious festival called the Ratha Yātra, or Chariot Pilgrimage, held in June or July, the images are placed on a large processional cart designed to look like a temple on wheels and pulled through the streets of Puri by several thousand temple servants. The Ratha of Jagannātha is some fourteen meters high, and has sixteen wheels, each over two meters in diameter. British observers mistook the name of the image for the name of the cart, hence the term "juggernaut" for a vehicle that is massive and difficult to stop. The British thought that the occasional death under the wheels of the cart was a ritual suicide by a devotee who wanted to die in God's auspicious sight (Darśana), but in actuality most may well be accidental. After a week residing about a kilometer from the temple, the images are put back on the carts and pulled back to the temple for reinstallation. Each year the Rathas are dismantled and the wood used for funeral pyres or in the temple kitchen, and periodically the images are replaced with new ones, the old ones being buried in the ground. The saint Caitanya (1486–1533 C.E.) lived at this temple for much of his adult life. (*See also* Caitanya; *Gītagovinda*; Jayadeva; Puri.)

⌘ JAIMINI ⌘

A sage and author who is particularly associated with the *Sāma Veda* tradition, in which several texts bear his name. The *Mīmāṃsā Sūtra* is also attributed to Jaimini. In the *Mahābhārata*, Jaimini is one of the Brahmin pupils of Vyāsa and is reputed to have recited the *Mahābhārata*. According to the *Mahābhārata* (1.57.74–75 and 12.314–315), Vyāsa divided the one Veda into four texts, and transmitted them along with the *Mahābhārata* as the fifth Veda through his five Brahmin disciples, without indicating clearly whether all five learned all the material or divided it between them. Purāṇas specify a division of labor among the disciples so that Jaimini learned the *Sāma Veda*. He is also credited with composition of the *Brahmāṇḍa Purāṇa*, which he recited to Hiraṇyanābha at the Naimiṣa Forest. It is by no means certain whether these are intended to be a single Jaimini or several. (*See also Mahābhārata*; Mīmāṃsā; Purāṇa; *Sāma Veda*; Veda; Vyāsa.)

⌘ JAINISM ⌘

Religion founded by Vardhamāna, known also by the titles Mahāvīra (Great Hero) and Jina (Conqueror). Probably an older contemporary of the Buddha in the sixth and fifth centuries B.C.E., the Jina promulgated a spiritual path of radical asceticism in which a renouncer was to wander naked and homeless until attaining liberation from rebirth through purification of bad Karma. He founded an order of monks and nuns that still exists in India, and while its following has never been large, Jainism was influential, especially before 500 C.E. in the north and before about 1000 C.E. in the south, its influence continuing in pockets since then. (*See also* Buddha; Saṃnyāsa.)

⌘ JAMADAGNI ⌘

Brahmin of the Bhārgava clan, son of Ṛcīka, and father of Paraśurāma. He married Reṇukā and had five sons. Angered at his wife, he demanded of his sons that one of them kill Reṇukā; only the youngest, Paraśurāma, would do so, after which her life was restored. Jamadagni was killed by Arjuna Kārtavīrya, a warrior king. Paraśurāma, an incarnation of Viṣṇu, took revenge by exterminating the warrior class entirely. (*See also* Bhārgava; Paraśurāma; Viṣṇu.)

⌘ JANAMAṢṬAMI ⌘

See Kṛṣṇa Janamaṣṭami.

⌘ JARJARA ⌘

Term used in the theatre for Indra's flagstaff, brought onstage ceremonially at the consecration of a theatre building and prior to every performance for ritual enactment of Indra's victory over the demons. As such, it represents Indra and his divine power, invoked for protection of the theatre and actors as they engage in a performance which, according to the *Nāṭya Śāstra*, is sacred and as meritorious as making sacrificial offerings (Yajña). (*See also* Indra; Indra-Dhvaja Festival; *Nāṭya Śāstra*.)

⌘ JĀTI ⌘

Sanskrit term for a subcaste group within the caste system. Jāti literally means birth, and refers to a birth-group or set of persons related by lineage and often sharing common customs, traditional occupation, and language. There are some 2,500 Jāti groups in India today. Each one of the Varṇa or caste groups (Brahmin, Kṣatriya, Vaiśya, and Śūdra) is subdivided into dozens of Jāti groups, each traditionally located in a particular region of India and each having certain unique customs. The status of each Jāti is based on the consensus of opinion of Hindu society on its practices, for example, adopting a vegetarian diet and religious practices that do not include offering blood sacrifice would be regarded highly. Over generations, the status of a Jāti may rise within its Varṇa category relative to other similarly ranked Jātis due to imitation of the behavior of high-status groups, a process known to anthropologists as Sanskritization (a term coined by M. N. Srinivas). Some of these groups apparently originated as occupationally based groups with a specific skill that is passed down from one generation to the next as trade secrets, as did guilds in medieval Europe. Many Jāti groups practice exogamy, so that women from one Jāti marry men from a particular other Jāti, and vice versa. Many Hindus continue to identify themselves as members of a particular Jāti today. (*See also* Caste; Dharma; Outcaste.)

⌘ JAYADEVA ⌘

Name of the author (twelfth century C.E.) of the Sanskrit text *Gītagovinda.* Legendary accounts of his life indicate that he was born into a Brahmin family in eastern India and had a traditional education that resulted in his mastery of Sanskrit. He became an ascetic renouncer (Saṃnyāsin) at a young age, staying nowhere two nights in a row. A Brahmin from Puri told Jayadeva that Jagannātha had ordained that he marry the Brahmin's daughter Padmāvatī, a temple Devadāsī, and she became his wife and his inspiration. His use of the term Jagadīśa (Lord of the World), synonymous with Jagannātha, in the refrain of the *Gītagovinda*'s first song (1.5–15) is an indication of his close association with the Jagannātha temple in Puri. His composition was regularly performed at the Jagannātha temple for centuries. (*See also* Devadāsī; *Gītagovinda*; Jagannātha; Puri; Kṛṣṇa; Rādhā; Vaiṣṇavism.)

⌘ JĪVA ⌘

Life; an individual person. Sometimes Jīva, more often the compound term Jīvātman, is used to refer to the individual soul or self, equivalent to Ātman. (*See also* Ātman; Puruṣa.)

⌘ JĪVAN-MUKTI ⌘

The state of being liberated from rebirth while still living. Most Hindu religious and philosophical traditions accept the possibility of one attaining liberation while living, so that one continues to live thereafter without generating any Karma. For example, in the Śaiva Siddhānta tradition, seven different varieties of Jīvanmukti are enumerated. In this regard, the Nyāya philosophical tradition is exceptional in that Nyāya does not admit the possibility of liberation until death. (*See also* Consciousness, States of; Kaivalya; Mokṣa; Rebirth; Samādhi.)

⌘ JÑĀNA ⌘

See Knowledge.

⌘ JÑĀNA MĀRGA; JÑĀNA YOGA ⌘

See Bhagavad Gītā; Path of Knowledge.

⌘ JONES, SIR WILLIAM ⌘

Sanskrit scholar and translator (1746–1794). Jones was employed in India as a judge, and when not performing his official duties he studied languages. He was the first to recognize the relationship between Sanskrit and the other Indo-European languages, especially classical Greek and Latin. He founded the Bengal Asiatic Society (now Royal Asiatic Society) in 1784 to bring together those who were interested in the intellectual heritage of India. Jones translated from Sanskrit the *Mānava Dharma Śāstra* as an aid to the administration of lands controlled by the British East India Company. He also translated Kālidāsa's *Abhijñānaśākuntala* and Jayadeva's *Gītagovinda*. He published the first edition of a Sanskrit text, the *Ṛtusaṃhāra*, attributed to Kālidāsa. His work laid the foundation for the fields of comparative philology and comparative Indo-European studies. (*See also* Indo-European; Indology; Sanskrit.)

— K —

⌘ KABĪR ⌘

North Indian saint who was and is claimed by both Hindus and Muslims as one of their own. Born into the weaver caste in

Vārāṇasī (Banaras) in the fifteenth century, he has a Muslim name, probably due to the mass conversion to Islam of his entire caste group shortly before his birth. Kabīr ridiculed institutionalized religion, both Hindu and Muslim, and emphasized that God cannot be named or described in any meaningful way. He is an exponent of what is known to Hindus as devotion to Nirguṇa Brahman, the impersonal Absolute that is beyond all limitation imposed by attributes, qualities, and names. He seems to have been influenced by, perhaps even been a practitioner of, Yoga of the Nāth tradition. Some of his poems have been preserved in the Sikh scripture entitled *Guru Granth Sahib*, others in Hindi language collections. (*See also* Nāths; Nirguṇa Brahman.)

⌘ KAILĀSA ⌘

Name of a mountain in the Himālayas, regarded as the site of Śiva's paradise. (*See also* Ellora; Śiva.)

⌘ KAIVALYA ⌘

Isolation. The term is used in the *Yoga Sūtra* of Patañjali to refer to the successful separation of the self or spiritual component of a person from the body or material component of a person, that is, autonomy from conditioned existence. This freedom of Puruṣa from Prakṛti is also the goal of the Sāṃkhya philosophical system. It is also known as Samādhi, and is equivalent to Mokṣa. (*See also* Consciousness, States of; Mokṣa; Samādhi; Sāṃkhya; Yoga; *Yoga Sūtra*.)

⌘ KĀLĀMUKHA ⌘

Black Face, the name of a south Indian sect of Śiva-worshipping Tantric ascetics who are of the Pāśupata tradition. The name comes from their practice of wearing a black mark on their foreheads. (*See also* Kāpālika; Pāśupata; Śiva.)

⌘ KĀLĪ ⌘

The Black Woman, name of the goddess of destruction. She is typically depicted as fierce in appearance, with a girdle of severed human hands, often holding a severed head and weapons in her hands, her long tongue smeared with blood. As such, she represents the destructive aspect of Mother Nature and does not tolerate evil, but also holds the promise of destroying the ignorance and the bonds of Saṃsāra. Her devotees also see her as the giver of life as well as its terminator, and she is often called Kālī Mā to emphasize her function as Mother of the World. Particularly within Tantric contexts, she is celebrated as the Absolute, but even there is often paired with Śiva as his Śakti, his feminine energy without which he would be inert. Offerings to Kālī often include blood offerings such as a goat, but may also include human sacrifice such as was practiced as recently as the nineteenth century by the Thugs, and is said still to occur occasionally. (*See also* Cāmuṇḍā; Caṇḍī; Durgā; Goddess; Kashmir Śaivism; Śakti; Thug.)

⌘ KALI YUGA ⌘

The fourth and final era in the series of eras in any Mahāyuga, or cycle of creation. It is an era of degeneration in human capabilities and lifespan, and a period of increasing chaos and deviance. Hindus view the world as now being in Kali Yuga of this cycle. According to chronologies in the Purāṇas, it began in 3102 B.C.E. with the end of the *Mahābhārata* war, and will last 432,000 years. It will end when the world can no longer be sustained and must be destroyed, making way for a new creation and new cycle of Yugas. (*See also* Kalkin; World Ages.)

⌘ KĀLIDĀSA ⌘

A poet and playwright widely regarded as the finest India has produced. He probably flourished during the reign of Candra Gupta II (375–415 C.E.) of the Gupta dynasty, also known as Vikramāditya. The name Kālidāsa means "servant of Kālī," but his works show an eclectic spirit in regard to religion, with praise of Śiva as the benedictions to his dramas and long narrative poems on the lineage of Rāma and the birth of Skanda or Kumāra. Little is known of his personal life. His works that are extant include the following dramas: *Abhijñānaśākuntala* (The recognition of Śakuntalā), *Mālavikāgnimitra* (Mālavikā and Agnimitra), and *Vikramorvaśīya* (Urvaśī won by valor). In addition to these, he is also credited with composition of a lyric monologue entitled *Meghadūta* (Cloud messenger), and two long lyric narratives entitled *Kumārasaṃbhava* (The birth of Kumāra) and *Raghuvaṃśa* (The lineage of Raghu). One other work, a poem entitled *Ṛtusaṃhāra* (Cycle of the seasons) may or may not have been composed by Kālidāsa; its language seems not to correspond to Kālidāsa's high standards, so if it is indeed his it may be an early work. The first six works listed show consistently brilliant and poetic use of language, to which the dramas add inventive plots that later playwrights took as their model for effective dramatic presentation. (*See also* Gupta; Jones, Sir William; Purūravas; Sanskrit; Urvaśī; Vikramāditya.)

⌘ KALKIN ⌘

Name of the tenth and final incarnation (Avatāra) of Viṣṇu. He is the Avatāra of the future, and will appear at the end of the Kali Yuga, the present World Age. At a time when chaos is unbearable, when illegitimate rulers preside over society and virtuous behavior is virtually unknown, Kalkin will appear as a warrior riding a white horse to destroy evildoers. He will restore order in society, reinstituting the four castes. As chaos subsides and order emerges, Viṣṇu will abandon the form of Kalkin and return to heaven and a new cycle of World Ages will begin with Kṛta Yuga, in which virtuous people with long lives will populate the earth. (*See also* Avatāra; Kali Yuga; Viṣṇu; World Ages.)

⌘ KALPA ⌘

See World Ages.

⌘ KĀMA ⌘

Desire, pleasure. The term is used particularly to refer to sexual fulfillment. Kāma is one of the Four Goals of Humanity (Puruṣārtha), one of the three worldly pursuits encouraged as appropriate for human beings. In that context, Kāma refers especially to sexual fulfillment through marriage and the enjoyment of family life. The term Kāma is also used, however, to refer to sexual desire, whether in the context of marriage or not. As such, it is one of the great temptations for the Yogī or practitioner of asceticism, one of the main obstacles to success in such an undertaking. Numerous myths revolve around a male ascetic's efforts to maintain his store of ascetic energy (Tapas) built up through celibacy, and a female, often a celestial nymph (Apsaras) sent by the gods to distract the ascetic from his austere practices and to reduce his store of Tapas so that he is less likely to threaten the position of the gods by his attainments. In this sense, Kāma and Tapas are traditionally seen as mutually exclusive opposites (though Tantric traditions endeavor to utilize both in attaining Mokṣa, liberation from rebirth). Similarly, Kāma and the two other worldly Goals of Humanity (Artha and Dharma) must be abandoned for successful pursuit of the fourth Goal, Mokṣa. Kāma is also the name of the God of Love, comparable to the West's Cupid, who pierces with his flower-arrows those whom he wants to fall in love. (*See also* Four Goals of Humanity; *Kāma Sūtra*; Prema; Tapas.)

⌘ *KĀMA SŪTRA* ⌘

A Sanskrit text, composed about 400 C.E. and attributed to Vātsyāyana, which treats the subject of Kāma (desire) in a scholarly fashion. In a style similar to Dharma Śāstra or Sūtra literature, the author classifies types of women and men and discusses their qualities, describes sexual positions and practices, and other topics. Given the obligation to pursue the Four Goals of Humanity, one of which is Kāma, cultivation of skill in lovemaking could be regarded as a socioreligious duty. While it has gained in the West in recent years the status of an underground classic, mentioned more often than actually read, the work's value to Indology is in what it reveals about social life in ancient India, primarily for the elite who had the leisure to enjoy very active social lives. (*See also* Kāma; Vātsyāyana.)

⌘ KĀÑCĪPURAM ⌘

Capital of the Pallava and Coḻa dynasties and the site of many temples. Kailāsanātha temple from the seventh century (dedicated to Śiva) and Vaikuṇṭha Perumal from the seventh and eighth centuries (dedicated to Viṣṇu) are among the earliest and most important. The Ekāmbara Nātha temple is unusual for its massive encircling stone wall and fifty-nine-meter-high Gopuram gateway, but especially for the huge mango tree that is regarded as a manifestation of Śiva and is claimed to be 3,500 years old. There are also many other temples. (*See also Mattavilāsa*; Temple.)

⌘ KANE, P. V. ⌘

Indologist (1880–1972). Born in the Ratnagiri district of Maharashtra, he was professor of law in the Government Law College and was granted the title Mahāmahopādhyaya ("great teacher") in 1942. He became vice-chancellor of Bombay University in 1947, and was honored with the Bhārat Ratna award in 1963. His *History of Dharmaśāstra* in five volumes is a major reference work. (*See also* Indology.)

⌘ KĀṆPHAṬA ⌘

Split-Ear, the name of a sect of Śiva-worshipping Tantric ascetics who wear large earrings and have split earlobes. Also known as the Nāth or Gorakhnāth sect, they practice Haṭha Yoga to develop their bodies as suitable vehicles for immortality and to acquire powers. (*See also* Gorakhnāth; Haṭha Yoga; Nāth.)

⌘ KANYĀKUMĀRĪ (CAPE COMORIN) ⌘

Virgin Maiden Cape, Land's End at the southern tip of India. It is a pilgrimage destination due to the myth of the Goddess doing ascetic practices here to win Śiva's hand in marriage; when he refused, she vowed to remain celibate. The Kumārī Amman temple commemorates her penances. There is also a memorial to Mahātmā Gāndhī where his ashes were kept prior to immersion in the ocean, and a memorial to Vivekānanda who meditated on an island offshore in 1892 before embarking on his religious mission. (*See also* Vivekānanda.)

⌘ KĀPĀLIKA ⌘

Name of a sect of ascetics devoted to Śiva. The name is derived from their custom of carrying a human skull (kapāla) as their begging bowl, out of which they ate and drank, a symbolic representation of the impermanence of life, and a very vivid reminder. They may have originated in south India in the first centuries C.E., and belong to the Tantric tradition, specifically the "Left-Hand" type who, as aids to the attainment of liberation, consume meat and wine and engage in ritual sexuality. The sect may have been absorbed into the Nāth sect. (*See also* Kālāmukha; Mattavilāsa; Nāth; Śaivism; Tantra.)

⌘ KARMA ⌘

Action; ritual act; religious observance. In the Vedic tradition, Karma referred to ritual actions. Brāhmaṇa texts generally envision a mechanistic world in which properly performed Karma necessarily produces the desired result, that is, that the gods are compelled to comply with the sacrificer's requests. The Upaniṣads present for the first time the idea of Karma as applying to all actions, not simply those performed in the context of sacrificial ritual, and as constituting a process in which good Karma results in a good rebirth, and bad Karma a bad rebirth. For example, *Bṛhadāraṇyaka Upaniṣad* 3.2.13 indicates that after death a man becomes something good from good Karma, and becomes something bad from bad Karma. The idea that one's actions affect the quality of one's rebirth took hold and became a powerful ethical guideline within Hindu religious traditions from about 500 B.C.E. onwards. Buddhism and Jainism also articulate the effects of one's actions upon oneself, and their advocacy of similar views certainly had the result of reinforcing within Hinduism the role of Karma. Hindu theistic traditions accept the idea of rebirth according to Karma, but typically emphasize the deity's power to prevent Karma's effect, that is, that the deity may choose to extend to a devotee his or her grace (Prasāda) and eliminate the effect of bad Karma. Liberation from rebirth (Mokṣa) is generally conceived as the elimination of all Karma, good and bad, so that one is not reborn in the human realm at all. (*See also* Mīmāṃsā; Path of Action; Rebirth.)

⌘ KARMA MĀRGA; KARMA YOGA ⌘

See Path of Action.

⌘ KĀRTTIKEYA ⌘

See Skanda.

⌘ KASHMIR ŚAIVISM ⌘

The inclusive term for several branches of Śaiva Tantrism, including the Kaula, Trika, and Krama schools. The Krama (Steps) school included a group of mystical cults of the Goddess Kālī, and probably originated in the Kashmir and Uḍḍiyāna areas of northwestern India. Their ritual practices feature deities garlanded with skulls and sometimes in animal forms, and have as their purpose to induce ecstatic expansion of the divine energy of Kālī within. Krama practitioners used prohibited substances and behaviors (the "Five M's") to attain liberation from convention and all restrictions imposed on consciousness by external values and whatever is not-Self. The Krama tradition has largely retained its identity within Śaivism. The Trika (Triad) tradition is a school that is ultimately monistic but includes devotion to three goddesses (Parā, a benevolent form, and two fierce forms, Parāparā and Aparā), who were regarded as emanations of Kālī. Rituals include the offering of the Five M's both to these goddesses and to human females as embodiments of the goddesses. Abhinavagupta initiated a mystical interiorization of the ritual practices, so that visualization and contemplation replaced physical performance of ritual actions in the higher stages of practice. The Trika school was largely absorbed within Kaula Tantrism after Abhinavagupta. (*See also* Abhinavagupta; Five M's; Kaula Tantrism; Left-Hand Tantra.)

⌘ KAULA TANTRISM ⌘

A tradition of "Left-Hand" Tantric practice. The goal of Kaula practice is to attain identity with Śiva, which is liberation from rebirth. One of the most important practices of Kaula Tantrics that aids in attaining liberation is the raising of Kuṇḍalinī Śakti (also known as Kula, hence the name of the tradition, Kaula, meaning, "concerning the Kula"). Another major component of Kaula worship is a meditation on desire (Kāmakalā) in which the female organ becomes (literally or figuratively) the object of meditation and ritual worship. This is said to be done in order to overcome sensuality in preparation for attaining liberation. Kaula rituals include the use of the Five M's, the five prohibited substances and behaviors that characterize "Left-Hand" Tantric practice. (*See also* Five M's; Kashmir Śaivism; Kuṇḍalinī; Left-Hand Tantra; Śrīvidyā Tantra; Tantra.)

⌘ KAURAVA ⌘

Descendant of Kuru, the most common name for the side of the Bhārata family led by Duryodhana, who were opposed to the Pāṇḍavas in the *Mahābhārata*.

⌘ KHAJURĀHO ⌘

The main temple complex of the Chandella dynasty of north-central India (tenth and eleventh centuries C.E.), and the site of well-preserved classical temples. The Khandariya Mahādeva temple is one of the finest examples of north Indian temple architecture extant, the main tower reaching some thirty-one meters above its platform, with 226 statues inside the temple and another 646 decorating the outside, including musicians, beautiful women, mythological beasts, ascetics, deities, and erotic couples united in acrobatic postures. Another Śiva temple, Viśvanātha, is also exceptional for its portrayal of daily life, women being especially prominent in its sculptures. A Hanuman temple has the oldest inscription at Khajurāho, dated to 922 C.E. It is likely that the erotic images for which Khajurāho is justly famous are due in large measure to Tantric religious traditions which were very influential in north India at the time, as well as to continuation of the social mores evident in the *Kāma Sūtra*. In addition to the Hindu temples dedicated to all the major deities, there is also a group of Jain temples in very similar style. (*See also* Konārak; Temple.)

⌘ KNOWLEDGE ⌘

Translates terms from Sanskrit such as Vidyā, or Jñāna. Most Hindu religious and philosophical traditions distinguish between two types of knowledge. The lower knowledge is informational, derived from study of texts or hearing of teachings; while it is useful, perhaps even indispensable, it must be brought to fruition with the higher knowledge, or wisdom. The higher knowledge (often called Prajñā) is typically derived from meditative insight, direct perception of reality, or the grace of God. (*See also* Consciousness, States of; Path of Knowledge; Yoga.)

⌘ KONĀRAK ⌘

Site of a large temple (thirteenth century C.E.) dedicated to the sun god Sūrya. The main building is constructed to represent Sūrya's chariot, with seven carved stone horses straining to pull it on its twenty-four massive wheels. Three large images of Sūrya are positioned to be lit by the sun's rays at dawn, noon, and sunset. As at Khajurāho, Konārak's sculptors decorated the temple with erotic couples. If the tower (Śikhara) actually had been completed, it would have reached some seventy meters in height; it is uncertain whether the sandy soil on which the temple was built could have supported that much weight. (*See also* Temple.)

⌘ KRISHNA ⌘

See Kṛṣṇa.

⌘ KRISHNAMURTI, JIDDU ⌘

Teacher of Hindu heritage (1895–1986). Born near Madras as the son of a Brahmin family, he came to the attention of the Theosophical Society when his father worked for the Adyār Library. He was educated in England and France, and made head of The Order of the Star in the East, which was to serve as the vehicle for his world mission of teaching. Krishnamurti had a profound spiritual experience in Ojai, California, in 1922, which he later referred to as "the process." Annie Besant, leader of the Theosophical Society, proclaimed him the Messiah, the next World Teacher, and Lord Maitreya in 1925, but in 1927 Krishnamurti repudiated the Society and dissolved the Order, announcing his intention to be an independent spiritual teacher, unaffiliated with any institutionalized religion. He often stated that no spiritual authorities could be relied upon, that the truth is not to be discovered by a prescribed path, and that the mind must free itself from constraints imposed on it by external forces to recover its inherent freedom. His teachings, presented in numerous lectures and publications, may be seen as generally in conformity to the Advaita Vedānta perspective. He died in Ojai in 1986. (*See also* Theosophical Society.)

⌘ KṚṢṆA ⌘

Black, or dark; the name of a manifestation of Viṣṇu, the eighth in lists of ten Avatāras. For many Hindus, particularly in north India, Kṛṣṇa is Ultimate Reality, all other forms of divinity including Viṣṇu being manifestations of Kṛṣṇa. Early literature depicts him as a warrior and sage who, as Arjuna's chariot driver, instructs Arjuna (in the *Bhagavad Gītā* and elsewhere in the *Mahābhārata*). There he reveals himself to be God, to whom all devotion goes and to whom devotees go at death. Yet even here there are indications that his childhood exploits in Vṛndāvana are known; for example, a rival warrior, Śiśupāla (clearly representative of Śiva, as he was born with four arms and three eyes!), belittles Kṛṣṇa's deeds, referring to his destruction of a wooden cart, killing Pūtanā and Kaṃsa, and lifting Mount Govardhana (*Mahābhārata* 2.38). Later literature (*Harivaṃśa, Bhāgavata Purāṇa, Gītagovinda*) amplifies on these stories of his childhood among the cowherding people of Vraja, emphasizing particularly his loving relationship with the Gopīs (cowherdesses, or milkmaids). According to these accounts, Kṛṣṇa was smuggled out of Mathurā to protect him from his evil and tyrannical uncle Kaṃsa, whom he later returned to kill, and he was raised in the pastoral setting of Vṛndāvana. There the Gopī women were enchanted with him and irresistibly attracted to him, leaving their husbands at the sound of Kṛṣṇa's flute to be with him in the forest. Of all the Gopīs, Rādhā was the favorite of Kṛṣṇa (particularly in the *Gītagovinda*) and had an especially intense relationship of love with him. Vaiṣṇava theologians have written that every human being should have an attitude of love toward God, and have described, based on these scriptures, four possible relationships one can have with Kṛṣṇa: as servant, parent, friend, and lover. Of these, the most intense and intimate is as his lover, a role that has appealed as a religious path not only to women such as Mīrā Bai, but to men such as Caitanya and Vallabha as well. The story of Kṛṣṇa's youth is immensely popular, celebrated in art, dance, drama, and song as well as texts and temple iconography. The festival Janamaṣṭami celebrates his birth and youth. Though the royal warrior-sage and the mischievous lover of milkmaids may originally have been distinct figures worshipped by different groups, later Hindu tradition has seen these as presenting a coherent account of one of the most important manifestations of the divine among humanity. (*See also* Arjuna; Avatāra; *Bhagavad Gītā*; Dvārakā; *Gītagovinda*; Gopī; Gosvāmin; Govardhana, Mount; Jagannātha; Kṛṣṇa Janamaṣṭami; Līlā; Mathurā; Rādhā; Vaiṣṇavism; Viṣṇu; Vṛndāvana.)

⌘ KṚṢṆA JANAMAṢṬAMI ⌘

Birth of the Eighth, name of a festival celebrating the birth of Kṛṣṇa, who was the eighth child of Devakī, and the eighth incarnation (Avatāra) of Viṣṇu. Held on the eighth day of the dark half of the month of Śrāvaṇa (July-August), the festival is celebrated by most Hindus, not Vaiṣṇavas only. A widespread practice is observing a fast on the day prior to the festival itself. The devotional sentiments of worshippers are expressed through auspicious viewing (Darśana) of images of the deity, beautifully dressed, and the sharing of blessed food that has been offered to the deity, Prasāda. Kṛṣṇa's birth was threatened by King Kaṃsa, who was killing all the babies born to his sister Devakī due to a prophecy that a son of hers would be his nemesis. At his birth, his father Vasudeva smuggled Kṛṣṇa across the river to the cowherding people of Vraja and exchanged him for a baby girl, whom Kaṃsa promptly killed. A voice from heaven announced that the girl was an incarnation of the Goddess Yoga-Māyā who had taken birth to protect Kṛṣṇa. The boy grew up among the herdsmen in the Vṛndāvana region and later returned to Mathurā and killed his uncle Kaṃsa. E. M. Forster's novel entitled *A Passage to India* contains a striking account of the festival in the "Temple" section. (*See also* Kṛṣṇa; Vaiṣṇavism; Vṛndāvana.)

⌘ KṢATRIYA ⌘

A member of the Warrior caste. Kṣatriyas are traditionally regarded as possessing the quality of Kṣatra (power, sovereignty), which, according to the *Ṛg Veda*, they share with the gods Indra and Varuṇa especially. Their particular social and religious duties (Dharma) included learning the art of weaponry so as to be able to protect those who needed protection and to fight other warriors, to learn how to rule, to donate to those who were deserving, and to study the Veda. (*See also* Caste; Dharma.)

⌘ KUMĀRA ⌘

See Skanda.

⌘ KUMBHA MELĀ ⌘

A religious festival held on a rotating basis every three years at these four pilgrimage sites: Hardwār; Nāsik; Ujjain; and Prayāga. According to legend, drops of the Elixir of Immortality (Amṛta) fell at these sites when the gods and demons churned the Ocean of Milk and fought over the Elixir. Pilgrims and renouncers (Saṃnyāsin) gather at each site every twelve years. The earliest historical evidence for such pilgrimages dates from the seventh century

C.E., when King Harṣa escorted a Chinese Buddhist pilgrim to one. (*See also* Amṛta; Hardwār; Nāsik; Prayāga; Ujjain.)

⌘ KUṆḌALINĪ ⌘

Something coiled, or circular; the term is a poetic way of referring to a snake. Kuṇḍalinī Yoga is a distinctive Tantric variety of Yoga in which bodily energy, conceived as a snake-like, coiled presence at the bottom of the spine, and as a divine feminine force (Śakti), is aroused and channeled to aid in the attainment of liberation from rebirth (Mokṣa). The image of the human body in Tantric groups practicing this form of Yoga includes the presence of six centers known as Cakras, arranged from the base of the spine to the forehead, and a seventh Cakra just above the crown of the head. These Cakras are linked by a channel known as Suṣumnā, the bottom entrance to which is blocked by the head of the serpent, the latent energy within the body. The purpose of Kuṇḍalinī Yoga practice is, through breathing exercises that stop energy circulation through other channels, to concentrate energy on the Kuṇḍalinī so as to awaken or arouse it, causing it to move up the Suṣumnā to activate each Cakra successively. When the Kuṇḍalinī/Śakti reaches the highest Cakra in the practitioner's head, it there unites with Śiva, bringing about the union of the feminine and masculine principles, Goddess and God, and resulting in liberation from rebirth. The human body is regarded as having within it these divine powers that correct practices of Yoga can activate, leading to Mokṣa. (*See also* Cakra; Śakti; Tantra; Yoga.)

⌘ KŪRMA ⌘

The Tortoise Avatāra of Viṣṇu, usually the second in lists of the ten incarnations. Viṣṇu took the form of the Tortoise so that the Gods and Demons could place on his back Mount Mandara to use as a churn in their effort to produce the Elixir of Immortality (Amṛta) by churning the Ocean of Milk. With Kūrma as the foundation for their activity, the gods and demons succeeded in producing Amṛta, over which they fought, the gods eventually gaining possession of it when Viṣṇu assumed the alluring form of Mohinī to distract the demons. This frequently told myth can be found in many texts; a fully elaborated version of the myth is in the *Mahābhārata* (1.15 to 1.17). (*See also* Amṛta; Avatāra; Viṣṇu.)

⌘ KURUKṢETRA ⌘

The Field of the Kurus. The location of the eighteen-day battle recounted in the *Mahābhārata*, north of Delhi.

⌘ KUŚA ⌘

Name of a variety of grass (*Desmostachya bipinnata*, or *Poa cynosuroides*), regarded as sacred. It is sometimes identified with, sometimes distinguished from, Darbha grass. In the Vedic sacrifice (Yajña), cut Kuśa grass was strewn around the altars and Vedi. Some ascetics have meditation mats made of Kuśa. (*See also* Darbha; Vedi; Yajña.)

⌘ KŪṬIYĀṬṬAM (KOODIYĀṬṬAM) ⌘

Acting Together, the name of a tradition of religiously significant theatre in Kerala, south India. For nine centuries since the reforms during the reign of King Kulaśekhara Varman, classical Sanskrit dramas have been enacted in the style known as Kūṭiyāṭṭam in Kerala. It is the only unbroken lineage of Sanskrit theatre performance in India. While performances once took place in the palaces, from about the thirteenth century through the late twentieth century performances were held within the compounds of the major Hindu temples of Kerala in specially constructed theatre buildings. Performers traditionally have been regarded as temple servants, a high-status social class, whose religious duty it is to perform; in fact, the actors (Cākyārs) receive the sacred thread at initiation as if they were Brahmins, though they do not learn the Veda. The dramas are performed as part of the temple calendar of festivals and offerings in honor of the gods. To a considerable extent, Kūṭiyāṭṭam performances in temples comply with the requirements specified in the Nāṭyaśāstra regarding purificatory rituals prior to performances, even adding more. Many of the dramas feature the appearance of one or more of the gods onstage, allowing the audience to experience the auspicious sight (Darśana) of God, much as is done in the temple with the icon. Dramas featuring Rāma are particularly popular, but dramas featuring Kṛṣṇa and based on the *Mahābhārata* are also performed regularly. The objective of the performance of such dramas is the same as for classical theatre in ancient times, namely, the evocation in audience members of the experience of Rasa (aesthetic enjoyment). The additional significance of Rasa as religious rapture, developed by the Vaiṣṇava Gosvāmin theologians is also well known to performers and an important objective. Actors say that performance is a religious duty (Dharma). Two peculiarities of performance style may be noted. One is that the presentation of extensive background, repetition of lines, and elaboration of their meaning through gesture and movement greatly lengthen performance time, so that a single act is the normal unit of performance, and it alone may well take over a week of nightly performance to complete. The other is that in dramas featuring the Vidūṣaka, a Brahmin buffoon, he will be given freedom to address the audience directly in the vernacular language of Malayalam, perhaps over several nights, on topics of contemporary social and political interest. Since the mid-1970s, due to land reforms led by the Communist Party, temples have lost much of their revenue and most have been unable to support their temple servants as they did in the past, so most performances in the Kūṭiyāṭṭam style have been held outside the temples for private patrons. (*See also* Darśana; Gosvāmin; Guruvayūr; Music; *Nāṭya Śāstra*; Pūjā; Rasa; Thrissur.)

— L —

⌘ LAKṢMAṆA ⌘

Name of the brother of Rāma in the *Rāmāyaṇa*. He represents the ideal younger brother, fulfilling his Dharma through service to his elder. He is regarded as a partial incarnation (Aṃśa-Avatāra) of Viṣṇu or sometimes the cosmic serpent Śeṣa or Ananta, associated with Viṣṇu. (*See also Rāmāyaṇa.*)

⌘ LAKṢMĪ. ⌘

See Śrī.

⌘ LAKULĪŚA ⌘

Name of the founder (probably second century C.E.) of the Pāśupata tradition. He is often regarded as an incarnation or manifestation of Śiva. He is typically represented as a naked Yogī with erect penis, holding a club. (*See also* Pāśupata; Śaivism; Śiva.)

⌘ LAW ⌘

See Dharma.

⌘ LAWS OF MANU ⌘

See Mānava Dharma Śāstra.

⌘ LEFT-HAND TANTRA ⌘

Term for traditions of Tantric practice in which social conventions are flouted purposefully. Left-Hand practices (Vāmācāra) include the use of prohibited substances and unsanctioned behavior, known as the Five M's (Pañca Makāra): Māṃsa (meat), Matsya (fish), Mudrā (parched or fermented grains), Mada (alcohol), and Maithuna (sexual intercourse). The rites are non-Vedic in content and purpose. This Left-Hand practice is contrasted with Right-Hand Tantric practice, which does not conflict with Vedic and Brahmanical traditions. The significance of the term "Left-Hand" is that the left hand is regarded as impure or inauspicious due to its use in cleaning oneself after a bowel movement, while the right hand is regarded as pure or auspicious. (*See also* Five M's; Kāpālika; Right-Hand Tantra; Tantra.)

⌘ LIBERATION ⌘

See Mokṣa.

⌘ LĪLĀ. ⌘

Play (both in the sense of a game and of a drama). Līlā is cited in the *Brahma Sūtra* and other works as the explanation for the creation of the world by God, who is omniscient, omnipotent, and self-sufficient and creates for the sake of enjoyment. The world is thus God's play. This has proven to be a fertile concept, particularly for Vaiṣṇava theologians, who have seen Līlā in the playful and erotic activities of Kṛṣṇa. The Gosvāmin theologians developed the idea of attaining liberation through adopting the persona and behavior toward Kṛṣṇa of one of his loving companions, especially the Gopīs who loved him most intimately. Līlā has also been seen in the activity of Śiva Nāṭarāja, whose dance of cosmic destruction and creation is a performance of unmotivated enjoyment. (*See also* Gopī; Gosvāmins; Kṛṣṇa; Nāṭarāja; Viṣṇu.)

⌘ LIṄGA (LIṄGAM) ⌘

The symbolic representation and aniconic form of Śiva. It has a phallic form, though Hindus generally do not regard it in this way. One myth of the origin of the Liṅga is as follows: Brahmā and Viṣṇu were disputing which was superior when a giant column of fire appeared. Unable to see either end of it, Viṣṇu assumed the form of a boar and dived downward, Brahmā assumed the form of a swan and flew upward to investigate. Neither found its end, at which point Śiva emerged from the column and proclaimed his superiority. Another myth recounts how Śiva found that there was no longer any need for his creative power, so he cut off his penis and stuck it in the ground where it stood upright and was worshipped by devotees. Both myths are frequently found in Purāṇas. Many scholars point to very similar phallic forms found in the ruins of the Indus Valley Civilization's cities as an indication of the archaic character of the Liṅga. One might also see similarity with the post (Yūpa) erected at every Vedic sacrifice for tethering animals. At Guḍimalla in Tamilnadu, an ancient Liṅga thought to date from the second century B.C.E. is still the object of worship in a Śiva temple; it has a clearly phallic form and a representation of Śiva as a warrior. The main image in most Śiva temples is a Liṅga, and many of the largest Śiva temples have naturally occurring stone Liṅgas. Twelve temples each have an image known as a Jyotir-Liṅga (Light Liṅga), regarded as inherently possessing divine power (Śakti) and as manifestations of the mythic column of fire. Liṅgāyat or Vīraśaiva sect members wear a small Liṅga on a cord around the neck as an indication of their religious affiliation. The Liṅga can be regarded as symbolically representing the power of sexuality and creativity held in restraint. (*See also* Liṅgāyat; Śaivism; Śiva.)

⌘ LIṄGĀYAT ⌘

Sect devoted to Śiva and known also as the Vīraśaiva. Founded in the twelfth century by Basava in what is now Karnataka, south India, it is a reformist movement with monotheistic and anti-caste attitudes. Members wear a Liṅga on a cord around the neck and regard themselves as belonging to Śiva. They do not participate in elaborate temple devotional rituals, as other south Indian Śiva worshippers do, and they do not accept the authority of Brahmins. They do not comply with the widespread pollution taboos associated with caste and gender distinctions. Śiva is regarded as the Absolute, and every human soul is identical with Śiva, but Māyā obscures this reality. The poems of praise to Śiva preserved in vernacular Kannadā language by this tradition emphasize having a personal relationship with Śiva. It is possible that Muslim influence can be found in the sect's disposal of the dead by burial rather than cremation, and in their egalitarian practices and monotheistic theology, but these may also be due to a reaction against dominant tendencies in mainstream Hindu traditions. (*See also* Basava; Liṅga; Mahādeviyakkā; Śaivism; Śiva.)

⌘ LOKA ⌘

Realm; world. A term used especially to refer to the heaven in which a particular god resides and rules. In Vedic literature there is frequent reference to the three realms of earth, atmosphere, and heaven. The term can also be used to refer to this world, as in the expression Lokapāla (World Guardians), a set of gods who are overseers of particular regions. (*See also* Śiva; Viṣṇu; World Guardians.)

⌘ LOKAPĀLA ⌘

See World Guardians.

⌘ LOMAHARṢAṆA SŪTA ⌘

One of the pupils of Vyāsa. According to the *Mahābhārata* (1.57.74–75 and 12.314–315), Vyāsa divided the one Veda into four texts, and transmitted them along with the *Mahābhārata* as the fifth Veda through his four Brahmin disciples plus his son Śuka, without indicating clearly whether all five learned all the material or divided it between them. Purāṇas specify a division of labor among the disciples so that Paila learned the *Ṛg Veda*, Vaiśaṃpāyana learned the *Yajur Veda*, Jaimini learned the *Sāma Veda*, and Sumantu learned the *Atharva Veda*, while Lomaharṣaṇa Sūta learned the Purāṇa and Itihāsa (historical) collections. In these accounts, Vyāsa's son Śuka is omitted, perhaps due to the fact that he is depicted in the *Mahābhārata* (12.310–320) as having attained liberation from rebirth and bodily disappeared from the earth. The son of Lomaharṣaṇa Sūta, Ugraśravas Sauti, is the reciter of portions of the *Mahābhārata*. The name "Lomaharṣaṇa" or its variant "Romaharṣaṇa" (Hair-Raiser) is indicative of his rhetorical skill. He is also described as a Sūta, a class of court attendants often regarded as descended from the union of a Brahmin and a Warrior, therefore having qualities of each; they functioned as court bards and attendants. (*See also* Itihāsa; *Mahābhārata*; Purāṇa; Sūta; Vyāsa.)

⌘ LOTUS ⌘

Aquatic plant (*Nelumbo nucifera*). It is regarded as an apt symbolic representation of the enlightened mind and of enlightenment, since it is rooted in mud but reaches up through water to the light above. Deities (especially Viṣṇu, Śrī, and Brahmā) and saints are often depicted in association with lotuses.

⌘ LOTUS POSTURE ⌘

The distinctive bodily position used for seated meditation. The posture is one in which the spine is straight, head upright, and the legs are crossed so that the right foot is placed on the left thigh and the left foot is placed on the right thigh. This posture is used in the practice of Yoga so that one can sit comfortably for a long period of time with minimal physical exertion. (*See also* Prāṇa; Yoga; *Yoga Sūtra*.)

⌘ LOVE ⌘

See Kāma; Prema.

— M —

⌘ MĀ ⌘

Mother. Used in reference to the Goddess, particularly when she is regarded as the Absolute, or Ultimate Reality. (*See also* Devī; Durgā; Goddess; Kālī.)

⌘ MADHVA ⌘

Founder of the tradition of Dvaita (dualistic) Vedānta. He was ordained as a member of the monastic tradition of Śaṅkara's Advaita (nondualistic) Vedānta, but developed his own theistic interpretation of the scriptures. Madhva wrote commentaries on major texts such as the *Bhagavad Gītā, Brahma Sūtra,* and some Upaniṣads. In Madhva's theology, Viṣṇu in the form of Kṛṣṇa is Ultimate Reality. He also accepts the orthodox Hindu perspectives on the cycle of rebirth and the possibility of liberation from rebirth. There is considerable controversy about the dates of Madhva's life: either 1238 to 1317, or 1199 to 1278 is usually advocated. (*See also* Advaita Vedānta; *Bhagavad Gītā; Brahma Sūtra;* Dvaita Vedānta; Vedānta).

⌘ MADRAS ⌘

Fourth-largest city in India, and capital of Tamilnadu. The first settlement of the British East India Company, it grew up around Fort Saint George (built in 1644) and was given a municipal charter in 1688. Among its many temples, two are most important. Kāpālīśvarar temple is an ancient Śiva temple in the Mylapore district, and Śrī Parthasarathy temple (Triplicane district) is a Kṛṣṇa temple built by the Pallava dynasty in the eighth century C.E. At the south end of the city is the headquarters of the Theosophical Society in Adyār. (*See also* British East India Company.)

⌘ MĀDRĪ ⌘

Name of the second wife of Pāṇḍu, and the sister of Śalya, in the *Mahābhārata.* She was the mother of the twin Pāṇḍava warriors Nakula and Sahadeva. Due to an ascetic's curse, Pāṇḍu died when he embraced Mādrī, and she insisted on commiting suicide on his funeral pyre as a Satī. (*See also* Pāṇḍava; Pāṇḍu; Satī.)

⌘ MADURAI ⌘

Major temple center in Tamilnadu, south India, dedicated to the divine couple of Mīnākṣī, the Fish-Eyed goddess, and Śiva. The annual celebration of the wedding of the goddess to Śiva, attended by Viṣṇu and other deities, is an event of great religious significance to devotees. The temple was founded in the thirteenth century under the rule of the Pāṇḍya dynasty, and expanded greatly in the seventeenth century. Its twelve Gopuram gateways tower forty-five to fifty meters high, and are covered with brightly painted images of deities. Each evening at 9:30 the image of Śiva (known here as Śrī Sundareśvara, The Beauty's Lord) is taken to Mīnākṣī's bedroom, where he stays until 6 a.m. The city is ancient, one of the oldest continuously inhabited sites in the world. (*See also* Mīnākṣī; Śiva; Temple.)

⌘ MAHĀBALIPURAM ⌘

See Māmallapuram.

⌘ *MĀHĀBHARATA* ⌘

The great epic of India and an important religious text for Hindus. The *Mahābhārata*, written versions of which in the Sanskrit language run to some 180,000 lines, is often cited as the world's longest poem. It is the product of a long oral tradition of recitation and elaboration over centuries, a process which continues to the present day; the story is also known in regional vernacular languages in India and Southeast Asia. Its reputed author Vyāsa, also known as Kṛṣṇa Dvaipāyana or Veda-Vyāsa, is depicted as a Brahmin sage who is also a prominent character in the story. The title, "The Great (Story) about the Bhāratas," refers to the Bhārata family, central characters in the narrative. The story can be summarized as follows. The ruling family of north-central India, the Bhārata clan, split into two groups in a dispute over succession to the throne: the Pāṇḍavas (five brothers, sons of Pāṇḍu who had ruled earlier), and their cousins the Kauravas (100 brothers, sons of Dhṛtarāṣṭra, who was ruling currently). The Pāṇḍavas had as their friend and ally Kṛṣṇa Vāsudeva, a prince from a nearby area who was also an Avatāra (God incarnate in human form), on earth to restore Dharma. At a Vedic ritual called Rājasūya (Royal Consecration), which would have declared the eldest Pāṇḍava Yudhiṣṭhira the emperor ruling over many kings, the Kauravas cheated at a dice match that was to have celebrated the conclusion of the rite, and the Pāṇḍavas were exiled with their wife Draupadī. After twelve years of exile in the wilderness, followed by a thirteenth year spent in disguise as they reentered society, the Pāṇḍava brothers returned to the kingdom to claim their share, but were rebuffed by their cousins. Both sides assembled their allies and met to fight a battle for sovereignty. After eighteen days of fierce fighting, the Pāṇḍavas won back the decimated kingdom, and ruled righteously for many years. The poem's characters are depicted as the gods and demons in human form, so that a character who represents a god is depicted in ways that remind the audience of that deity. The characters and the situations they are involved in are regarded by many Hindus as providing guidelines on how they should live their own lives, even today. The *Mahābhārata* also includes many passages that explicitly teach religious and philosophical doctrines, the most significant of which is the *Bhagavad Gītā* (Song of the Blessed One), the most widely known Hindu religious text. The story is so popular that the Government of India's television network Doordarshan chose the *Mahābhārata* as the subject for a weekly serial in 1988 and 1989. Peter Brook produced a play based on the story; it was staged in Britain, France, the United States, and Australia, and its enactment was filmed. (*See also* Avatāra; *Bhagavad Gītā*; Draupadī; Kṛṣṇa; Pāṇḍavas; Rājāsūya; Vyāsa.)

⌘ MAHĀDEVA ⌘

Great God. The term is usually employed to refer to Śiva, particularly when he is regarded as the Absolute. (*See also* Śaivism; Śiva.)

⌘ MAHĀDEVIYAKKĀ ⌘

Twelfth-century female saint of south India. She was so devoted to Śiva that she rejected a royal marriage to wander as a homeless, naked ascetic, singing of her devotion to her true husband Śiva. She is revered by the Liṅgāyat sect. (*See also* Liṅgāyat; Śiva.)

⌘ MAHĀKĀLA ⌘

Great Time; a name for Śiva in his capacity as destroyer. (*See also* Nāṭarāja; Śiva.)

⌘ MAHĀRĀJ JI, GURU ⌘

Leader of the Divine Light Mission since the death of his father Shri Hans Mahārāj Ji in 1966. Born Prem Pāl Singh Rawat in 1957, he moved to the United States in 1971. His marriage to an American woman in 1974 and a public estrangement with his mother led to a loss of his following. (*See also* Divine Light Mission.)

⌘ MAHARISHI MAHESH YOGI (MAHARṢI MAHEŚA YOGĪ) ⌘

Teacher of a meditation technique known as Transcendental Meditation, or the Science of Creative Intelligence. Born in 1911 as Mahesh Prasād Varma, he earned a degree in physics from Allahabad University in 1942. He studied under a meditation master named Swāmī Brahmānanda Saraswati, also known as Guru Dev (1869–1953). On the death of his Guru, Mahesh went into the Himālayas for a meditation retreat from which he emerged in 1958 with plans to transform the world. He founded several organizations that have brought this simple approach to calming meditation to the West, where he and his associates have initiated several million Westerners. (*See also* Transcendental Meditation.)

⌘ MAHĀSABHĀ ⌘

See Hindu Mahāsabhā.

⌘ MAHĀŚIVARĀTRI ⌘

Great Night of Śiva. Name of the annual festival dedicated to Śiva, held on the thirteenth night and fourteenth day of the dark half of the month of Phālguna (February-March). The festival is very widely celebrated, so that even those who are not devotees of Śiva often take part. Devotees typically fast all day, and the festival begins with an all-night vigil of temple visitation, devotional song, and Pūjā offerings. Auspicious viewing (Darśana) of temple images of Śiva, often the Liṅga form, are an important aspect of the festival. The Liṅga is likely to be decorated with sandalwood paste, flower petals, and bilva leaves, and bathed in milk and honey, in honor of Śiva. The following day features feasts and celebrations of all kinds. A tale recounted in several Purāṇas reveals the mythic origin of this festival. An evil hunter once unintentionally dropped water on a Śiva Liṅga, caused some bilva leaves to fall on it, and stayed awake all night, going without food for a day while hunting. In doing so, he honored Śiva, however inadvertantly, and as his reward he went to heaven after death.

Should others of better character and better Karma similarly honor Śiva, the account says, they will be rewarded as well. The festival follows the pattern established in the myth. The thirteenth night and fourteenth day of each month is sacred to Śiva and is celebrated in a similar fashion, but on a smaller scale, by devotees as Śivarātri. (*See also* Liṅga; Śaivism; Śiva.)

⌘ MAHĀTMĀ ⌘

One who has a great soul. The term is a title often given to or used by individuals regarded as saintly by Hindus. Mohandās Gāndhī is an example in recent times of a person widely regarded as saintly and as deserving of this title, traditionally reserved for a leader whose leadership is based on explicitly religious grounds, usually a Saṃnyāsin. (*See also* Ātman; Gāndhī, Mohandās.)

⌘ MAHENDRA ⌘

A variant of the name Indra (Mahā + Indra), meaning Great Indra.

⌘ MAHENDRAVIKRAMA VARMAN ⌘

Name of a king of the Pallava dynasty who probably reigned about 600 to 630 C.E. from his capital of Kāñcīpuram. He is credited as the author of the play entitled *Mattavilāsa* (The drunken farce). (*See also Mattavilāsa*.)

⌘ MAHIṢA, MAHIṢĀSURA ⌘

Name of a demon (Asura), whose form was that of a water buffalo but who could assume other forms as well. He conquered the entire world and fought against the gods, who could not defeat him thanks to the boon he had received that no man could kill him. The gods determined that a woman must be found to kill this demon. They combined all their energy (Tejas) in the form of Devī, the Goddess, or Durgā, who immediately rushed off and killed Mahiṣa. The appearance of the Buffalo Demon was the occasion for the origin of the Goddess, according to this myth, which gave the Goddess a place in the Brahmanical pantheon of gods. (*See also* Devī; Durgā; Goddess.)

⌘ MAJUMDAR, R. C. ⌘

Indologist (1888–1980). Born in Faridapur district of eastern Bengal, he received a Ph.D. from Calcutta University and became professor of history at Dhaka University. His monumental *History and Culture of the Indian People* was completed just before his death. (*See also* Indology.)

⌘ MĀLĀ ⌘

Rosary; garland. The term is used especially to refer to a string of beads used to keep count of recitations of a Mantra or prayer. (*See also* Bhakti.)

⌘ MĀMALLAPURAM ⌘

A temple complex on the beach south of Madras in Tamilnadu, site of a provincial capital of the Pallava dynasty (fifth through eighth century C.E.). Built by the Pallavas in the seventh century C.E., the small temples and shrines are carved out of rock. There are eight halls (Maṇḍapam), two of which were left unfinished; the most interesting is the Kṛṣṇa Maṇḍapam which features a sculpture of him holding Mount Govardhana to shelter the cowherds from Indra's rain. There are also eight Rathas, miniature temples in various styles, five of which are named after the Pāṇḍavas, the heroes of the *Mahābhārata*. The Shore Temple is a beautiful full-size temple, unusual for having comparable shrines to both Śiva and Viṣṇu; it has been declared a World Heritage protected site in an effort to aid preservation. The site also features a cliffside bas-relief of a very elaborate sculpture depicting the descent of the Ganges from heaven, apparently combined with a representation of Arjuna's penance. In January-February there is an annual dance festival that lasts a month.

⌘ MAMMAṬA ⌘

Scholar and literary critic who lived about 1100 C.E. in Kashmir. He wrote a work on poetics and aesthetics entitled *Kāvya Prakāśa*.

⌘ MANASĀ ⌘

Goddess worshipped especially in Bengal and other parts of northeastern India. She is a goddess of snakes and their poisons.

The Jhapan festival in her honor occurs in monsoon season, when her devotees gather cobras which they handle and allow to bite them so as to demonstrate their faith in and total reliance on the grace of the goddess in this life and the afterlife. (*See also* Nāga; Viṣṇupur.)

⌘ *MĀNAVA DHARMA ŚĀSTRA,* or *MANUSMṚTI* ⌘

Name of the most important text on the social and religious obligations (Dharma) of Hindus. The work was composed in Sanskrit, probably about the first century B.C.E. or first century C.E., and has some 2,685 verses. Within a few centuries, this text had become, and has since remained, the definitive and authoritative teaching on Varṇāśramadharma, the social and religious obligations based on one's caste and stage of life. Almost half the verses of this text attributed to the sage Manu are found also in the *Mahābhārata*'s twelfth and thirteenth books, though it is unclear which text has borrowed from the other. Manu deals with topics such as the following: how a king should rule his kingdom, the punishments appropriate to specific crimes, taxation, inheritance, rites of passage (Saṃskāra) such as marriage, relationships between married couples, and the duties of individuals of various caste groups and the four stages of life. These rules are set within the context of a clearly articulated worldview. Chapter 1 relates the creation of the cosmos and the divinely ordained place of humanity in the world. The text devotes a great deal of its attention to the unique position and status of Brahmins, insisting that they are to be treated with the utmost respect and rewarded for their vital contributions to the welfare of society. British officials in the nineteenth century established Manu's text as the primary guide to Hindu legal traditions in their colonial administration. (*See also* Caste; Dharma; Four Goals of Humanity; Four Stages of Life; Jāti; Manu; Marriage; Saṃskāra.)

⌘ MAṆḌALA ⌘

A meditation diagram. These usually consist of squares, concentric circles, and/or interlocking triangles focussing on a central point. Sometimes they are abstract forms, sometimes they have representations of deities on them. They are used in the practice of Yoga as an aid to concentration, helping the meditator focus the mind on one thing. They are most effectively used by visualization rather than by looking at a physical image. (*See also* Yantra; Yoga.)

⌘ MĀṆIKAVĀCAKAR ⌘

Ninth-century Brahmin Nāyanār saint who composed and sang devotional songs to Śiva in Tamil. His poetic composition *Tiruvācakam* (Blessed Utterance) may have been influenced by the example and concepts of the *Bhagavad Gītā*, but the object of his devotion is Śiva. His work is still sung in rituals of devotion at Śiva temples in Tamilnadu. (*See also* Nāyanār; Śiva.)

⌘ MANTRA ⌘

A sound, word or words used as an aid to meditation or in religious observances. Repeated recitation of a Mantra regularizes the breath. In Yoga practice, they may also be used to focus the mind. The most well known Mantra is Oṃ (or Auṃ), but there are many, some of which are quite long. All Mantras are regarded by those who use them as having meaning, but some have a clear and obvious meaning based on their grammar and syntax. The Veda Saṃhitās are also known as Mantra Saṃhitās, the verses regarded as Mantras. (*See also* Oṃ; Saṃhitā; Yoga.)

⌘ MANU ⌘

Name of a progenitor of humanity in various texts. Manu is associated with the Fish (Matsya) Avatāra of Viṣṇu as the human being who survives the flood and repopulates the earth. To Manu is attributed the legal text *Mānava Dharma Śāstra* (Laws of Manu), the most important and certainly best-known Hindu text on Dharma (duty, law). The text includes such matters as the duties incumbent upon the social classes or castes and the four stages of life, and how people in such categories should interrelate; domestic rituals and rites of passage; inheritance laws, and other topics. (*See also* Dharma; *Mānava Dharma Śāstra*; Matsya).

⌘ MARĀṬHAS ⌘

Name for a group of people from Mahārāṣṭra who were successful warriors. They rose to prominence in the late seventeenth century under the leadership of Śivāji, who remains a hero in the state today. His martial exploits against the militarily superior Mughal authorities are legendary. He used guerrilla tactics frequently and well, eventually controlling most of central India's Deccan plateau and heavily pressuring Emperor Aurangzeb. After his death in 1680, the Marāṭhas were commanded by leaders known as Peshwas, headquartered at Pune, who continued the expansionist policy of Śivāji until their defeat in 1761 at Panipat by a Muslim army. The last Peshwa surrendered to British authorities only in 1818, ending Marāṭha independence. (*See also* Pune; Śivāji.)

⌘ MĀRĪCA ⌘

Name of the uncle of Rāvaṇa, according to the *Rāmāyaṇa*. He was a demon who practiced austerities in a forest hermitage. Rāvaṇa persuaded his uncle to aid in his plan to abduct Rāma's wife Sītā by disguising himself in the form of a deer to lure away Rāma and Lakṣmaṇa so that Rāvaṇa would find Sītā alone. Mārīca was shot by Rāma and died, but the plan succeeded. (*See also* *Rāmāyaṇa*; Rāvaṇa.)

⌘ MĀRKAṆḌEYA ⌘

A Brahmin sage and ascetic descended from Bhṛgu. He was granted a vision of the cataclysmic flood that ended the world (Pralaya). Adrift on the waters, he saw an infant from which light was streaming; he was inhaled by the infant, and saw the entire universe, the gods and demons, and all the elements of creation. He was exhaled by the infant, whom he then knew to be Mahāviṣṇu, the Absolute in the form of an infant. This myth reflects the general Hindu view of time as cyclical, and of the world as being repeatedly created and destroyed. One of the eighteen major Purāṇas is named after Mārkaṇḍeya. (*See also* Creation; Pralaya; Viṣṇu; World Ages.)

⌘ MARRIAGE ⌘

One of the most important rites of passage (Saṃskāra), regarded as a sacrament. The traditional Vedic ceremony includes the husband and wife walking around a fire seven times as they affirm their marriage vows to the accompaniment of verses from the Veda. Marriage is expected and encouraged, both as a means of having offspring to continue the lineage so the ancestral offerings will not cease, and for the sake of pleasure (Kāma). The practice of arranging marriages of females while they are still children is an ancient one, supported by the *Mānava Dharma Śāstra* (9.88–94) and other legal texts, where it is envisioned that a man of thirty marry a girl of twelve. Widow remarriage was a contested matter, the legal authorities differing widely on its admissibility. The *Mānava Dharma Śāstra* (5.156–64) forbids a second marriage for widows of consummated marriages. It seems generally to have been envisioned that marriage did not pertain only to one lifetime, but the linking of one's Karma with another's had profound impact on the afterlife and future lives as well, hence the reluctance to allow remarriage, and the widespread support for the practice of widow immolation, or Satī. (*See also Mānava Dharma Śāstra*; Saṃskāra; Satī.)

⌘ MARUTS ⌘

Sons of Rudra; deities of storm in the Veda. Invoked often in the *Ṛg Veda* (1.85–88, and 7.56–59, for example), especially with Indra, they are celebrated as young warriors who drink Soma, and are asked to protect those who worship them. They are often praised for bringing rain. (*See also* Indra; Rudra; Soma.)

⌘ MATHURĀ ⌘

Ancient cultural and religious center in Uttar Pradesh. It is particularly associated with Kṛṣṇa, who is reputed to have been born here: Śrī Kṛṣṇa Janmabhūmi, his birthplace, is a small room resembling a prison cell in the ruins of the ancient Keśava Deo temple (which was destroyed by the Mughal emperor Aurangzeb in the late seventeenth century). Temples to Kṛṣṇa abound, often honoring Rādhā as well. Mathurā is just a few miles south of Vṛndāvana (Vrindāban) where he spent his youth with the cowherds and milkmaids as celebrated in the *Bhāgavata Purāṇa*, *Gītagovinda*, and other texts. (*See also* Govardhana, Mount; Kṛṣṇa; Pilgrimage; Vṛndāvana.)

⌘ MATSYA ⌘

The Fish Avatāra of Viṣṇu, first of the ten incarnations. Once a small fish approached Manu and asked for protection from larger fish. Manu took the fish and placed it in a pot, moving it to larger pots, a pond, and finally the Ganges River as the fish grew. Out of gratitude, the fish told Manu that soon there would be a great flood that would cover the whole earth, and that he should build a boat to save himself. Manu gathered the seven Ṛṣis (representative of the seven Brahmin clans that created and transmitted the majority of the *Ṛg Veda*) in the boat as the rain began to fall. The level of the water rose and covered the earth. As the boat floated on the water, the fish appeared and, by means of a horn on its head, pulled Manu's boat to the one remaining mountain peak that was not covered by water. Manu tied the boat to the peak, and as the water receded, Manu and the sages emerged to repopulate the earth. In this fashion Manu became the progenitor of humanity and saved the Vedas from extinction, thanks to the advice of Viṣṇu in the form of a fish. Variant versions of this myth are found in many Purāṇas (for example, *Matsya Purāṇa* 1.11–34, and 2.1–19). One version in the *Śatapatha Brāhmaṇa* (1.8.1) does not identity the fish as any god's incarnation, and another version in the *Mahābhārata* (3.185) identifies the giant fish as Brahmā the Creator, which may indicate that the myth was originally not identified with either god, but eventually the miraculous manifestation of the fish came to be seen as the salvific work of Viṣṇu. (*See also* Avatāra; Manu; Viṣṇu; World Ages.)

⌘ MATSYENDRANĀTH ⌘

Founder of the Nāth sect in the tenth century C.E. It is said that, in the form of a fish (matsya), he overheard Śiva teaching his wife Pārvatī, and transmitted these teachings to humanity. (*See also* Nāth.)

⌘ *MATTAVILĀSA* ⌘

The Drunken Farce, the name of a play attributed to King Mahendravikrama Varman of the Pallava dynasty, in the early seventh century C.E. The setting is Kāñcīpuram, at the time of the play's composition. The play revolves around the antics of Kāpālin, a Śiva-worshipping ascetic of the Kāpālika sect, and his female disciple Devasomā, who have lost the skull that functions as their begging bowl. Their search for it brings them into contact with members of various other religious orders then current, including a degenerate Buddhist monk named Nāgasena, a Pāśupata devotee, and a lunatic. They eventually find that the skull has been taken away by a dog. The drama presents caricatures of the religious traditions of that time, ridiculing the pretensions and hypocrisy of those who fall far short of their professed ideals. A small portion of the script, where Kāpālin performs a dance, is still enacted in the Kūṭiyāṭṭam tradition of Kerala. Here the character is regarded as Śiva in disguise, and the performance is a solemn religious event, traditionally enacted within the compound of a Hindu temple in the context of a religious festival as a devotional offering to the deity. (*See also* Kāñcīpuram; Kāpālika; Kūṭiyāṭṭam; Mahendravikrama Varman.)

⌘ MAURYA ⌘

Name of the first imperial dynasty of India (321–180 B.C.E.). Founded by Candragupta Maurya just after the appearance in northwest India of Alexander the Great, the Mauryan state was a highly centralized bureaucracy with a large standing army. Candragupta's grandson was the famous Aśoka.

⌘ MAYA ⌘

A Dānava (demon) who is a great architect and builder. He is credited with construction of Indraprastha, city of the Pāṇḍavas in the *Mahābhārata*. Purāṇa traditions attribute the building of Tripura, the demons' city, to him also.

⌘ MĀYĀ ⌘

Illusion; magic; creative power. The term appears in the *Ṛg Veda* and later literature as the power of a god (or even a demon) to create. The world was seen as the manifestation of this power, Māyā. Its most important usage is found in the Advaita Vedānta philosophical system as articulated by Śaṅkara, where Māyā refers to the illusory nature of the phenomenal world. According to Śaṅkara, the world is not unreal but we misperceive it because of our ignorance, and because of the power of Māyā. We see the world, and ourselves, as separate entities having particular names and forms, when in reality all is Brahman. Thus, the world is illusory, unreal in an ultimate sense because its manifestations are impermanent, and reality is Nirguṇa Brahman, Ultimate Reality beyond all attributes and qualities. Māyā is the force that enmeshes and binds us to Saṃsāra, the cycle of rebirth from which we seek liberation (Mokṣa). Seeing through Māyā and overcoming ignorance lead to liberation. In some theistic traditions, Māyā is seen as the creative power of Ultimate Reality, the feminine force (Śakti) that creates the world, either in the sense of the feminine consort of God or as the Goddess who is Ultimate Reality in her own right. (*See also* Advaita Vedānta.)

⌘ MĀYĀPUR ⌘

Town in West Bengal that is the site of a very large Kṛṣṇa temple operated by the Hare Krishna movement, or the International Society for Krishna Consciousness. (*See also* Hare Krishna Movement.)

⌘ MEDITATION ⌘

See Kuṇḍalinī; Tapas; Yoga.

⌘ MERIT ⌘

Translation of the Sanskrit term Puṇya, equivalent to good Karma. Actions that are beneficial and ethical, such as making pilgrimages or donating food to ascetic renouncers, are regarded as generating merit for the person who performs them, leading to better rebirth. (*See also* Karma.)

⌘ MERU, MOUNT ⌘

Mythic mountain thought to reside at the center of the world, supporting heaven. The gods are regarded as residing on Meru and its associated peaks. Also sometimes called Sumeru, it is the center around which the continents and oceans are arranged in imaginative geographies and cosmologies preserved in the *Mahābhārata* and Purāṇas. A number of different peaks, from the source of the Ganges to Iran, have been identified as Meru. (*See also* Creation; Kailāsa.)

⌘ MĪMĀṂSĀ ⌘

The philosophical tradition of Enquiry, one of six philosophical schools regarded by Hindus as orthodox. This tradition is also known as Pūrva Mīmāṃsā (Earlier Enquiry), in contrast with Uttara Mīmāṃsā (Later Enquiry) or Vedānta, the philosophical school with which it is paired as most similar. They have in common that each has created a theology from analysis of scriptural statements. Mīmāṃsā is largely based on Jaimini's *Mīmāṃsā Sūtra*, a work perhaps datable to about 200 B.C.E. The school's focus is on the Vedic literature and the sacrificial rituals that literature enjoins one to perform. Statements made in the Vedic texts that indicate a specific action one should perform are regarded by the Mīmāṃsā school as obligatory and as leading to absolute happiness if correctly performed. Other portions of the Veda that do not relate to sacrifice are regarded as irrelevant. Hence the accurate interpretation of the Vedic texts is crucial, and this school has accordingly devoted great attention to grammar and linguistic analysis. The Vedic texts themselves are regarded as eternal and infallible, not created by human beings (apauruṣeya). Correctly performed sacrificial rituals are held to lead inevitably to the desired result of heaven for the patron. The tradition continues today, for example, in the curriculum of the monastic schools of Śaṅkara's Advaita Vedānta tradition. (*See also* Philosophical Schools; Śabara; Vedānta.)

⌘ MĪNĀKṢĪ ⌘

The Fish-Eyed Goddess, to whom the Madurai temple is dedicated. She is said to have been born with long, fish-shaped eyes, a fishy odor, and three breasts. She became a great warrior and had many victories until Śiva (Śrī Sundareśvara, The Beauty's Lord) appeared, whereupon her third breast disappeared, as did her fishy odor and warrior nature, signifying that Śiva was her lord. Their marriage was arranged but her maternal uncle (or brother) was late; the marriage was held without him. Each year the festival occurs in the month of Caitra (March-April) and the wedding of the goddess is celebrated, even though he (understood to be Viṣṇu) is late again, delayed by a tryst with a Muslim princess at a nearby mosque! The divine couple are housed in separate shrines, but each evening at 9:30 Śiva's image is carried to her bedroom and the two images cohabit until the following morning at six. The two are regarded as a married couple. (*See also* Goddess; Madurai; Śiva.)

⌘ MĪRĀ BAI ⌘

Female saint (1498–1550 C.E.). She was a princess of a powerful Rājput clan in western India who fled an arranged marriage to devote herself to worship of Kṛṣṇa. Her songs of love and longing for her divine lover, composed in vernacular Hindi, continue to have appeal throughout northern India; indeed, her poems may well be the most often quoted of any north Indian saint. Few of her poems appear in writing before the eighteenth century, however, causing some scholars to question whether many of the poems traditionally attributed to her were actually authored by her. One is included in the Sikh scripture entitled *Guru Granth Sahīb*. That others might want to attribute their poetry to her is an indication of the power of the account of her saintly life. She patterned her love for Kṛṣṇa on the relationship of the Gopīs to him, and said that in a former life she had been a Gopī who had loved Kṛṣṇa. She lived as an ascetic Saṃnyāsin and travelled widely singing God's praises. She is said to have been a disciple of Ravidās. To experience the bliss of Kṛṣṇa's presence as fully as possible, she lived for years in Vṛndāvana, scene of the earthly youth and loveplay with the Gopīs. A temple there, built in the nineteenth century by the chief minister of the princely state of Bikaner in Rajasthan, has an image of Mīrā standing next to Kṛṣṇa and Rādhā. (*See also* Gopī; Kṛṣṇa; Ravidās; Vṛndāvana.)

⌘ MITRA ⌘

One of the twelve Ādityas. The name means "friend" or "companion" and emphasizes his companionship both with his human worshippers and certain of the gods of the Veda. Invoked often in the *Ṛg Veda*, Mitra is usually paired with Varuṇa (as in 5.62 through 5.72, and 7.60 through 7.66) or with Aryaman (as in 5.67). Mitra and Varuṇa are celebrated for their sovereignty over the world and especially for being guardians of cosmic order (Ṛta). In *Ṛg Veda* 3.59, Mitra is invoked alone, where he is praised for summoning human beings to activity, sustaining the world, and looking upon human activity unceasingly. (*See also* Āditya; Aryaman; Ṛta; Varuṇa.)

⌘ MOHENJO-DARO ⌘

Major city of the Indus Valley Civilization, sometimes also known as the Harappan Civilization. It flourished from about

2500 B.C.E. until about 1700 B.C.E. It was located toward the southern end of the Indus River, in what is now the Pakistani province of Sind. The city had a population of some 40,000 to 50,000 people, making it one of the largest cities of the ancient world at the time. (*See also* Harappa; Indus Valley Civilization.)

⌘ MOHINĪ ⌘

Female form of Viṣṇu. When the gods and demons quarrelled over possession of the Amṛta (elixir of life), Viṣṇu assumed the form of a beautiful female to distract the demons, allowing the gods to take possession of the elixir. (*See also* Amṛta.)

⌘ MOKṢA ⌘

Liberation. The term is used to refer to liberation from Saṃsāra, the cycle of rebirth. Mokṣa is a state free from all suffering and sorrow, often described as infinitely blissful. Theistic traditions typically depict Mokṣa as proximity to God so that loving devotion can be expressed, but not a merging with God. For example, Vaiṣṇava traditions generally regard Mokṣa as being in the presence of Kṛṣṇa or Viṣṇu in a heavenly realm, while Śaiva Siddhānta envisions Mokṣa as attaining equality with, but not identity with, Śiva. Monistic traditions such as Advaita Vedānta regard Mokṣa as union with Ultimate Reality (Brahman), a state of unlimited being, awareness, and bliss in which the limitations of one's individuality and personality are transcended so that one merges with Brahman. However conceived in any particular tradition, Mokṣa is the goal of every Hindu religious tradition. (*See also* Bhakti; Consciousness, States of; Jīvan-mukti; Rebirth; Saṃsāra.)

⌘ MUDRĀ ⌘

A position in which the hands are held that communicates symbolically a particular meaning. A Mudrā can be used iconographically, as a pose in which a deity is depicted so as to communicate a message such as "have no fear." A Mudrā may also be used by a Tantric meditation practitioner as a posture that is regarded as powerful and transformative because a deity also adopts that posture; identification with that deity is facilitated by imitation of the posture. Over a hundred different Mudrās are used in Hindu iconography. (*See also* Darśana; Mūrti; Tantra.)

⌘ MUKTĀNANDA, SWĀMĪ ⌘

Guru in Siddha Yoga tradition of Tantric Kuṇḍalinī practice (1908–1982). A disciple of Swāmī (or Bhagwān) Nityānanda, Muktānanda inherited the movement his Guru had founded, the Siddha Yoga movement. After meeting his Guru in 1947 at the age of thirty-eight, Muktānanda was awakened and came to the United States in 1970 to initiate followers. He had remarkable success, and left an organization with hundreds of meditation centers worldwide. The tradition is based on Kashmir Śaivism. (*See also* Kashmir Śaivism; Siddha Yoga.)

⌘ MÜLLER, FRIEDRICH MAX ⌘

(also spelled MUELLER). Philologist, orientalist, and historian of religions (1823–1900). Born in Dessau, Germany, as the son of poet Wilhelm Müller, he studied at Leipzig and Berlin, where he became fascinated with the recently deciphered language of Sanskrit. He went to Paris to study with Eugène Burnouf, and there began to prepare an edition of the *Ṛg Veda*. Müller went to London to examine manuscripts obtained by the British East India Company, and in 1847 the Company commissioned him to edit and publish the text, which appeared in installments from 1849 to 1874. He was appointed Taylorian Professor of Modern Languages at Oxford University in 1854, then professor of comparative philology at Oxford from 1868 onwards, the first such chair in Britain. He wrote many works on comparative religions and mythology, Hinduism, and language, as well as producing translations of various Sanskrit texts. He also edited the fifty-one-volume series *Sacred Books of the East*, a groundbreaking effort that is still useful today. (*See also* Indology; Sanskrit.)

⌘ MUNI ⌘

Sage. In the *Ṛg Veda* (as in 10.136), a Muni is a sage who performs ascetic practices. In later Hindu traditions, a Muni is particularly a sage who has taken a vow of silence.

⌘ MŪRTI ⌘

Form, especially the divine form as represented in iconography. (*See also* Darśana; Mudrā; Pūjā; Trimūrti.)

⌘ MURUGAN (MURUKAN) ⌘

Name in Tamil of the god of war, Skanda, known also as Kārttikeya or Kumāra. (*See also* Skanda.)

⌘ MUSIC ⌘

In Hinduism, music has a religious significance. The recitation of the Veda, particularly in the *Sāma Veda* tradition, is highly musical. Classical Indian music developed many of its complex rāgas in the context of devotional offerings to the gods. Music was always an integral part of dramatic enactment, as clearly indicated in the *Nāṭya Śāstra* of Bharata and in the Kūṭiyāṭṭam form of theatre, preserved in Hindu temples for centuries. Popular enactments of stories from the *Mahābhārata*, *Rāmāyaṇa*, and Purāṇas usually include music as well. Devotional songs (Bhajans) such as those sung by Mīrā Bai or the Nāyanār poets express religious sentiments in vernacular languages that are readily understood. Music has even been spoken of by performers as their means of liberation, because they transcend their limitations and become vehicles for divine inspiration as they perform. As with all art in traditional India, the artists were generally regarded not as creators of their art but as vehicles for the expression of already existing truths. (*See also Nāṭya Śāstra.*)

— N —

⌘ NĀGA ⌘

Snake. Serpents have received worship in South Asia for many centuries, where they have been regarded as guardians of the life-giving powers of the waters in springs, pools, and wells. They have long been venerated as powerful beings who guard fields. Their association with water and soil has led to Nāgas being worshipped for fertility, prosperity, and the healing of illness. They figure prominently in village life throughout India, and shrines to Nāgas can be found under trees, near water, or at the temples of the gods. Viṣṇu is often depicted with a protective canopy of cobra hoods above him, as he lies on the coils of Śeṣa the multi-headed cosmic serpent. Śiva is usually associated with Nāgas in his iconic representations as well. Goddesses are also often depicted with Nāgas as attendant or guardian figures; Manasā in Bengal is regarded as the Mother of Serpents and is worshipped by her devotees who handle snakes to show their reliance on the goddess's grace. Nāgas can change shape, and are often depicted in iconography as having human faces. Nāgas are often regarded as living in a netherworld called "Pātāla."

⌘ NĀGĀ ⌘

Name of an order of naked ascetics from castes other than Brahmins. Since Brahmins were ideally not supposed to use violence, even in their own defense, Nāgā ascetics fought to protect them. They have particularly been affiliated with the Daśanāmi order founded by Śaṅkara, and have engaged in pitched battles with both Muslim forces and rival Hindu ascetic orders, which also had renounced warriors. (*See also* Daśanāmi.)

⌘ NAIMIṢA ⌘

A forest famous as a place of pilgrimage. It was the site of a twelve-year-long Vedic sacrifice held by Śaunaka at which the *Mahābhārata* (1.1) was recited by Ugraśravas Sauti, son and pupil of Lomaharṣaṇa Sūta, who had heard it at Janamejaya's sacrifice being recited by Vaiśaṃpāyana, Vyāsa's pupil. (*See also* Lomaharṣaṇa; *Mahābhārata*; Sūta; Vyāsa.)

⌘ NAMBŪTIRI (NAMBOODIRI) BRAHMINS ⌘

A lineage of Brahmins in Kerala, south India. They may well have arrived in Kerala in the first few centuries B.C.E. They are distinctive for recognizing only three Vedas (not the *Atharva*), and for a peculiar style of recitation of the Veda with accompanying hand gestures (Mudrā) and head movements (used as mnemonic devices for accents). In the history of Kerala, Nambūtiri Brahmins have been granted extraordinary privileges because of their learning and the desire on the part of rulers to support Brahmanical culture, which they were seen to embody. (*See also* Brāhmaṇa; Brahmin; Trayī Vidyā.)

⌘ NAMMĀḺVĀR ⌘

South Indian saint, who probably lived in the eighth century C.E. One of the Āḻvārs, he was born a Śūdra (the serf or servant caste), but despite his low status in conventional social terms, his poems became tremendously popular throughout the region in which Tamil was spoken. They were collected in a text known as the *Tiruvāymoḻi* and have been used in temple rituals since about the tenth century along with other devotional poems, the entire collection known as the *Prabandham* or *Nālāyira Divya Prabandham* (Composition of Four Thousand Poems). His poems reveal a very emotional devotion to Viṣṇu. His use of the vernacular language of Tamil had the effect of broadening the audience for his work within Tamil society, appealing to people of all social classes, but also limited the circulation of his poems to the region of south India where Tamil was understood. His work is one of the earliest examples of Bhakti (devotional) poetry in vernacular languages, and has had great influence. Some of his poems continue to be recited by devotees to the present day. (*See also* Āḻvārs; Bhakti; *Tiruvāymoḻi*; Vaiṣṇavism.)

⌘ NAMUCI ⌘

A demon whom Indra killed. The *Ṛg Veda* makes only passing reference to the event (for example, 8.14.13), but the story is elaborated in later literature where Namuci is said to have received the boon that he could be killed neither in day nor night, and neither by anything wet nor dry. Indra caught Namuci at sunset and killed him with seafoam, thereby complying with the conditions of the boon. (*See also* Indra; Narasiṃha.)

⌘ NĀNAK ⌘

Founder of Sikhism (1469–1539). Born of a Hindu Kṣatriya family near Lahore, he made a living as an accountant. After a religious experience he travelled widely in India before settling in Kartarpur, Punjab, where he attracted disciples. He praised the One God in devotional songs, and fused elements of Hindu and Muslim belief and practice. He accepted Hindu ideas such as rebirth according to Karma, and liberation from rebirth, but rejected the authority of the Vedas and Brahmins, as well as the worship of any of the Hindu deities and the caste system. His poems are preserved in the *Ādi Granth*, compiled in 1604 as the first sacred text of the newly emergent Sikh community.

⌘ NANDA GOPA ⌘

Foster father of Kṛṣṇa. (*See also* Kṛṣṇa.)

⌘ NANDI ⌘

Joyful. Name of the bull who is Śiva's vehicle (Vāhana). Typically depicted as a powerful white bull, Nandi represents natural strength and instinct tamed and channelled. (*See also* Śiva.)

⌘ NARA ⌘

See Nārāyaṇa.

⌘ NĀRADA ⌘

A Brahmin sage who appears remarkably often in the Purāṇas. He frequently serves as a message bearer, informing human beings of some event or of the meaning of something having to do with the gods. He also receives teachings frequently, serving as a substitute for the human audience as, for example, when Viṣṇu reveals the power of Māyā to Nārada. His earliest appearance in literature may be in the *Chāndogya Upaniṣad* (7.1), where he is presented as a learned Brahmin who knows the Vedas and has other knowledge, but does not know the self, and is then instructed by Sanatkumāra.

⌘ NARASIṂHA ⌘

The Man-Lion Avatāra of Viṣṇu, fourth of the ten incarnations. The demon Hiraṇyakaśipu hated Viṣṇu and sought all means to harm him. He practiced austerities and won a boon from Brahmā that he could not be killed by any animal or human or god. A son named Prahlāda was born to Hiraṇyakaśipu and angered him greatly by being a devotee of Viṣṇu. Hiraṇyakaśipu abused Prahlāda until Narasiṃha burst out of a pillar and killed Hiraṇyakaśipu, thereby complying with the conditions of the boon by being neither animal nor man nor god. The myth illustrates the saving power of Viṣṇu, and has parallels with the myth of Namuci being killed by Indra. (*See also* Avatāra; Indra; Namuci; Viṣṇu.)

⌘ NĀRĀYAṆA ⌘

"Son of the Primordial Man" (Nara). Nara and Nārāyaṇa are associated with one another from the Veda onward. Nārāyaṇa is the seer (Ṛṣi) credited with *Ṛg Veda* 10.90, the Puruṣa Sūkta (Hymn of the Primordial Man), in which creation takes place by sacrifice of Puruṣa, who pervades the universe and extends beyond. Nara and Nārāyaṇa are regarded as a pair of gods or sages or yogins. Nārāyaṇa comes to be identified with Viṣṇu from early times. In the *Śatapatha Brāhmaṇa* (13.6), Puruṣa Nārāyaṇa is said to have performed a Pañcarātra (five-day) sacrifice, and the *Taittirīya Āraṇyaka* (10.1.6) identifies Nārāyaṇa with Viṣṇu. In the *Mahābhārata*, the names are used interchangeably, and Arjuna is regarded as an incarnation of Nara, and Kṛṣṇa an incarnation of Nārāyaṇa, continuing the theme of their inseparability. (*See also* Kṛṣṇa; Puruṣa; Viṣṇu.)

⌘ NĀSATYA ⌘

A name for the twin Vedic gods the Aśvins, with the meaning "helpful" or "kindly." (*See also* Aśvins.)

⌘ NĀSIK ⌘

City in Mahārāṣṭra at which, every twelve years, the Kumbha Melā festival is held. It is on the bank of the Godāvarī River, which is lined with bathing Ghāṭs (stairs down to the water) and some 200 temples and shrines. (*See also* Kumbha Melā.)

⌘ NĀSTIKA ⌘

Literally, one who says "it is not." The term is applied by orthodox Hindus to atheists and those who are not orthodox, particularly those who repudiate the authority of the Vedas, such as Buddhists, Jains, and Cārvākas.

⌘ NĀṬARĀJA ⌘

Lord of Dance, a name for Śiva in the form of a dancer. The iconographic image features a four-armed, but otherwise human, figure encircled in a ring of flame. Śiva is standing on his left foot, the right one raised as he whirls around. In one right hand he holds a small, two-headed drum traditionally used by Indian dancers to mark time as they dance. In one left hand he holds fire, the other being held out for balance. His remaining right hand is held up in the Mudrā, or gesture, indicating that one should have no fear, that he is approachable. He stands on a dwarfish figure who represents ignorance, which he is crushing, a destructive act in a sense, but one that liberates as well; Śiva grants knowledge and eliminates ignorance, thereby making liberation from rebirth possible. The drum and fire can both be regarded as symbolic representations of creation and destruction. The drum indicates the passage of time, so that with each beat of the drum a world is destroyed, and with the next beat a world is created. The fire represents both the destruction it can effect and the creation that such destruction makes possible. In addition, the fire is seen as a creative force, associated with the heat of life itself, the heat of passion that creates new life, and the fire of the Vedic sacrifice through which the sacrificer creates a new relationship with the gods, even a new self. The center of the cult of Śiva as Nāṭarāja is the temple of Cidambaram, and the image is particularly often found in south India, where brilliantly executed bronze statues of this form are often seen in temples. As Lord of Dance, Śiva is not only the master of the stage but also of the cosmos. (*See also* Cidambaram; *Nāṭya Śāstra;* Śiva.)

⌘ NĀTH ⌘

Name of a north Indian sect of Tantric Śaivism, also known as Kāṇphaṭa Yogīs. The founders of the sect appear to have been Matsyendranāth and Gorakṣanāth or Gorakhnāth (probably tenth century C.E.), who are widely credited with the development of Haṭha Yoga. Both are also regarded as Siddhas, perfected human beings who have achieved liberation from rebirth and have supernormal powers, including immortal bodies. This sect accepted members from all caste groups and has enjoyed considerable prominence in north India. (*See also* Gorakṣanāth; Haṭha Yoga; Kāṇphaṭa; Kuṇḍalinī; Matsyendranāth.)

⌘ NĀTHDWĀRA ⌘

Site of Śrī Nāthji, an image of Viṣṇu. The image, of black stone, was brought to Nāthdwāra (forty-eight kilometers north of

Udaipur in Rajasthan) in 1669 from Mathurā to prevent its destruction by Aurangzeb's Mughal forces.

⌘ NĀṬRĀJ ⌘

See Nāṭarāja.

⌘ *NĀṬYA ŚĀSTRA* ⌘

The Science of Drama. This Sanskrit text, attributed to the sage Bharata, presents in some 5,600 verses an analysis of the dramatic arts in a comprehensive fashion, with attention to language, makeup, costuming, music, the stage, and other features of performance. One of its most important contributions is the presentation of the theory of Rasa (particularly in chapters 6 and 7), the dominant aesthetic theory for the evaluation of both drama and poetry. The text begins with a description of the origin of drama, in which creation of drama is attributed to the creator god Brahmā, who taught Bharata this material as "the fifth Veda." Such a statement indicates a desire to invoke authority in support of the teachings presented, and to link the teachings to Vedic and Brahmanical tradition. It is stated that the first dramatic presentation was an enactment of the battle between gods and demons, at which depiction the demons took offense and disrupted the performance. It was determined that a theatre building would be needed as a proper setting for performance, and the text describes the extensive procedure for building a theatre and consecrating it by asking the Gods to inhabit and protect the structure. Brahmā is to be center stage and an array of gods as World Guardians (Lokapāla) are to be around the sides of the stage. All performances are to include ritual worship of the gods to insure success. Ritual procedures include the enactment onstage of Vedic mythic themes such as the use of a flagstaff that is called Indra's thunderbolt weapon (Vajra, and in the theatre Jarjara) and is used to break a waterpot onstage, so that the water flows over the stage, recalling Indra's mythic deed that made life possible. Worship of the gods is called Pūjā, reflective of the influence of devotional (Bhakti) traditions. The *Nāṭya Śāstra* thus represents a synthesis of ancient and more modern Hindu religious traditions, probably due to the desire both to preserve ancient traditions and to adapt to changing religious practices. The text has served as the measure of aesthetic quality for classical theatre ever since its composition, perhaps in the second century C.E. (*See also* Kūṭiyāṭṭam; Music; Nāṭarāja; Pūjā; Rasa; World Guardians.)

⌘ NAVARĀTRĪ PŪJĀ ⌘

Nine nights' worship, the name of a festival of devotion to the Goddess Durgā, also known as Daśahrā. This festival is celebrated all over India, but primarily in the north, around October 1. (*See also* Daśahrā; Durgā; Pūjā.)

⌘ NĀYANĀR ⌘

Saint in the Tamil tradition of Śaivism. The name means Leader, and along with the Vaiṣṇava saints known as Āḻvārs, they were venerated in the context of devotional (Bhakti) cults in south India. The Nāyanār poets of the sixth through eighth centuries C.E. composed songs of praise to Śiva, many of them highly emotional expressions of their love for God. Sixty-three poet-saints are revered in the Tamil tradition of śaivism, their biographies recounted in a text entitled *Periya Purāṇam* (Great history), composed in the twelfth century C.E. The Nāyanār poets include a woman, kings, Brahmins, men of low and Outcaste social status, and even a former Buddhist monk who had converted to Śaivism. Socially diverse groups such as this are a characteristic feature of Bhakti traditions, and indicate not only the inclusive nature of the community of devotees but also the concept that all human beings are capable of expressing their love for and devotion to God. Reverence for these saints, whose lives embody the ideals of devotion to which all devotees aspire, continues to be central to Tamil Śaivism. (*See also* Bhakti; Civavākkiyar; Māṇikavācakar; Śaiva Siddhānta; Śaivism; Śiva.)

⌘ NEHRU, JAWAHARLAL ⌘

The first Prime Minister of the Republic of India (1889–1964). Nehru was born in Allahabad to a wealthy Brahmin family originally from Kashmir; his father was an attorney. His early schooling was at the exclusive English school Harrow, and at Cambridge University. He returned to India and began to practice law in 1912, but became an activist in the Indian independence movement and was imprisoned repeatedly by British authorities for participating in civil disobedience campaigns led by Mohandās Gāndhī. Throughout his adult life, Nehru was skeptical of the spiritual aspects of Gāndhī's approach to political mobilization because of his distrust of religious orthodoxy, yet became one of Gāndhī's most trusted associates. Imprisoned for most of World War II because of his attempt to secure Britain's promise of independence after the war for India's cooperation during the war, Nehru wrote his book entitled *The Discovery of India* in jail. With the partition and independence in 1947, Nehru became the first Prime Minister of India, and his insistence on India being a secular state in which citizens of all religious groups could freely interact was vital to the establishment of that tradition. He was also a leader of international stature, the driving force behind establishment of the Non-Aligned Movement of nations seeking an alternative to membership in either the Western or Communist camps during the Cold War. He died in office, having set precedents for the Government of India as a secular and democratic institution. (*See also* Gāndhī, Mohandās.)

⌘ NEPAL ⌘

The world's only Hindu monarchy. A nation of some twenty million people, Nepal lies along the Himālaya Mountain range between India and Tibet (now part of China). Hinduism is the official state religion, though Buddhism is a visible presence in Nepal as well, and there is some intermixture of the two. Nepal, an absolute monarchy until 1990, at that time adopted a parliamentary form of government, the king becoming a largely ceremonial position as head of state, but retaining the power to dissolve Parliament at any time.

⌘ NEW DELHI ⌘

See Delhi.

⌘ NIMBĀRKA ⌘

Name of the twelfth-century-C.E. founder of a north Indian sect of Vaiṣṇavism devoted to Kṛṣṇa and Rādhā. Nimbārka developed a school of Vedānta interpretation known as Bhedābheda Advaita (simultaneous difference and nondifference between the human soul and God). This theology is a theistic Vedānta in which devotion to Kṛṣṇa and Rādhā leads to liberation from rebirth. (*See also* Kṛṣṇa; Rādhā; Vaiṣṇavism; Vedānta.)

⌘ NIRGUṆA BRAHMAN ⌘

Brahman Without Qualities, that is, the impersonal Absolute. It is particularly Śaṅkara and his Advaita Vedānta tradition that expounds the ultimacy of Nirguṇa Brahman and the identity of the individual self (Ātman) with it. For him, all forms and attributes are limitations imposed by ignorance and Māyā on what is in reality without attributes and limitations. Rāmānuja's Qualified Nondualism (Viśiṣṭha-Advaita) theology accepts the ultimacy of Nirguṇa Brahman but asserts also the reality of the personal form of Īśvara as well. Other formulations of the relation between Brahman and various manifestations of Brahman have been numerous. (*See also* Advaita Vedānta; Brahman; Guṇa; Saguṇa Brahman.)

⌘ NIRṚTI ⌘

The Vedic goddess of misfortune and destruction. In Vedic sacrifices (Yajña), offerings are made to appease her and keep her away from the sacrificial site. She is mentioned in the *Ṛg Veda* (7.37.7, and 7.104.9) occasionally as an ominous presence that the sacrificer wants to avoid.

⌘ NYĀYA ⌘

The philosophical tradition of logical analysis, one of the six schools of thought regarded as orthodox in Hinduism. It is typically paired with Vaiśeṣika, the tradition to which it is considered to be most similar. Nyāya is more than simply a means of analyzing arguments and employing reason for the sake of attaining correct knowledge. It is also a philosophical and metaphysical system in which the correct use of logical analysis is held to lead to liberation from rebirth. Perhaps the most significant advance in Nyāya thought came in the twelfth century with Gaṅgeśa's *Tattvacintāmaṇi*, a work so revolutionary that later tradition refers to his school of thought as Navya-Nyāya (New Nyāya). The interest of Navya-Nyāya is in epistemology, specifically, valid means of cognition (pramāṇa), that is, methods of attaining the truth, of which four are acknowledged: (1) sense perceptions (pratyakṣa), from information provided by one's senses; (2) inference (anumāna), reasoning from cause to effect, or the reverse, or from shared characteristics; (3) analogy (upamāna), knowledge of a thing based on its similarity to another, known thing; and (4) the authoritative teachings of scriptures (śabda), particularly the Vedic literature. Through knowing reality truly, liberation results. Nyāya maintained that liberation could be experienced only after death, not while living, contradicting most other schools of philosophical thought and most Hindu religious traditions. Nyāya refined its analytical techniques in debates with Buddhists (through about the twelfth century, until their disappearance), and with other Indian schools of thought. (*See also* Philosophical Schools; Vaiśeṣika.)

— O —

⌘ OLCOTT, HENRY STEELE ⌘

Hindu advocate (1832–1907). Cofounder of the Theosophical Society (with Helena P. Blavatsky), and its first president. He served in the U.S. Army, attaining the rank of colonel, then became a successful attorney and journalist before meeting Madame Blavatsky in 1875. While primarily an advocate of Buddhism, Olcott also drew upon Hindu religious thought in the formulation of the Theosophical Society's doctrines. He travelled extensively in India and had a role in stimulating English-educated Hindus to value their own religious and philosophical heritage more highly. (*See also* Blavatsky, Helena Petrovna; Theosophical Society.)

⌘ OṂ ⌘

Mantra also written as Auṃ. The *Chāndogya Upaniṣad* begins with a long discussion of the sound Oṃ, where it is held to represent all sound, to be the essence of the Veda and the key to immortality and union with Brahman. The mantra has figured prominently in meditation and Yoga practices of all kinds. In the form Auṃ, three sounds blended into one, Hindus have seen an auditory representation of the three realms (earth, atmosphere, and heaven) as a unified cosmos. Oṃ has also been taken into

Buddhism, where it is used in many meditative traditions, for example, as the most often chanted Mantra in Tibetan Buddhism (Oṃ maṇi padme huṃ), and in the name of the controversial Japanese cult Auṃ Shinrikyō. (*See also* Mantra; Yoga.)

⌘ OSHO ⌘

See Rajneesh, Bhagwan.

⌘ OUTCASTE ⌘

Term for an individual or group excluded from the caste system of social organization. They are regarded by members of the caste system as having very low status, and they traditionally performed the least desirable functions in society, such as handling dead bodies, cleaning latrines, etc. Such people are the "Untouchables," so named because a person of caste status would be regarded as ritually polluted by their touch. Some groups may have been classified as Outcaste because they were tribal groups not assimilated by Brahmanical culture; others may once have been in the caste system but lost their status because of failure to perform appropriate rituals or to observe social strictures. Traditionally, Outcastes were required to announce their presence by means such as making loud noises so that higher-status people could avoid them. Even in the twentieth century, Outcastes were denied entry into many Hindu temples. Today probably about ten per cent of the population of India is composed of people of Outcaste status. Mahātmā Gāndhī termed Outcastes the Harijan (Children of God) in an effort to emphasize their humanity and encourage Indian society to accept and integrate them. India's Constitution, since its adoption in 1950, has made discrimination based on one's caste or outcaste status illegal. The Government of India, in an effort to improve the socioeconomic status of Outcastes, has reserved a percentage of places in colleges, universities, and government service for members of Backward Classes, a category that includes Outcastes and Śūdras (Serfs). (*See also* Ambedkar, Bhīmrao; Caṇḍāla; Caste; Dharma; Gāndhī, Mohandās; Harijan; Jāti.)

— P —

⌘ PADMANĀBHI ⌘

Lotus-Navel; an epithet of Viṣṇu that describes the following popular iconographic image. Viṣṇu is depicted reclining on his coiled serpent Śeṣa (Ananta) as a bed, as Viṣṇu floats on the cosmic ocean, dreaming the universe into existence, a lotus growing from his navel, on which sits Brahmā who will create at the behest of Viṣṇu. (*See also* Thiruvanantapuram.)

⌘ PADMĀSANA ⌘

See Lotus Posture.

⌘ PAILA ⌘

One of the Brahmin pupils of Vyāsa. According to the *Mahābhārata* (1.57.74–75, and 12.314–315), Vyāsa divided the one text of the Veda into four, and transmitted them along with the *Mahābhārata* as the fifth Veda through his five Brahmin disciples, without indicating clearly whether all five learned all the material or divided it between them. Purāṇas specify a division of labor among the disciples so that Paila learned the *Ṛg Veda*. (*See also Mahābhārata*; Purāṇa; *Ṛg Veda*; Vyāsa.)

⌘ PALLAVA ⌘

The name of a powerful south Indian dynasty ruling from Kāñcīpuram in Tamilnadu, third through ninth centuries C.E. They may have been Pāhlava (Parthian, Persian) in origin. Under their patronage the temples and shrines of Māmallapuram were constructed.

⌘ PAÑCAMAKĀRA ⌘

See Five M's.

⌘ PAÑCARĀTRA, or PĀÑCARĀTRA ⌘

Name of an early sect devoted to Viṣṇu. The name (meaning Five Nights) may be derived from a reference in the *Śatapatha Brāhmaṇa* (13.6) in which Puruṣa Nārāyaṇa is said to have performed a five-night sacrifice. The tradition had a doctrine of the manifestation of Viṣṇu in the world with his full nature and attributes, the Vyūha doctrine, in which Viṣṇu appears as Vāsudeva, Saṃkarṣaṇa, Pradyumna, and Aniruddha. From the Pañcarātra perspective, an Avatāra is a lesser manifestation of God. The sect's Āgamas, texts dedicated to specifying correct ritual procedures for worship, contributed to the standardization of images of the gods and incorporated many Tantric Mantras for recitation in addition to Vedic Mantras. The Pāñcarātra tradition initiated and accepted members from all social groups and both genders. Though the sect was previously widely dispersed throughout India, by about the tenth century it was being absorbed into various Vaiṣṇava devotional movements and sects. (*See also* Avatāra; Bhāgavata; Śrīvaiṣṇava; Vaiṣṇavism; Viṣṇu; Vyūha.)

⌘ PĀṆḌAVA ⌘

Name of those descended from Pāṇḍu, particularly the five brothers who are the heroes of the *Mahābhārata*: Yudhiṣṭhira, Bhīma, Arjuna, Nakula, and Sahadeva. (*See also* Arjuna; Draupadī; *Mahābhārata*; Vyāsa.)

⌘ PAṆḌIT; PUNDIT ⌘

From the Sanskrit Paṇḍita (learned one), a scholar educated in the traditional manner; a Brahmin who is learned in the Sanskrit texts.

⌘ PĀṆINI ⌘

Author of the work *Aṣṭādhyāyī*, the first linguistic description of the Sanskrit language. In approximately 4,000 short statements, in which the letters of the Sanskrit alphabet are used to represent categories (such as all vowels, or all long vowels), he lists rules that apply to the formation of linguistic units such as verbs, adjectives, etc. The text presents the alphabet in a logical order based on where in the mouth one pronounces the sounds. He is often cited as the world's first linguist, and his text is the world's first grammar in any language. It is thought that he may have lived about 400 B.C.E., and legends associate him with the university at Taxila (Takṣaśila) in northwest India. (*See also* Patañjali; Sanskrit.)

⌘ PARAMAHAṂSA YOGĀNANDA ⌘

See Yogānanda, Paramahaṃsa.

⌘ PARAMPARĀ ⌘

Series. The term is used especially to refer to an unbroken lineage of Guru-pupil relationships in which a subject is taught. (*See also* Guru.)

⌘ PARĀŚARA ⌘

Brahmin sage, son of Śakti, grandson of Vasiṣṭha, with whom he is mentioned in *Ṛg Veda* 7.18.21. He is a Ṛṣi credited with composition of *Ṛg Veda* 1.65 through 1.73, poems which invoke Agni. In the *Mahābhārata* (1.99), he is the father of Kṛṣṇa Dvaipāyana Vyāsa by Satyavatī, who conceives in a boat in the middle of the Yamunā River and gives birth to Vyāsa on an island. Parāśara seems to have no role in the raising of his son. (*See also* Vasiṣṭha; Vyāsa.)

⌘ PARAŚURĀMA ⌘

Rāma with a battle-axe, one of the incarnations of Viṣṇu, usually listed sixth of the ten Avatāras. He is celebrated for saving the Brahmin class by annihilating the Warrior class (Kṣatriya). Paraśurāma was a Brahmin of the Bhārgava clan (descendants of Bhṛgu), the son of Jamadagni and Reṇukā. Angered with his wife, Jamadagni once asked each of his sons to cut off their mother's head, but all refused until Paraśurāma, the youngest, immediately complied. His father asked him what boon he wanted as his reward, and he asked that his mother's life be restored, which it was. For generations Jamadagni's clan had been the gurus of the Heheya dynasty. King Arjuna Kārtavīrya of that dynasty killed Jamadagni and took away his cow Kāmadhenu. Paraśurāma vowed revenge, killing the Warrior class twenty-one times over. The story is one of a series involving enmity between Bhārgava Brahmins and the Warrior class. (*See also* Avatāra; Bhṛgu; Bhārgava; Viṣṇu.)

⌘ PARIVRĀJAKA ⌘

Wanderer. The term is used for a religious mendicant, a renouncer (Saṃnyāsin) who has entered the fourth stage of life. (*See also* Four Stages of Life; Saṃnyāsa.)

⌘ PĀRVATĪ ⌘

Mountain Woman, the name of Śiva's wife, daughter of Parvata of the Himālaya region. She is also frequently called Umā or Devī. While she is usually depicted as benign and gentle, in various traditions she is also identified with Durgā and Kālī as well.

Pārvatī is the mother of Gaṇeśa (Gaṇapati) and Skanda (Kārttikeya, Kumāra), who form a family with Śiva. Gaṇeśa was produced by the Goddess alone, through rubbing off her body some unguent from which she fashioned a human figure to keep her company in the absence of Śiva. On his return, Śiva attempted to pass by Gaṇeśa, who had been commanded by Pārvatī to guard her door, and a great fight ensued between Śiva and Gaṇeśa. Śiva beheaded Gaṇeśa, but Pārvatī insisted that he be brought back to life, so the first available head was placed on his body, the head of an elephant, and Gaṇeśa was made the leader of Śiva's host of followers. Their other son Skanda was born from Śiva's seed and adopted by Pārvatī. Many of the Śaivite Purāṇas, and particularly the Tantras, have as their frame story that the teachings presented in the text were first taught by Śiva to Pārvatī. (*See also* Durgā; Gaṇeśa; Kālī; Śiva; Skanda.)

⌘ PĀŚUPATA ⌘

Name of an early religious tradition devoted to the worship of Śiva. The name is derived from Śiva's epithet Paśupati (Lord of Creatures). The tradition attributed its foundation to Śiva himself manifest as Lakulīśa (Lord with a Club); modern scholarship regards him as an ascetic of the second century C.E. Pāśupatas believed that the world consists of Paśu (creatures), Pāśu (bondage), and Pati (the Lord, Śiva). Liberation is to be attained by meditation, reciting Mantras, rubbing ashes on the body as a reminder of life's impermanence, and other practices. One's own efforts and the frace of Śiva are both important in attaining liberation from rebirth. The Pāśupata system, which died out about the fifteenth century C.E., is very similar to the Śaiva Siddhānta, which seems to have been influenced by it. (*See also* Śaiva Siddhānta; Śaivism; Śiva.)

⌘ PĀTĀLA ⌘

Nether region. The name is often used particularly for the region of the Nāga (serpent) beings. It is sometimes used more generally to refer to the nether regions, including the residences of assorted demons and the hells in which those suffering the effects of their bad Karma reside. (*See also* Creation.)

⌘ PĀṬALIPUTRA ⌘

Capital of the Māgadha Empire after Ajātaśatru moved the capital from Rājagṛha in the fifth century B.C.E. The Mauryan Empire (fourth to second centuries B.C.E.) had its capital here as well. The ruins are being excavated, and remains of a palace, a brick Buddhist monastery, and city walls have been uncovered in the southern portion of the modern city of Patna, capital of Bihar state.

⌘ PATAÑJALI ⌘

Name of an author who composed the *Yoga Sūtra*, perhaps datable to the first century B.C.E. through second century C.E. Also, the name of an author, perhaps second century B.C.E., who composed the commentary *Mahābhāṣya* on Pāṇini's grammatical work *Aṣṭādhyāyī*. (*See also* Pāṇini; Sanskrit; *Yoga Sūtra*.)

⌘ PATH OF ACTION ⌘

The religious practices of devotion centering on fulfilling one's social and religious obligations (Dharma) and making offerings to the gods. Within the context of this way of being religious, emphasis falls on correct performance of action (Karma). In the Vedic tradition, performance of the sacrificial ritual in the specified manner, particularly the sacrifice of animals accompanied by poems in praise of the gods, so that the offerings will be pleasing to the gods, is the essential feature. Sacrifice was regarded as maintaining the cosmic order and the relationship between human beings and their deities, as well as benefitting the sacrificer in the afterlife. The later Hindu tradition elaborates upon these ideas and practices, modifying but not abandoning the concept of sacrifice. For example, as presented in the *Bhagavad Gītā*, fulfilling the social and religious obligations incumbent upon one according to one's caste and stage of life (Varṇāśrama-dharma) is vital, and is conceived as a sacrifice of one's self-interest; one acts without attachment to the fruits of one's actions. Worship is primarily in the form of Pūjā offerings made to God (or the gods) in one's home or at a temple, usually not involving the sacrifice of animals, but continuing the pattern of sacrificial offerings. Properly performed action is regarded as conducive to liberation from rebirth (Mokṣa). (*See also Bhagavad Gītā*; Dharma; Karma; Mokṣa; Pilgrimage; Pūjā; Yajña.)

⌘ PATH OF DEVOTION ⌘

The religious practices of devotion (Bhakti) to a deity. The first use of the term Bhakti may well be the concluding statement of the *Śvetāśvatara Upaniṣad*, where Rudra-Śiva is the object of devotion. The fullest early articulation of Bhakti as a way of being religious is the *Bhagavad Gītā*, where Kṛṣṇa presents devotion as the highest and most effective means of religious practice, overarching and encompassing the Path of Action and the Path of Knowledge. From south India arose a wave of highly emotional, loving devotion in the form of poems sung in worship of Viṣṇu by the Āḻvārs and in worship of Śiva by the Nāyanār saints. North India soon saw a similar upsurge of devotion focussing on love of the Lord, particularly for the Avatāras Kṛṣṇa and Rāma. In contrast to these movements, in which the specific charming and lovable qualities of God are celebrated, north India also saw the development of devotion to God conceived as formless and as transcending all qualities (Nirguṇa Brahman), such as in the poems of Kabir and Nanak. Most devotional traditions insist that the devotee does not seek and cannot attain union with God; the goal is proximity to God so as to serve God with loving devotion eternally. Worship on the Path of Devotion may be conducted in the privacy of the home or in the public setting of a temple; in either case, Pūjā offerings are made to God along with prayers and songs of devotion. Devotional traditions tend not to emphasize the importance of caste hierarchy in the context of worship. An important component of devotional worship is making pilgrimages to sacred places associated with the deity worshipped. (*See also* Āḻvārs; Avatāra; *Bhagavad Gītā*; Bhakti; Mokṣa; Nāyaṉār; Nirguṇa Brahman; Pilgrimage; Pūjā; Saguṇa Brahman; Śaivism; Temple; Vaiṣṇavism.)

⌘ PATH OF KNOWLEDGE ⌘

The religious discipline that eliminates ignorance and results in knowledge (Jñāna), particularly knowledge of Brahman, leading to liberation from rebirth. The Path of Knowledge is articulated especially in the Upaniṣads, where the earlier texts emphasize the liberating power of knowledge of Brahman. Later texts specify Yoga as the method for attaining knowledge of Brahman. The Upaniṣads generally present a monistic worldview, in which Brahman is the only reality, but ignorance prevents our correct perception of the truth that the individual, embodied self (Ātman) is actually no different from Ultimate Reality (Brahman). The disciplined practice of Yoga aids in perceiving reality and knowing oneself to be Brahman, by establishing an ethical lifestyle and cultivation of physical and mental calmness and control, leading to mystical insight. The Vedānta traditions elaborate on the Upaniṣadic teachings in a variety of ways, both monistic and theistic. The leading exponent of the monistic interpretation of the Upaniṣads, and founder of a monastic order that embodies those teachings, is Śaṅkara. Vedānta traditions emphasize the important role of scriptural authority in attaining knowledge of Brahman or God that brings liberation from rebirth (Mokṣa), including the Vedic literature, particularly the Upaniṣads, but also the *Bhagavad Gītā* and *Brahma Sūtra*. (*See also* Advaita Vedānta; *Bhagavad Gītā*; Brahman; *Brahma Sūtra*; Mokṣa; Śaṅkara; Upaniṣads; Vedānta; Yoga.)

⌘ PAṬṬADAKAL ⌘

Site in northern Karnataka of temples built by the Cālukya dynasty (seventh-eighth century C.E.). The two major temples here are the Mallikārjuna, the sculptures of which depict the instruction of Arjuna by Kṛṣṇa in the *Bhagavad Gītā*, and the Virupākṣa or Lokeśvara temple, sculptures of which illustrate episodes from the *Mahābhārata* and *Rāmāyaṇa*. (*See also* Aihole; Bādāmī; Temple.)

⌘ PHILOSOPHICAL SCHOOLS ⌘

Six philosophical points of view (Darśana) are recognized by Hindus as orthodox. They are so regarded because each accepts the authority of the Vedic literature, seeing it as revealed truth. Each school of thought is a means to liberation from rebirth, in that each teaches a means to the disciplined use of reason leading to correct perception of reality and experience of Brahman. The six traditions regarded as orthodox are as follows: Nyāya (Logical Analysis), Vaiśeṣika (Distinctionism), Sāṃkhya (Enumeration), Yoga (Application), Mīmāṃsā (Enquiry), and Vedānta (End of the Veda). Schools of thought regarded as unorthodox include Buddhism, Jainism, Cārvaka (Materialism), and others. (*See also* Cārvaka; Mīmāṃsā; Nyāya; Sāṃkhya; Vaiśeṣika; Vedānta; Yoga.)

⌘ PILGRIMAGE ⌘

A common practice in Hinduism, with a long history. Sacred places to which devotees make pilgrimage (translating the Sanskrit Yātra) include not only temples, but also the Himālaya Mountains, and specific spots on riverbanks (a Tīrtha, or ford, crossing-point) or lakes. The Tīrtha is a crossing-point in the sense that here one can metaphorically cross over the dangerous flux of life to the security of the world beyond, the heavenly reward so often cited as the result of such pilgrimages. Places associated with a deity, such as Rāma's Ayodhyā or Kṛṣṇa's Vṛndāvana, are regarded as sacred by devotees of that god, who travel there to walk where he did and experience his sacred presence. The *Mahābhārata* (3.80–153) has a long catalogue of the merits to be attained from pilgrimage to particular places, frequently indicating that the good Karma from going to or bathing at a specific site would be equal to that of ten Horse Sacrifices or would result in rebirth in a heavenly realm. This shows that already by the time of the composition of that text (by 400 C.E.), pilgrimage was a well-established tradition. Indeed, Buddhists were making pilgrimage to the holy sites associated with the birth, enlightenment, first teaching, and death of the Buddha very shortly after his lifetime (fifth or fourth century B.C.E.), and it may well be that Hindus then were also making pilgrimage to sites they held sacred. Pilgrimage is closely associated with the Path of Devotion (Bhakti), in that no one is excluded from making pilgrimage to a sacred site; indeed, even a serf (Śūdra) who bathes at Puṣkara is assured that he or she will not be reborn in lower forms (*Mahābhārata* 3.80.51–52). The tradition of pilgrimage continues to be important to the present day; in fact, with the advent of modern modes of transportation, even more people have the opportunity to reach sacred places than ever before. (*See also* Ayodhyā; Bhakti; Hardwār; Kumbha Melā; Path of Devotion; Prayāga; Puṣkara; Rāmlīlā; Temple; Tīrtha; Vārāṇasī; Vṛndāvana.)

⌘ PITṚ ⌘

Father; used in reference to the deceased ancestors as a group. Sacrificial offerings (Śrāddha) are regularly to be offered to the

Viśvedevas, divine protectors of the ancestors, then to the Pitṛs themselves, then to Viṣṇu. The practice includes the offering of balls of rice or grain (Piṇḍa) to the deceased. The World of the Ancestors (Pitṛ-Loka) is a heaven inhabited by the deceased; in the Vedic era it was apparently regarded as lasting as long as ancestral rites continued, but in later times was regarded as lasting only as long as the effects of one's good Karma. (*See also* Ancestral Rites; Death; Funeral; Rebirth; Śrāddha.)

⌘ PONGAL ⌘

A festival celebrated in Tamilnadu in mid-January. Pongal is a mixture of rice, dhal, milk, and sugar, cooked together in a pot and symbolic of abundance and prosperity. The four-day festival celebrating a good harvest includes the washing and decorative painting of cattle, who are fed Pongal.

⌘ POONA ⌘

See Pune.

⌘ POONJAJI (POONJA, HARILAL W.) ⌘

Name of a Guru (1910–1998) who has become very popular with Western spiritual seekers, including former followers of Rajneesh. Born in the Punjab to a sister of a famous saint named Swāmī Rāma Tīrtha, he experienced his first profound spiritual state of Samādhi at age nine. He met Ramana Maharṣi and became his disciple in 1944. Poonjaji is unusual in some respects, having renounced the world yet having also had a family and, until his retirement in 1966, a career. His family home, after the partition, is in Lucknow, capital of Uttar Pradesh, and he regularly holds teaching sessions in his home or another, larger one, in that neighborhood. (*See also* Rajneesh, Bhagwan; Ramana Maharṣi; Saṃnyāsa.)

⌘ PRADAKṢIṆA ⌘

See Circumambulation.

⌘ PRAJĀPATI ⌘

Lord of Creatures. Creator god often referred to in Vedic literature, particularly the Brāhmaṇas and Upaniṣads, there often described as the grandfather of the gods and demons. In this literature, he is frequently depicted as granting a boon to the demons or a particular demon, which then must be circumvented so that the gods prevail. He later comes to be identified with Brahmā, though they were apparently often regarded as distinct personalities in the Brāhmaṇa literature. (*See also* Brahmā; Creation; Dhātṛ.)

⌘ PRAKRIT (PRĀKṚTA) ⌘

Unrefined; natural. The term is used for vernacular speech in ancient times in India, and is contrasted with Sanskrit (Saṃskṛta), the refined and perfected speech of well-educated people. Prakrit is an Indo-European language, essentially cognate with Sanskrit. Four dialects of Prakrit are usually recognized: Śaurasenī, Māhārāṣṭrī, Apabhraṃśa, and Paiśācī. Authors of classical Sanskrit dramas and literature utilized Prakrit dialects for the speech of women and characters of low social standing, while Sanskrit was used for Brahmins, kings, and gods. This both reflects historical reality (the upper classes studied and spoke Sanskrit) and allows authors to indicate the social status of individuals in their works. Prakrit dialects, at one time regional, vernacular languages of the Indian subcontinent paralleling Sanskrit, became stylized literary languages, while spoken vernaculars continued to evolve into Hindi, Marathi, Bengali, etc. (*See also* Sanskrit.)

⌘ PRAKṚTI ⌘

Nature; Matter. The term is used especially in the Sāṃkhya philosophical tradition to refer to the material world as distinct from spirit or the self (Puruṣa). Prakṛti evolves into some twenty-four elements or components, from which Puruṣa is separate but in which it becomes entangled, in the process losing awareness of its distinctness. Liberation for Puruṣa consists in developing the ability to discriminate clearly between the eternal spirit and the constant flux of material forms. Prakṛti is grammatically feminine, while Puruṣa is grammatically masculine, which was productive of much thought about feminine and masculine principles in the human and divine realms, influencing numerous philosophical and religious traditions. Prakṛti is at times equated with Māyā as the means by which one is bound within Saṃsāra. (*See also* Māyā; Puruṣa; Sāṃkhya.)

⌘ PRALAYA ⌘

Cosmic dissolution. The term is used to refer to the cataclysmic end of the world at the end of Kali Yuga. At the end of each set of four World Ages, when the creation can no longer be sustained, destruction takes place. Pralaya is usually regarded as the special time of Śiva's activity. The end of the world is often described in accounts in the Purāṇa literature as destruction by fire, followed by flood, the world dissolving into the primeval chaos out of which creation takes place periodically. The period in which the universe in unmanifest is the night of Brahmā, and when it again becomes manifest is the day of Brahmā. (*See also* Creation; Śiva; World Ages.)

⌘ PRĀṆA ⌘

Breath. In the Upaniṣads and all systems of Yoga, Prāṇa is the energy of the body, related to the breath and the process of respiration. Prāṇa is generally regarded as existing in the form of five specific life-breaths: (1) Prāṇa, the ascending breath, which includes both inhalation and exhalation; (2) Apāna, the descending breath, associated with the lower half of one's body; (3) Vyāna, the diffused breath, present and circulating throughout the entire body; (4) Udāna, the upward breath, associated with belching, speech, and the turning of one's energy to higher states of consciousness; and (5) Samāna, the breath of the abdomen, associated with digestion. These energies or life-breaths circulate through channels in the human body, and their departure takes place at the moment of death. (*See also* Kuṇḍalinī; Prāṇāyāma; Yoga.)

⌘ PRĀṆĀYĀMA ⌘

Control of life-breaths. Exercises that manipulate and control the breathing process are very important in all systems of Yoga. In Patañjali's exposition of Yoga, Prāṇāyāma is the fourth element of his system. Holding the breath, neither inhaling or exhaling, is one of the principal exercises of breath control. It is often asserted that complete quiescence, neither inhaling nor exhaling, is the moment at which enlightenment or union with Brahman occurs. Holding the breath is thought to lengthen one's life. Yoga practitioners use breath control as a means of controlling the activity of the mind. (*See also* Kuṇḍalinī; Prāṇa; Yoga.)

⌘ PRASĀDA ⌘

Grace. The term is used in theological contexts to refer to the grace of God, whereby a devotee is liberated from rebirth. The term is used in the context of devotional worship (Pūjā) to refer to offerings made to the icon of the deity which then are offered to devotees as representative of God's grace. Such offerings may include food and drink which, offered before God's image, are regarded as the blessed remains of God's meal which devotees consume so as to make the blessing part of themselves. Prasāda may also include burning lamps, camphor, or incense which are brought from the presence of the divine image and offered to devotees, who perform acts such as inhaling the fragrant smoke and holding their hands over the burning substance, then touching their heads with their hands to transfer the blessing. (*See also* Path of Devotion; Pūjā; Temple.)

⌘ PRAYĀGA ⌘

Name of an ancient city and place of pilgrimage at the confluence of the Ganges and Yamunā Rivers. Hindus traditionally regarded it as the spot where the invisible river Sarasvatī also joins the other two. The place is revered as the site of Brahmā's first sacrifice, and one of four places where drops of the Elixir of Immortality (Amṛta) fell when the gods and demons churned the Ocean of Milk and fought over the Elixir. Every twelve years, this event is memorialized with a Kumbha Melā at Prayāga, attended by some two million pilgrims; in the years 2001 and 2013 Prayāga will host the event. Prayāga is often called Tīrtha Rāja (King of Pilgrimage Sites). There is a column erected by Aśoka in the third century B.C.E., to which Samudra Gupta added an inscription of his own, brought here from nearby Kauśambī and placed in a fort built by Akbar. The city was sacked by Muslims and a new city built there named Allāhābād; many Hindus call it Ilāhābād and think of that as a corruption of the name Ilāvāsa (Home of Ilā, an early queen). (*See also* Ganges River; Kumbha Melā; Pilgrimage; Tīrtha; Yamunā River.)

⌘ PREMA ⌘

Love. In Vaiṣṇava theology, Prema is contrasted with Kāma (desire), Prema being regarded as a pure, spiritual love, as in devotional love for God, while Kāma is regarded as mundane, physical love. (See also Kāma.)

⌘ PRETA ⌘

The spirit of a deceased person. A Preta is sometimes called a hungry ghost because it requires offerings of food and water (Śrāddha ceremonies) in the afterlife. Performance of proper ceremonies will result in the Preta moving on to other realms and eventual rebirth. (*See also* Ancestral Rites; Death; Funeral; Pitṛ; Śrāddha.)

⌘ PṚTHIVĪ ⌘

See Earth.

⌘ PŪJĀ ⌘

Reverence; honoring. The term is used to refer to the act of venerating or honoring highly respected persons such as one's Guru or elders, or for the act of worshipping God or gods. In either case, hospitality toward honored guests provides the pattern. Pūjā can be contrasted with Yajña, the Vedic sacrifice, which it ultimately replaced but from which much of the ritual structure was derived. Pūjā is mentioned in the *Ṛg Veda* (8.17.12 is the only occurrence). Brāhmaṇa texts that treat the Vedic sacrifice in great detail, however, do not discuss Pūjā offerings at all. The term is used in the *Gṛhya Sūtra* (domestic ritual) texts to refer to rites of hospitality for Brahmin guests in one's home. Use of the term Pūjā to refer to worship of deities occurs perhaps for the first time in an inscription from the second century B.C.E. in regard to the Bhāgavata-Pañcarātra deities Vāsudeva and Saṃkarṣaṇa. Mayrhofer, in his etymological dictionary, points to Dravidian roots as the most likely source for the term. Whatever the origin of the term and practices, Pūjā has been the dominant means by which

Hindus have expressed their religious sensibilities in the past 2,000 years. Pūjā slowly came to be recognized and encouraged by Brahmanical authorities both for domestic rites and for the large-scale public ritual activities at temples. The *Mānava Dharma Śāstra*, however, reflects the early Brahmanical tradition's hesitancy in endorsing Pūjā, insisting that temple priests who conduct Pūjā services be excluded from Vedic offerings to gods and deceased ancestors (3.152). Pūjā rituals reflect their origin in hospitality practices, the whole series of actions demonstrating respect and service of an honored guest. Central to Pūjā rituals is the use of an image (Mūrti) of the deity or deities being honored. Typical of Pūjā practices are invocation of the deity, offering of a seat, offering of water to wash the feet and hands and to rinse the mouth, bathing of the image of the deity, offering of fresh clothing, and the offering of sandalwood paste and other unguents. Incense, flowers or flower petals, lit lamps, food and drink, and other paraphernalia are offered the deity as well. Throughout the ritual, Mantras are recited, and sometimes prayers as well. Food and water presented to the deity, and the water and other liquids used to bathe the image of the deity, are offered to the devotees as blessed substances indicative of the deity's grace (Prasāda), and are usually ingested by devotees to receive the benefit; similarly, the burning incense, camphor, and lamps may be circulated among devotees to distribute the deity's blessings. The deity in the form of the image is regarded as granting to devotees an auspicious sight (Darśana) of himself or herself, and devotees assemble to receive Darśana. Some temples annually or periodically take the images of deities out of the temple on procession through the surrounding area, for example, as the Jagannātha temple of Puri does in large carts pulled through the city streets by temple servants. Pūjā rites in the home are similar to temple rituals in every respect, but on a smaller scale. (*See also* Bhakti; Darśana; Mūrti; Path of Devotion; Prasāda; Temple; Yajña.)

⌘ PUNDIT ⌘

See Paṇḍit.

⌘ PUNE (POONA) ⌘

A large city in western Mahārāṣṭra, birthplace of the great Marāṭha leader Śivāji. Often described as the state's cultural capital, it has become India's college town, with such major institutions as Poona University and Deccan College. It is also an important center of traditional and Western-style scholarship on Sanskrit literature, and is the site of the Bhandarkar Oriental Research Institute. At the south end of town on a hilltop is a Pārvatī temple, and nearby the Saras Baug Gaṇeśa temple. In western Pune is the Pātāleśvara Temple, a small rock-cut shrine dedicated to Śiva that dates from the eighth century. Northern Pune is the site of the Osho Commune International, formerly known as the Rajneesh Ashram, a major center of Western spiritual seekers, and a place where New Age ideas and practices and being blended with traditional Hindu religious ideas and practices. (*See also* Gaṇeśa; Rajneesh, Bhagwan; Śivāji.)

⌘ PUṆYA ⌘

See Karma; Merit.

⌘ PURĀṆA ⌘

Ancient Tales. The term is used to refer to a class of texts that date in their written form to perhaps the fourth century C.E. and later, but which also contain in many cases material that may be a thousand years older than that. Preserved for centuries as oral traditions, they were written down, perhaps partly in response to the written scriptures of Buddhism and Jainism. Purāṇas contain vast amounts of mythology, but also accounts of kings and their historical records, pilgrimage sites, religious teachings on Dharma (social and religious obligations) and Mokṣa (liberation from rebirth), and many other subjects. Purāṇa texts fall into the category of Smṛti (Remembered Tradition) rather than Śruti (Revelation), so have been preserved with less fidelity than the Vedic texts, so there are numerous variations between manuscripts and orally transmitted versions. Some Purāṇas have attained a status and authority comparable to the Vedas or even exceeding the Vedas, notably the *Bhāgavata Purāṇa* in Vaiṣṇava devotional groups. (*See also* Scripture; Smṛti; Śruti.)

⌘ PURI ⌘

Coastal city in Orissa, and a major pilgrimage site. The Jagannātha temple, built in 1198, houses images of Kṛṣṇa, his brother-

and fellow Avatāra Balarāma, and their sister Subhadrā, who married Arjuna. The annual Ratha Yātra, or Chariot Festival, takes place in June or July. Jayadeva, author of the *Gītagovinda*, apparently lived in Puri, and Caitanya, the fifteenth-century saint, lived in the Jagannātha temple for much of his adult life. Puri is also the site of Vimalā Pīṭha, one of four monasteries of the Daśanāmi Order founded in the ninth century C.E. by Śaṅkara. (*See also* Caitanya; Daśanāmi Order; Jagannātha; Jayadeva.)

⌘ PUROHITA ⌘

The One Placed in Front. The term is used for the Brahmin priest of a king, his royal chaplain.

⌘ PURŪRAVAS ⌘

Name of an ancient king, about whom a legend is told in *Ṛg Veda* 10.95. He fell in love with Urvaśī, a celestial nymph (Apsaras) who had been temporarily banished from heaven and forced to live on earth. She set as conditions for her living with him that he care for her two rams, and that she never see him naked. After four years, celestial musicians (Gandharvas) decided to bring her back to heaven and brought about the violation of her agreement. They stole one of her rams one night, and when Purūravas jumped out of bed to rescue it, they caused lightning to flash, revealing a naked Purūravas to her. She vanished from his sight and he searched for her in vain. Finally she pitied him and returned, bearing him a son named Āyus (Life), who continued his royal lineage. The story is related in later literature as well, including the *Śatapatha Brāhmaṇa*, *Mahābhārata*, several Purāṇas, and the drama by Kālidāsa entitled *Vikramorvaśī*, which presents the most elaborate version of the tale. (*See also* Kālidāsa; Urvaśī.)

⌘ PURUṢA ⌘

Person. The Cosmic Person of *Ṛg Veda* 10.90, described there as the whole universe; "a quarter of him is all beings, three-quarters of him is immortal." From the sacrifice and dismemberment of Puruṣa come all phenomena, including the hierarchically ordered classes of society, a system of social organization we now call the caste system. It is said in this Vedic poem that the Brahmin class was produced from Puruṣa's head or mouth, indicating both their preeminence among Āryan groups and their preoccupation with intellectual and vocal matters; they learned the Veda and recited it to make the sacrificial rituals effective. The Warrior (Rājanya or Kṣatriya) class is said to have been produced from Puruṣa's arms, symbolically representative of the physical power of the warrior. The Commoner (Vaiśya) class was produced from the thighs of Puruṣa, the proximity to the organs of procreation indicating their function as society's producers of food and wealth, especially cattle. The group of lowest status, the non-Āryan Serf (Śūdra) or servant class, was produced from the feet of Puruṣa, representing their function as those who serve the Āryan classes. The term Puruṣa was later used as equivalent to either Ātman (the individual self or soul, as in the Sāṃkhya or Yoga philosophical schools) or Brahman (Ultimate Reality, the Absolute, as in the Upaniṣads). Theistic traditions use the term Puruṣottama (Supreme Person) to refer to God, a usage particularly often seen in Vaiṣṇava literature. (*See also* Brahman; Caste; Prakṛti; Puruṣottama; Sāṃkhya; Yoga.)

⌘ PURUṢĀRTHA ⌘

See Four Goals of Humanity.

⌘ PURUṢOTTAMA ⌘

Best of Persons. The term can be used for a perfected saint, but is often applied to the Supreme Lord, particularly by Vaiṣṇavas in regard to Viṣṇu or Kṛṣṇa.

⌘ PŪRVA MĪMĀṂSA ⌘

See Mīmāṃsā.

⌘ PŪṢAN ⌘

Nourisher. One of the twelve Ādityas, the bringer of prosperity and guardian of men and animals. He is invoked in *Ṛg Veda* 6.53 through 6.56. (*See also* Āditya.)

⌘ PUṢKARA ⌘

Blue Lotus. Also, the name of a famous place of pilgrimage (Pushkar or Pokkhar in Rajasthan, western India, near Ajmer) where, according to the *Mahābhārata* (3.80.41–60) Brahmā is continually present. The good Karma of bathing here is said to be equivalent to that of performing ten Horse Sacrifices, and even a Serf (Śūdra) who bathes here will not be reborn in a lower form. The gods are said to have attained insight through Yoga here, and twelve years' residence brings rebirth in Brahmā's world. Even going to Puṣkara mentally equals the merit of going to all pilgrimage sites. One of the very few temples dedicated to Brahmā in all of India is here. Puṣkara hosts an annual Camel Festival featuring some 50,000 camels on the full-moon day of Kārttika (October-November). (*See also* Brahmā; Pilgrimage.)

— Q —

There are no entries for Q.

— R —

⌘ RĀDHĀ ⌘

Prosperity. The name of a Gopī who was Kṛṣṇa's favorite lover. Though her name is absent from early accounts of his youth in Vṛndāvana, Rādhā appears as Kṛṣṇa's beloved particularly in the twelfth-century poem *Gītagovinda,* where their love in all its moods is recounted. Rādhā is depicted as a married woman, their love illicit and therefore her devotion to him is all the more intense. Rādhā, to many Vaiṣṇavas, represents the human soul in relation to God, longing for the presence of God and surrendering all pretense, abandoning all social conventions to attain union with God. Rādhā is, in this sense, the ideal devotee and all should strive to be like her. Vaiṣṇava theologians advocate emulation of her emotional state, and some traditions include the practice of imitating Rādhā and the Gopīs even to the extent of taking on female attire and mannerisms in the context of worship. For other Vaiṣṇavas, Rādhā and Kṛṣṇa are not only earthly lovers but together constitute Ultimate Reality. The saint Caitanya of the sixteenth century was such an impassioned devotee of the divine pair that his followers have ever since regarded him as an incarnation of Rādhā and Kṛṣṇa in a single body. As a goddess, Rādhā is unusual in that she does not function independently, and does not receive reverence as a divine Mother or in a fierce form, but only in association with her divine lover. (*See also* Caitanya; Gītagovinda; Gopī; Gosvāmin; Kṛṣṇa; Vallabha.)

⌘ RADHAKRISHNAN, SIR SARVEPALLI ⌘

Indian philosopher and diplomat (1888–1975). Born at Tiruttani, near Madras, he was educated at Madras Christian College, eventually becoming a professor at universities in Mysore, Calcutta, and Oxford. In 1936 Radhakrishnan became Spalding Professor of Eastern Religions and Ethics at Oxford University. He served as an Indian delegate to the League of Nations from 1931 to 1939, and was India's chief delegate to UNESCO (United Nations Educational, Scientific and Cultural Organization) in 1946, becoming chairman of UNESCO in 1949. He was the first ambassador from India to the Soviet Union in 1949, was vice president of India from 1952 to 1962, and president from 1962 to 1967. His many published works include studies of Indian philosophy and a translation of the major Upaniṣads. (*See also* Indology.)

⌘ RĀDHĀSOĀMĪ SATSANG ⌘

"The True Fellowship of Rādhā's Lord," a religious movement founded in 1861 by Swāmī Shiv Dayal Singh (1818–1878) in the city of Agra. The teachings of this organization are largely based on those of Hindi-speaking saints of north India such as Kabīr and Nānak. A central tenet is that the soul in bondage is liberated through love of God as taught by the spiritual master (Guru). There is a strong emphasis on morality, vegetarianism, discipline, and meditation.

⌘ RAGHAVAN, V. ⌘

Indologist (1908–1990). Born at Tiruvarar in Thañjavūr district of Tamilnadu, he was educated at Presidency College in Madras. He was appointed professor of Sanskrit at Madras University, and authored many works on Indian literature and drama. (*See also* Indology.)

⌘ RĀHU ⌘

The name of the demon of eclipse. He is thought to swallow the sun during an eclipse, only to release it due to divine intervention. Myths of the churning of the Ocean of Milk to produce the Elixir of Immortality (Amṛta) often include reference to Rāhu swallowing the sun and being forced to relinquish it by Viṣṇu, and of his swallowing the Amṛta, for which his head was cut off but, having tasted the Elixir, is now immortal. When the gods and demons struggled for possession of the Amṛta pot, four drops of it fell to earth, and at those four spots the Kumbha Melā (Pot Festival) is celebrated on a rotating basis on a twelve-year cycle. (*See also* Amṛta; Kumbha Melā.)

⌘ RAI, LALA LAJPAT ⌘

Indian nationalist (1865–1928). Born in the Punjab, Rai became prominent in the independence movement. He lived in New York for three years and, in 1915, founded the journal *Young India*, which he published until 1919 when Mohandās Gāndhī took over the roles of editor and publisher. Rai was injured while participating in a protest march in Lahore in 1928, and died as a martyr to the cause of independence. (*See also* Gāndhī, Mohandās; Rāj.)

⌘ RĀJ ⌘

Reign; the term is used especially to refer to the period of British dominance, mid-eighteenth through mid-twentieth century, the British Rāj. The term Rāj is derived from the Sanskrit word Rājā (King) and Rājya (Reign). The British began their presence in India in 1600, with the British East India Company engaging in trade. The Company progressively expanded the area in its control, winning from the Mughal emperor the right to collect tax revenue in Bengal, a portion of which was to be sent to the emperor. In effect, Bengal became a colony of the Company, and by the mid-nineteenth century most of coastal India was under Company control. In 1857, Indian soldiers in the Company's army, known as Sepoys, rebelled against their employer and fought against British troops and administrators. Known as the Mutiny of 1857 (to the British) or the Rebellion of 1857 or the War of Independence (to the Indians), this event caused the government of Britain to reconsider how India was administered, and the decision was made to dissolve the British East India Company in 1858, all its assets and holdings becoming possessions of the government, and the land controlled in India becoming a Crown

Colony. In the late nineteenth and early twentieth centuries, the independence movement gained strength, particularly under the inspiring leadership of Mohandās Gāndhī, and with the end of World War II the decision was made to grant independence to India. Because of Muslim concerns about their safety and degree of representation in a largely Hindu India, the territory was partitioned into two nations, India and Pakistan, which became independent in 1947, ending the British Rāj. Among the major effects on Hinduism of the British Rāj were the presence in India of Christian missionaries who criticized aspects of Hindu religious tradition, and British judges who outlawed such practices as Satī (widow immolation) and human sacrifice by the Thugs. The British presence and administrative control certainly stimulated efforts at reform from within Hinduism. (*See also* British East India Company; Gāndhī, Mohandās; Ghadr Movement; Rai, Lala Lajpat; Satī; Thugs.)

⌘ RĀJASŪYA ⌘

Consecration of the King, the name of an important Vedic ritual. Filled with symbolic proclamations of the ruler's sovereignty, the ritual had as its purpose to install a new king or to reconfirm the sovereignty of a ruler, and to demonstrate the loyalty of his subjects. The ritual was structured as five Soma sacrifices with interspersed Iṣṭi offerings, the whole of it taking about two years to complete. The king was to take a step in each of the four directions, symbolically conquering all surrounding territory. He was to mount his chariot and ride off to shoot arrows at the effigy of a rival warrior, thereby enacting his military prowess in a symbolic fashion. A chariot race, and the king's enthronement and Abhiṣeka (anointment) were also part of the ritual sequence. In addition, the story of Śunaḥśepa was to be recited, in which a Brahmin boy, bound as a sacrificial offering to Varuṇa, praised the God and attained freedom. The rite was to end with a dice match in which the ruler was to throw a winning roll of the dice, thereby demonstrating his good fortune and that the gods were on his side. The ritual provided the structure for the narrative of the second book of the *Mahābhārata* (Sabhā Parvan, the Book of the Meeting Hall), in which these elements of the ritual were used as narrative motifs in the epic account. (*See also* Horse Sacrifice; Vājapeya; Yajña.)

⌘ RAJNEESH, BHAGWAN (RĀJANĪṢA, BHAGAVAN) ⌘

Guru who led a movement popular among Westerners. Also known as Osho, he began in the 1960s to attract followers to his center in Pune (Poona), a city in western India, after leaving a career as a professor of philosophy. At the height of his popularity in the late 1970s and early 1980s, Rajneesh had several thousand followers living in Pune at a time, and thousands more abroad. An initiated follower was regarded as a "sannyasi" or renounced ascetic, though the traditional meaning of the term did not apply to these individuals. In the early 1980s, Rajneesh and a group of disciples left Pune and established Rajneeshpuram, a center for meditation and communal living near Antelope, Oregon. In 1985, however, Rajneesh was indicted and deported from the United States for immigration fraud, and returned to Pune. His eclectic teachings drew upon traditional Hindu and especially Tantric vocabulary and practices of Yoga, but included also elements of Buddhism and other religions, as well as incorporating such symbolic representatives of joyful release as Zorba the Greek. Sexuality was an important aspect of Rajneesh's teachings. His technique called The Mystic Rose (a regimen of laughing for three hours each day for a week, then crying for three hours each day for a week, then silent sitting for three hours a day for a week) was, Rajneesh felt, the most important breakthrough in meditation in twenty-five centuries. Rajneesh himself was regarded by his followers as an enlightened, and even divine, being. Devoted followers donated lavishly to support the organization and Rajneesh himself, who was often seen in expensive automobiles. His death in 1990 and the conviction of several of his closest disciples on various charges led to the organization becoming much less visible, as did the decision to abandon their orange robes and prayer beads (Mālā) with the picture of Rajneesh. The center in Pune, renamed the Osho Commune International, still has thousands of visitors and residents each year who take courses on meditation, healing, and other topics. All who want to be residents at the commune must take a blood test on site that shows them to be HIV-negative. (*See also* Guru; Poonjaji; Pune; Saṃnyāsa; Yoga.)

⌘ RĀKṢASA ⌘

A demon of vile habits, given to devouring human beings, disrupting the sacrifices of Brahmins, and roaming through the forests at night. (*See also* Daitya; Dānava; Demon.)

⌘ RĀM ⌘

Hindi language version of the name Rāma.

⌘ RĀMA ⌘

Prince of Ayodhyā and hero of the *Rāmāyaṇa, Rām Carit Mānas,* and other works. He is depicted as a human hero and as an Avatāra or incarnation of Viṣṇu, usually counted as the seventh incarnation in lists of ten. He married Sītā and was to assume the throne but, due to palace intrigue, was exiled to the forest, where he was accompanied by his wife and younger brother Lakṣmaṇa. There they experienced many adventures, including the abduction of Sītā by Rāvaṇa, who carried her off to his capital Laṅkā. With the aid of Hanuman and an army of forest-dwelling monkeys, Rāma rescued Sītā and they returned to Ayodhyā where Rāma was crowned king. Rāma is traditionally understood as an exemplar of Brahmanical values and the maintenance of Dharma. Rāma's birth is celebrated in the annual festival of Rāmnavamī, and his heroic deeds are enacted in the Rāmlīlā drama. The name, in its Hindi language form Rām, is often regarded in northern India as a name for the Absolute, or God, and recited repeatedly as a Mantra. (*See also* Avatāra; Ayodhyā; Dharma; Hanuman; *Rām Carit Mānas*; *Rāmāyaṇa*; Rāmlīlā; Rāmnavamī; Sītā; Viṣṇu.)

⌘ RĀMAKRISHNA ⌘

Religious name of the mystic and holy man (1836–1886) who was the inspiration for the founding of several modern religious movements. Born as Gadadhar Chatterjee in the Hooghly District of Bengal to a Brahmin family, he took religious instruction from Gurus of several different traditions and adopted the ascetic way of life (Saṃnyāsa). He became a priest at the Dakṣiṇeśvar temple near Calcutta, a temple dedicated to the goddess Kālī, on whom he meditated and to whom he sang devotional songs. He began to have visions of Kālī as the Mother, and went into profound trances or states of mystical absorption (Samādhi). He was removed from his office as temple priest, apparently because temple administrators regarded him as ill, insane, or derelict in his duty. His family arranged for him to be married to a child of a neighboring village, but he immediately returned to the temple of Kālī where he lived for the next quarter-century; after coming of age, she lived with Rāmakrishna, but their marriage was never consummated. The intensity of his meditations and visions increased as he dedicated himself to his spiritual practices. He took a female Tantric practitioner as his Guru, learning Kuṇḍalinī Yoga and other Tantric methods of spiritual discipline. He also learned from an Advaita Vedānta monk the bliss of knowledge of Brahman, and from a Vaiṣṇava teacher the devotional love of Kṛṣṇa by taking on the role of Rādhā in the imaginative world of Bhakti. He learned about Islam and Christianity as well in the multireligious society of nineteenth-century Bengal. As his fame grew, he began to attract both householder devotees who viewed him as a saint and renounced ascetics who took him as their Guru. Despite his eclectic interests, he remained very much a devotee of Kālī. Shortly after his death in 1886, one of his leading disciples, Vivekānanda, founded three organizations dedicated to continuing the religious fervour Rāmakrishna had inspired: the Rāmakrishna Order, a monastic organization; the Rāmakrishna Mission, a social service organization; and the Vedānta Society, founded in New York in 1895 to transmit to the West the ideas of Rāmakrishna and Advaita Vedānta Hinduism. (*See also* Advaita Vedānta; Kālī; Kuṇḍalinī Yoga; Tantra; Vivekānanda.)

⌘ RAMANA MAHARṢI ⌘

Saint in south India (1879–1950). He was born some thirty miles south of Madurai, Tamilnadu, in a middle-class family. When Ramana was twelve, his father died, and the family moved to Madurai where Ramana learned English at a mission school. At age seventeen he had a powerful experience of the difference between the body and the spirit, or Ātman, which helped him to decide to renounce his social position for a life as a Saṃnyāsin to dedicate himself to religious pursuits. He left his home for the mountain temple of Aruṇācala, where he spent the rest of his life. He became renowned as a profoundly spiritual person and his presence was widely regarded as sacred. His perspective could best be described as Advaita Vedānta monism, the view that the Ātman is no different from Brahman, the Absolute. He is famous for asking of those who came to him, "Who are you?" to force examination of one's self and life. This question also was the title of one of the short works he wrote during his life, the other entitled *Self-Enquiry*. His presence over half a century made the remote mountain in Tamilnadu that was his residence a place of pilgrimage for devout Hindus and Western seekers. (*See also* Advaita Vedānta; Poonjaji.)

⌘ RĀMĀNANDA ⌘

Religious name of a Vaiṣṇava saint and ascetic of the fourteenth and/or fifteenth century. Born in Prayāga (Allāhābād), early in his life he was a high-ranking member of Rāmānuja's Śrīvaiṣṇava movement but was regarded as ritually polluted by his practices as a wandering ascetic (Saṃnyāsin). He departed from that order and founded his own order (now known as the Rāmānandi Saṃpradāya) devoted to Rāma with his main center in Vārāṇasī (Banaras). He preached against caste restrictions and hierarchy, saying that all were equal before God. His charisma, his use of the vernacular language of Hindi, and his appeal to the common person won him a large following in north India. The female saint Mīrā Bai was a disciple of his, and he is thought to have influenced both Kabīr and Nānak as well. (*See also* Bhakti; Mīrā Bai; Vaiṣṇavism.)

⌘ RĀMĀNUJA ⌘

Organizer and saintly leader of Śrīvaiṣṇavism in the eleventh and twelfth centuries C.E. His dates are traditionally given as 1017 to 1137, but scholars often regard 1077 to 1157 as more likely correct. Rāmānuja was a Brahmin who sought initiation in the Śrīvaiṣṇava tradition and renounced his married state to become an ascetic. He was invited to assume leadership of the Śrīvaiṣṇava community and administrative control of their large temple at Śrīraṅgam. He reorganized the temple's administration, achieving the cooperation of groups of Brahmins from several different subcastes, as well as non-Brahmins, in temple activities. This illustrates the relatively liberal attitude toward status distinctions within the community, particularly during Rāmānuja's lifetime. He was very successful in winning converts to Śrīvaiṣṇavism in south India, making that tradition one of the largest devotional movements in India. For Rāmānuja, Ultimate Reality is a personal Lord who reveals himself to those who are devoted and acknowledge their dependence on God. His interpretation of the Vedānta texts incorporates knowledge of Brahman as salvific, as did the well-established monistic Advaita tradition as championed by Śaṅkara, but also included performance of one's social and ritual duties, all of which were secondary means of attaining liberation from rebirth. The primary means of liberation for Rāmānuja, however, was devotion to God (Bhakti). The devotee who seeks God's presence in his or her life discovers that God needs the loving devotion of his devotee as well. Bhakti is thus the mutual participation of God and his devotees. Since the twelfth century, Rāmānuja has been regarded as the most authoritative teacher of the Śrīvaiṣṇava tradition who, through his teachings preserved in written form and the temple he reorganized and supervised, has made salvation available to a whole community. His articulation of a theistic interpretation of Vedānta, known as Viśiṣṭha-Advaita (Qualified Nondualistic) Vedānta, made devotion a path acceptable to even the most orthodox Brahmins. (*See also* Bhakti; Śrīvaiṣṇavism; Vaiṣṇavism; Vedānta; Viśiṣṭha-Advaita Vedānta.)

⌘ RAMANUJAN, A. K. ⌘

Indologist (1929–1993). Born into a Tamil Śrīvaiṣṇava family living in Mysore, he earned an M.A. in English at the University of Mysore. He taught English literature at colleges in Quilon, Kerala; in Madurai, Tamilnadu; in Belgaum, Karnataka; and in Baroda, Gujarat. He studied linguistics at Deccan College in Poona, then at Indiana University, earning a Ph.D. in 1963. He was appointed to the faculty of the University of Chicago in 1962, where he taught south Asian studies and linguistics until his death. He wrote numerous translations and studies of Dravidian literature and Indian folktales, and his own poetry in English and Kannada. (*See also* Indology.)

⌘ *RĀMĀYAṆA* ⌘

Long poem attributed to the Brahmin sage Vālmīki. Datable to about the second century B.C.E. through the second century C.E., the work is often described in Western scholarly literature as "epic poetry," but in India it is regarded as the first work of true poetry or belles lettres (Kāvya). It seems likely that there was an oral tradition for some centuries before the written text appeared; oral and written versions have existed ever since. The story centers on the hero Rāma, a prince of Ayodhyā, who married Sītā and was about to become king when he was forced into exile in the forest by intrigue in the palace. His wife and younger brother Lakṣmaṇa accompanied him into the forest. Sītā was abducted by the Demon King Rāvaṇa, taken to his home of Laṅkā and held captive there while Rāvaṇa tried to persuade her to marry him. Rāma assembled an army of allies made up of residents of the forest, including the monkey Hanūmān. They attacked Rāvaṇa's army and succeeded in killing Rāvaṇa and liberating Sītā, reuniting her with Rāma. To the question whether she had been faithful to Rāma in captivity, she called on the gods to bear witness to her truthfulness, which they did. Rāma and Sītā returned to Ayodhyā, where they ruled for many years and had two sons. Finally, the kingdom's populace began to question her faithfulness and she called upon the Goddess Earth to open up and receive her. The work is widely regarded as a narrative embodying Hindu values and concerns still valid to the present day. When Doordarshan, the Indian government television network, decided in the 1980s to produce a series that would be both entertaining and culturally significant, the *Rāmāyaṇa* was chosen as the first such series, and was immensely popular. The story is also well known throughout Southeast Asia, where dramatic enactments of it are popular. (*See also* Avatāra; Ayodhyā; Rāma; *Rām Carit Mānas*; Rāmlīlā; Rāvaṇa; Sītā; Vālmīki.)

⌘ *RĀM CARIT MĀNAS* ⌘

The Lake of Rāma's Deeds, the name of a sixteenth-century text in the Hindi language by Tulsīdās. The work tells the story of Rāma, and in many respects follows the story as found in the much older Sanskrit text of the *Rāmāyaṇa* by Vālmīki, but also contains some additional episodes not in the *Rāmāyaṇa*. The *Rām Carit Mānas* also is regarded by Hindi speakers as more effectively conveying the emotional significance and thereby evoking the devotional response than the text of Vālmīki. For example, while often in Vālmīki's text an action takes place without Rāma's knowledge, in Tulsīdās's text Rāma is consistently depicted as divine and therefore omniscient, the purpose being to encourage devotion to Rāma and reliance on his divine grace for liberation from rebirth. His work is much beloved and frequently quoted by

Hindi speakers. The use of language by Tulsīdās set a standard of excellence for Hindi that encouraged other authors to strive for similar effects in using the widely understood north Indian vernacular. (*See also* Rāma; *Rāmāyaṇa*; Tulsīdās.)

⌘ RĀMEŚVARAM (RAMESHWARAM) ⌘

An important place of pilgrimage in southern Tamilnadu for Vaiṣṇavas and Śaivas, where Rāma worshipped Śiva. Numerous events in the story of Rāma are associated with this spot. The Rāmanāthaswāmy temple commemorates Rāma's worship of Śiva after defeating Rāvaṇa and regaining Sītā, and was built in the twelfth century. Later additions have raised the height of its Gopuram gateways to some fifty-three meters. Kothandaraswāmy temple marks the spot where Vibhīṣaṇa, brother of Rāvaṇa, surrendered to and worshipped Rāma. A hill at the edge of town has a shrine containing the footprints of Rāma in stone. (*See also* Rāma; *Rāmāyaṇa*.)

⌘ RĀMLĪLĀ ⌘

The Play of Rāma. The name refers to the dramatic enactment of the story of Rāma, usually about the time of the Daśaharā (Dassehra) festival, September-October. The most famous and spectacular Rāmlīlā occurs over a month-long period in and around the town of Rāmnagar, across the Ganges River from Vārāṇasī (Banaras). There the dramatic enactment takes place over several square miles, in the open, with a crowd of many thousands watching and participating in the event. Women of the audience sit with Sītā in captivity, men accompany Rāma as his army to attack Laṅkā, and everyone obtains Darśana (auspicious sight) of the divine in the form of Brahmin boys who are regarded as embodying, for the duration of the Rāmlīlā, Rāma and Sītā. Pilgrims travel long distances to attend this event. (*See also* Avatāra; Līlā; Pilgrimage; Rāma; *Rāmāyaṇa*; Vārāṇasī.)

⌘ RĀMNAVAMĪ ⌘

Rāma's Birth Festival. Held in the month of Caitra (March-April) on the ninth day of the bright half, the festival celebrates the birth of Rāma at Ayodhyā. As one of the Avatāras of Viṣṇu, Rāma is revered for establishing a reign of perfect harmony that has been remembered as the ideal society and is still cited today as such. During the festival, devotees fast and bathe in the sacred rivers, particularly the Sarayū and Narmadā, associated with his life. Visits to Rāma temples, and the auspicious viewing (Darśana) of divine images of Rāma, are very important. Singing devotional songs, and hearing recitation of the *Rām Carit Mānas* or *Rāmāyaṇa*, are activities devotees particularly relish. Recently it has become popular to attend showings of films based on the life of Rāma, or to view videotapes of the television series based on his life, these being regarded as Darśana also. (*See also* Avatāra; Ayodhyā; Darśana; Rāma; *Rāmāyaṇa*; *Rām Carit Mānas*; Rāmlīlā.)

⌘ RASA ⌘

A theory of aesthetics first articulated in the *Nāṭya Śāstra* of Bharata (perhaps second century C.E.) in regard to drama, later applied to poetry as well. In the Rasa theory, a dramatic or poetic work of art is a precondition, presentation of which allows the audience member to experience, not merely a personal emotional state (Bhāva) tied to specific personal experiences, but a generalized state of emotional consciousness (Rasa) that is joyful aesthetic appreciation. According to Bharata, eight Rasas can be experienced: passionate love, humor, sorrow, anger, heroic perseverence, fear, disillusionment, and amazement. Later theorists add a ninth Rasa: spiritual peace. Aesthetic theorists and dramatists had long regarded śṛṅgāra (passionate love) as the most effective primary Rasa for a work of art. The spectator was to relish the state of consciousness evoked, appreciating the interplay of emotional states in a detached, almost meditative way. Indeed, the aesthetic theorist Abhinavagupta wrote that the Rasa experience was analogous to the attainment of Mokṣa, but only temporary, lasting as long as the drama that was its catalyst, whereas liberation was eternal. The religious significance of the Rasa theory was fully realized when it was used by the Bengali Vaiṣṇava Gosvāmins to develop a theology of devotion to Kṛṣṇa. (*See also* Abhinavagupta; Gosvāmins; *Nāṭya Śāstra*; Kashmir Śaivism.)

⌘ RĀṢṬRĪYA SVAYAMSEVAK SANGH ⌘

The National Volunteer Association, a Hindu nationalist organization. Founded in 1925 by K. V. Hedgewar (1890–1940), it is a controversial and influential political force, and one of the major anti-Muslim institutions in modern India. The R.S.S. violently opposed the partition of British India into the nations of India and Pakistan after World War II, and was probably responsible for many of the deaths that occurred during that difficult period. One disgruntled R.S.S. member, Nathurām Godse, murdered Mahātmā Gāndhī because he thought Gāndhī was too sympathetic toward Muslims and had condoned the partition. Muslims, Christians, and Communists have all been specifically named by the R.S.S. as non-Hindu, and therefore to be excluded from citizenship if the R.S.S. program were to be implemented throughout India. R.S.S. volunteers are subjected to intensive training, both physical and mental, to prepare them for their mission to awaken the Hindu people. Most of the leadership has been unmarried men who can devote themselves without distraction to the movement. Membership in the 1980s and 1990s appears to be about five million, though many other Hindus sympathize with at least some part of the R.S.S. message. (*See also* Bhāratīya Janatā Party; Hindu Mahāsabhā; Savarkar, Ganesh Damodar; Vishva Hindu Parishad.)

⌘ RĀVAṆA ⌘

Demon King of Laṅkā and the villain of the *Rāmāyaṇa*. Rāvaṇa is depicted as having ten heads, and as having received boons from Brahmā for his practice of asceticism, so that the gods are unable to kill him. He abducts Sītā while she is in exile with her husband Rāma in the forest, and carries her off to his homeland, Laṅkā. There he tries to persuade her to marry him, to no avail. Rāma arrives with an army of allies and Rāvaṇa fights until he dies at Rāma's hands. Recently, Rāvaṇa has been seen in a more positive light by political activists in south India as a tragic hero and defender of southern, Dravidian culture against Brahmanical culture from the north. (*See also* Dravidian; Hanuman; Rāma; *Rāmāyaṇa*; *Rām Carit Mānas*; Sītā.)

⌘ RAVIDĀS ⌘

Name of a mystic and saint of the fifteenth and sixteenth centuries. Born in Vārāṇasī (Banaras), apparently to an Outcaste cobbler family, he became a member of the Sant tradition of north Indian devotional poets. He ridiculed institutionalized Hindu traditions of temple worship, caste restrictions, and hierarchy, and emphasized the importance of devotion to the One God. He may have been influenced by Nāth traditions of Yoga, as well as the mystical Sufi traditions of Islam. Some forty-one poems attributed to Ravidās are included in the Sikh scripture entitled *Guru Granth Sahīb*. In the nineteenth and twentieth centuries, followers of Ravidās have established a new religious movement in which Guru Ravidās is worshipped, and his birthday is celebrated as a religious event, in temples in the Punjab region and in Banaras. (*See also* Nāth; Sant.)

⌘ REBIRTH ⌘

Hindus generally believe that after death, a human being is reborn in accordance with the actions (Karma) performed in life, so that good actions lead to a good rebirth and bad actions to a bad rebirth. Rebirth as a human being is not the only possibility, as all forms of animal life, as well as deities and various other lifeforms such as demon, Nāga, Apsaras, and Gandharva are all within the rebirth cycle (Saṃsāra). Most Hindus would exclude from Saṃsāra only the God whom they regard as the Absolute, or Ultimate Reality, which differs from one Hindu religious tradition to another; that deity is regarded as the creator and supervisor of the world, including the cycle of rebirth. Liberation from the cycle of rebirth is possible, the various religious traditions differing on the means of liberation. All theistic traditions agree that God may grant liberation to a devotee as a result of divine grace. Nontheistic traditions such as Advaita Vedānta or Sāṃkhya emphasize the human effort required in attaining liberation through the Path of Knowledge or the practice of Yoga. While Hinduism is characterized by widespread acceptance of rebirth, or reincarnation, this was not always the case. In the Vedic period (perhaps 1500 to 700 B.C.E.), prior to the composition of the Upaniṣads, there was apparently no concept of rebirth. The individual after death was memorialized by periodic rituals called Śrāddha in which rice balls (Piṇḍa) were offered to three generations of paternal and maternal ancestors; the first Śrāddha ceremony performed for a deceased ancestor placed that person among the Pitṛs (forefathers) in the celestial realm of Pitṛ-Loka. This afterlife was one that in the Vedic era did not include the possibility of rebirth as a human being. The Upaniṣads first introduced the concept of rebirth according to one's Karma, and the possibility of liberation from rebirth, as in *Bṛhadāraṇyaka Upaniṣad* 4.4.5–7, and *Chāndogya Upaniṣad* 8.15.1. (*See also* Creation; Death; Karma; Mokṣa; Pitṛ; Preta; Saṃsāra; Śrāddha; Upaniṣads.)

⌘ REINCARNATION ⌘

See Rebirth.

⌘ RENOUNCER ⌘

See Saṃnyāsin.

⌘ RENUNCIATION ⌘

See Saṃnyāsa.

⌘ *ṚG VEDA* ⌘

The Veda of Hymns of Praise. The first collection (Saṃhitā) of Vedic poems, probably compiled between 1200 and 1000 B.C.E., it consists of 1,028 poems ranging in length from fifty-eight verses to a single verse. Averaging ten verses each, the collection has over 10,000 verses in various metrical patterns, a total of some 432,000 syllables. The work's structure reveals conscious editing along rational principles, including having each book begin with a poem to Agni (except Book 8, a miscellany, and Book 9, which is dedicated to Soma), and in series of poems invoking a particular god the poems are arranged in order of length, longest first. For the great majority of its history this text was not in written form, but was transmitted exclusively orally and by memorization. It is widely regarded as the most accurately preserved of all ancient texts in the world. For any particular Vedic verse or poem, modern scholars do not know the place or date of its composition, and while there is at least one name associated with each poem as its seer (Ṛṣi), there is little information available about these individuals. The poems are quite diverse, containing praises of the Vedic gods, references to their myths, requests to the gods for desired benefits for the reciters and their patrons, references to historical events and persons, and details about ancient Āryan society. The *Sāma Veda* and *Yajur Veda* were compiled utilizing the poems of the *Ṛg Veda* in different order for different priests during the sacrifice; about ninety per cent of each text is *Ṛg Veda* verses. The *Mahābhārata* credits Vyāsa with dividing what had been one Veda into four texts (*Ṛg*, *Yajur*, *Sāma*, and *Atharva*) and teaching his disciples his edited version; Purāṇas credit each pupil with learning one of the Vedas, Paila transmitting the *Ṛg Veda*. (*See also Atharva Veda*; *Mahābhārata*; Nambūtiri Brahmins; Paila; Ṛṣi; Ṛta; *Sāma Veda*; Saṃhitā; Scripture; Śruti; Trayī Vidyā; Veda; Vyāsa; *Yajur Veda*.)

⌘ *RIG VEDA* ⌘

See Ṛg Veda.

⌘ RIGHT-HAND TANTRA ⌘

English translation of the Sanskrit term Dakṣiṇācāra. Some Tantric traditions distinguish Right-Hand and Left-Hand practices on the basis that Left-Hand practices utilize prohibited substances (Pañcamakāra, the Five M's) and behaviors that are controversial, while Right-Hand practices do not conflict with conventional moral standards and internalize the worship so that the practices are visualized rather than physically enacted. Right-Hand traditions of Tantra are therefore more socially acceptable than Left-Hand traditions generally are. The significance of the term "right-hand" is that the right hand is regarded as pure or auspicious, in contrast to the left hand which is used to clean oneself after a bowel movement and is, therefore, widely regarded as impure or inauspicious. (*See also* Five M's; Left-Hand Tantra; Tantra.)

⌘ RISHI ⌘

See Ṛṣi.

⌘ RISHIKESH ⌘

(ṚṢIKEŚA or corrupted from HṚṢĪKEŚA). An important place of pilgrimage in northern Uttar Pradesh, in the foothills of the Himālaya Mountains. The Ganges River flows through Rishikesh, and numerous temples and Yoga Āśramas line the banks. The oldest temple is the Bhārata Mandir. The nearby Triveṇi Ghāṭ at dawn is the site of milk offerings to the river goddess, and at sunset small oil lamps are set adrift on the water in a ceremony of Gaṅgā worship. (*See also* Pilgrimage.)

⌘ RITA ⌘

See Ṛta.

⌘ ROY, RĀM MOHUN ⌘

Bengali Brahmin (1772–1833) who founded the Brahmo Samāj in Calcutta in 1828. A dedicated student of languages, Roy gained facility in Sanskrit, Arabic, Persian, and Hebrew, as well as English and his native Bengali. He was familiar with Christianity from his employment with the British East India Company, his contact with missionaries in India, and his trip to Britain, and found much to admire in Christianity and Western humanistic traditions. Roy encouraged Hindus to avail themselves of Western-style education, but not to abandon their heritage either. He sought to establish journalism and a free press in Bengal, both in Bengali and in English. He regarded certain aspects of Hinduism, notably the practice of Satī (widow immolation), the use of images in worship, polytheism, animal sacrifice, and the social rules of caste, as later accretions that should be eliminated to return Hinduism to its original form. For Roy, true Hinduism was to be found in the Upaniṣads, which he interpreted as revealing the one God, though many names were used for God. His perspective was largely in conformity with Advaita Vedānta; his major contribution was in applying that religious perspective to his society. He used his expertise in Sanskrit to argue that the ancient scriptures did not insist upon the use of images in worship, or the practice of Satī. The movement he founded attained popularity only with the social elite, particularly in Bengal, but it is likely that support among Hindus for reform of Hindu practices such as Satī encouraged the British authorities to outlaw Satī in 1829. (*See also* Ārya Samāj; Brahmo Samāj; British East India Company; Indology; Rāj; Satī; Upaniṣads; Vedānta.)

⌘ ROYAL ASIATIC SOCIETY ⌘

(*See* Jones, Sir William; Sanskrit.)

⌘ ṚṢI ⌘

A Vedic seer or sage. The verses of the Vedic Saṃhitās are attributed to inspired sages who "saw" the eternal truths and have transmitted these on to later generations, as so described in the *Nirukta* of Yāska (2.11), a commentary on Vedic language. Later sages are often described as Ṛṣis, for example, Vyāsa in his composition of the *Mahābhārata*. (*See also Atharva Veda; Ṛg Veda; Sāma Veda*; Saṃhitā; Śruti; Veda; Vyāsa; *Yajur Veda*.)

⌘ R.S.S. ⌘

See Rāṣṭrīya Svayamsevak Sangh.

⌘ ṚTA ⌘

Cosmic order, as conceived in the Vedic literature. Ṛta is separate from the Devas, who did not create it, though certain of the Vedic gods are praised as guardians of the cosmic order, particularly Varuṇa and Mitra. Both these Devas were invoked to oversee agreements, and if the terms of the agreement were violated they were to punish the violator. While Ṛta was conceived as operating impersonally and without regard to any appeals, the poems to Varuṇa and Mitra feature frequent requests that these gods intercede and prevent punishment. Ṛta is closely related to truth, as is evident, for example, in *Ṛg Veda* 7.64 through 7.66, where Varuṇa and Mitra are asked to preserve cosmic order and punish the untruthful. *Ṛg Veda* 4.23, a poem to Indra, shows the close relationship between Ṛta and the Vedic sacrifice, which upholds cosmic order when performed correctly. Its opposite, Anṛta, carries the meanings of untruth and unreality. Ṛta is a term and concept that, for all its importance in the Vedic period, ceases to be used thereafter, but related terms and concepts such as Dharma and Karma continue certain features of Ṛta. (*See also* Dharma; Mitra; Varuṇa.)

⌘ RUDRA ⌘

Name of a Vedic god later known as Śiva. In the *Ṛg Veda* (1.114, 2.33, and 7.46, for example), Rudra is described as providing healing medicines to humanity, but is also fierce and his wrath is feared. Rudra is the father of the Maruts (or Rudras), deities of storm associated with rain and Indra. He is usually invoked separately from other gods and very rarely praised in a group of the gods, a feature unique to Rudra (though he is invoked with Soma in *Ṛg Veda* 6.74, an exception). Offerings to Rudra are to be made outside of the sacrificial compound so that he will stay away from the sacrifice. Rudra is often regarded as the god of wild places such as forests and mountains, away from settled villages and farmland, and the god of crossroads where dangerous bandits lurk. In the *Śvetāśvatara Upaniṣad,* Rudra is identified with Śiva and is described as the Lord, the embodied form of Brahman, the One who is beyond all the multiplicity of forms, and Puruṣa; the text (6.23) encourages devotion (Bhakti) to Rudra and to one's Guru, apparently the first textual use of this important term. (*See also* Bhakti; Maruts; Śaivism; Śiva; *Śvetāśvatara Upaniṣad.*)

⌘ RUDRĀKṢA ⌘

The seed of a shrub (*Elæocarpus ganitrus*) used as beads for rosaries by devotees of Śiva (Rudra), used in counting the number of recitations of a Mantra or the deity's name. The name means "Rudra's eye," and some devotees regard the seeds as Rudra's tears. (*See also* Bhakti; Rudra; Śaivism; Śiva.)

— S —

⌘ ŚABARA ⌘

Author of the *Śābara-bhāṣya,* the most extensive and important commentary on Jaimini's *Mīmāṃsā Sūtra.* He may have written in the first century B.C.E. (*See also* Jaimini; Mīmāṃsā.)

⌘ SACRED THREAD ⌘

Investiture with the sacred thread of sacrifice was originally called Yajñopavīta; later, the sacred thread itself took on this name. Persons of the three upper castes (Brahmin, Kṣatriya, Vaiśya) traditionally received the sacred thread in their youth in a ceremony of initiation supervised by their Guru. Such a ceremony is one of the twelve rites of passage (Saṃskāra) incumbent on the three upper castes. Properly initiated persons are called "twice-born" because they have received a new identity through the ritual. The *Mānava Dharma Śāstra* (2.44) specifies that the sacred thread of a Brahmin should be made of cotton; of a Kṣatriya, hemp fibers; and of a Vaiśya, wool. In ancient times, the sacred thread was worn only during the actual performance of ritual ceremonies. In recent centuries it has become customary for women no longer to receive the sacred thread, and for only male Brahmins to wear it throughout their lives. Cākyārs, temple servants in Kerala whose Dharma is to perform Kūṭiyāṭṭam dramas as devotional offerings to the temple's deities, receive initiation and wear the sacred thread throughout their lives, though they do not study the Veda and do not preside at sacrificial rituals. The thread is worn over the left shoulder and hangs under the right arm. (*See also* Saṃskāra; Twice-Born; Upanayana.)

⌘ SACRIFICE ⌘

See Yajña.

⌘ SĀDHANA ⌘

Practice; spiritual discipline. The term is used especially for procedures and techniques of worship involving ritual performance and meditation. (*See also* Sādhu; Tantra.)

⌘ SĀDHU ⌘

A word meaning successful, excellent, proper, or having reached the goal. The word is used particularly to refer to a holy man or saint. (*See also* Sādhana.)

⌘ SAGUṆA BRAHMAN ⌘

The Absolute with Attributes. The term refers to Ultimate Reality or God conceived as a being with particular qualities, personality, and form, such as Śiva or Viṣṇu. (*See also* Guṇa; Nirguṇa Brahman.)

⌘ SAHAJA ⌘

Innate; natural. The term is used by Tantrics of Sahajīya sects to refer to the innate and natural characteristics and tendencies of human beings, which are regarded as sacred. Such natural, innate characteristics as the sex drive are not to be suppressed, but are to be experienced, and one should learn to control and use the power they hold. Doing so is held to lead to ecstatic transformation and liberation from rebirth. (*See also* Sahajīya; Tantra.)

⌘ SAHAJĪYA ⌘

A Tantric movement that crossed boundaries between traditions, including Bāuls, Śāktas, Vaiṣṇavas, and Buddhists. The movement probably began about the eighth century C.E. in eastern India, especially in Bengal and Bihār. Sahajīyas held that the human body has characteristics and qualities that are innate and natural (Sahaja), such as sexuality. To try to suppress or eliminate such an aspect of being human would be painful and futile; instead, one should experience and use the power available to us as embodied creatures. Sahaja is equated with Ātman of Vedāntic thought, and like Ātman is identical with the Absolute, Brahman. Techniques of Tantric Yoga, including sexual practices designed to promote ecstatic transformation, are regarded as leading to liberation from rebirth. Vaiṣṇava Sahajīyas saw the relationship between Kṛṣṇa and Rādhā as the divine pattern for their own spiritual endeavors. (*See also* Bāuls; Sahaja; Tantra.)

⌘ ŚAIVA SIDDHĀNTA ⌘

The Truth about Śiva. This is the name of a sect that is dominant in Tamilnadu, south India. The theology developed by this tradition about the thirteenth century C.E. gave systematic doctrinal and ritual expression to the powerfully emotional devotion of the Nāyanār poets of earlier centuries, and seems to have largely absorbed and replaced the once widespread Pāśupata tradition. Śaiva Siddhānta is theistic or dualistic, and emphasizes the eternal distinction between Śiva as the Absolute and human souls, which are Śiva's creation. Souls exist typically in bondage, but can be transformed through the grace of Śiva so as to exist in communion and equality with Śiva, but not identity with Śiva. In Śaiva Siddhānta, initiation and the performance of daily rituals are vital components of the path to liberation, its ritual tradition being based on the Śaiva Āgama texts. (*See also* Kashmir Śaivism; Nāyanār; Pāśupata; Śaivism; Śiva.)

⌘ ŚAIVISM ⌘

The worship of Śiva. The complex figure of Śiva may represent the confluence of several streams of tradition. The people of the Indus Valley Civilization may have worshipped a god with qualities similar to Śiva. The Vedic Āryans worshipped a god named Rudra (Howler, perhaps) who was regarded as a god of wild places and is celebrated in some poems of the *Ṛg Veda* (2.33, for example) for his healing medicines and his dreaded power. Rudra comes to be called Śiva (Auspicious) in the *Śvetāśvatara Upaniṣad*, where he is regarded as the creator of the world, to be worshipped with devotion (Bhakti), and to be the object of meditation that will bring knowledge of Śiva and liberation from rebirth. Practitioners of Yoga are directed to model themselves on Īśvara (The Lord), one of the names used most often for Śiva. He is the archetypal Yogī and is frequently depicted in later literature such as the *Mahābhārata*, *Rāmāyaṇa*, and Purāṇas as the Yogī among the gods. Śiva is often represented symbolically by the Liṅga, a phallic form that communicates great creative power. The paradoxical combination of austere asceticism and potent sexuality is a feature of Śiva's mythology, in which he is depicted oscillating between the solitary, celibate life of the Yogī and the settled life of the householder married to Pārvatī and father of Gaṇeśa and Skanda. Śiva thus is the locus of a great deal of Hindu thought about the competing demands of spiritual life and domestic life. Sects devoted to worship of Śiva began to appear perhaps about the second century C.E. The Pāśupata (devotees of Paśupati, Lord of Creatures) tradition is the first to emerge, and identifies itself with the Brahmanical heritage as represented particularly by the *Śvetāśvatara Upaniṣad*. Offshoots of the Pāśupatas are less concerned with accommodating to Brahmanical norms, and include the radically ascetic Kāpālika, Lākulīśa, and Kālamukha sects which have many features of Tantra. The Liṅgāyat or Vīraśaiva sect is somewhat antithetical to the Brahmanical tradition. Devotion to Śiva as a personal Lord who can grant liberation developed particularly in south India, where the Nāyanār poets sang of their devotion in the vernacular language of Tamil in the seventh through ninth centuries C.E. Their songs of emotional devotion have become the basis of south Indian Śaivism, as embodied in the Śaiva Siddhānta sect. Worship of Śiva is a prominent feature of Tantric traditions, in which the Absolute is often conceived of as the union of Śiva and Śakti, God and Goddess. The annual festival in celebration of Śiva is Mahāśivarātri. (*See also* Kāpālika; Kashmir Śaivism; Liṅga; Liṅgāyat; Mahāśivarātri; Nāṭarāja; Nāyanār; Pāśupata; Rudra; Śaiva Siddhānta; Śakti; Śiva; Tantra; Yoga.)

⌘ ŚĀKTA ⌘

A person or tradition devoted to Śakti as the Goddess.

⌘ ŚAKTI ⌘

Power. Personified as the Goddess, Śakti is conceived as the female principle of the universe, or as the Absolute. Śakti can be the creative and energetic consort of any god, but is particularly associated with Śiva. Tantric traditions often regard the union of Śakti and Śiva as the Absolute (as in Kuṇḍalinī Yoga), but in Śākta traditions she alone is the Absolute. She is Śiva's power; without her he would be lifeless. Just as the word Śiva written without the mark for the letter "i" would be Śava (a corpse), the short "a" being assumed present unless another vowel is specified, so too Śiva would be a corpse without the enlivening presence of his Śakti. (*See also* Cakra; Durgā; Goddess; Kuṇḍalinī; Śiva; Tantra.)

⌘ *SĀMA VEDA* ⌘

One of the three Veda Saṃhitā collections; a text composed largely of selections from the *Ṛg Veda*, with instructions on how to sing the verses. It is the special ritual function of the Udgātṛ priest to sing these verses during a sacrifice. Melody and correct pronunciation are emphasized. It may have been compiled about 900 B.C.E. The *Mahābhārata* credits Vyāsa with dividing what had been one Veda into four texts (*Ṛg*, *Yajur*, *Sāma*, and *Atharva*) and teaching his disciples his edited version; Purāṇas credit each pupil with learning one of the Vedas, Jaimini transmitting the *Sāma Veda*. (*See also* Jaimini; Saṃhitā; Trayī Vidyā; Udgātṛ; Veda; Vyāsa.)

⌘ SAMĀDHI ⌘

Completion; contemplation; absorption. The eighth and final element in the practice of Yoga as described in the *Yoga Sūtra* of Patañjali and other classic sources. It is a state of higher cognition in which union with Brahman is attained, Karma is eliminated, and the practitioner is guaranteed of no further rebirths after death in this lifetime; it is thus equivalent to the attainment of Mokṣa or liberation from rebirth. Samādhi is the same as the state of Kaivalya (isolation) in which the self or spiritual component is isolated from or becomes independent of the body or material component of a person. A Samādhi is also the tomb of a saint. (*See also* Consciousness, States of; Kaivalya; Mokṣa; Yoga; *Yoga Sūtra*.)

⌘ SAṂHITĀ ⌘

Literally, "collection." The term is used particularly in reference to the Mantra texts of the Veda, that is, the *Ṛg*, *Yajur*, *Sāma*, and *Atharva Veda* texts, without their appended Brāhmaṇa, Āraṇyaka, or Upaniṣad texts. (*See also Atharva Veda*; *Ṛg Veda*; *Sāma Veda*; Veda; *Yajur Veda*.)

⌘ ŚAṂKARA ⌘

See Śaṅkara.

⌘ SĀṂKHYA ⌘

Enumeration. One of the six philosophical schools recognized by Hindus as orthodox. Sāṃkhya is traditionally regarded as first articulated by Kapila (perhaps 500 B.C.E.). It is a dualistic philosophical perspective, positing two eternal principles, Puruṣa (Spirit) and Prakṛti (Nature; Matter). Sāṃkhya enumerates the twenty-four elements or evolutes of Prakṛti in which the Puruṣa becomes enmeshed, thereby forgetting its true nature as a spiritual entity entirely free of entanglement in matter. The twenty-four evolutes of Prakṛti are as follows: Buddhi (Intellect), which produces Ahaṃkara (Ego), which in turn produces Manas (Mind), the five senses, and the five bodily functions. From Manas also evolve the five sensory objects and the five gross elements from which all matter is produced. Sāṃkhya also analyzes the creativity of Prakṛti as the activity of the three Guṇas, namely, Sattva (purity), Rajas (energy), and Tamas (inertia), varying proportions of each being present in all material forms. Liberation consists in the Puruṣa recognizing the entangling nature of Prakṛti and distinguishing between the pure consciousness of Puruṣa and the sensory information and bodily activity of Prakṛti, so that the Spirit attains Kaivalya or isolation from Matter, total freedom. It is an atheistic system, in which no god figures. Thus, as with other Hindu philosophical schools, it envisions liberation from rebirth as the outcome of valid cognition and disciplined action. Sāṃkhya is paired with Yoga, the philosophical school with which it is most compatible, Sāṃkhya providing the metaphysical foundation for the practices developed by Yoga. It has been a very influential tradition, appearing in the *Bhagavad Gītā* and elsewhere in the *Mahābhārata* as a discipline leading to valid cognition of reality, and has been widely utilized in theistic and Tantric contexts. (*See also* Philosophical Schools; Prakṛti; Puruṣa; Yoga.)

⌘ SAṂNYĀSA ⌘

The state of being an ascetic who has renounced social position and obligations. It is a tradition that became widespread and largely accepted by about the sixth century B.C.E., in both Brahmanical and non-Brahmanical religious groups in northern India. Renunciation calls into question the value of Brahmanical institutions such as marriage and family life, sacrificial rituals, and the social hierarchy of the caste system. Renouncers can be contrasted with the householder who performs his social and religious obligations, raises a family, performs rituals, etc. The renouncer has abandoned or transcended those obligations and lives an ascetic life, usually receiving donations of food from householders. Efforts to make renunciation more socially acceptable include the system of four stages of life (Āśrama), so that renunciation would take place only late in life after all social obligations have been fulfilled. It is traditionally a state into which one enters by a ritual that formally changes one's social status. Though women can become renouncers, it is widely regarded as a difficult life suitable only for extraordinary women. Buddhist, Jain, and some Hindu traditions have orders of nuns. Renouncers leave their social position as determined by caste; they vow celibacy and poverty, dedicating themselves to the effort to attain liberation from rebirth. Usually the renouncer marks his adoption of this way of life by shaving the head, wearing an ocher (orange-red) robe or in some cases no clothing at all, and by performing rites for deceased ancestors, then lastly for himself as if he had died. He then abandons ritual performance altogether, disposing of ritual implements and internalizing the fire, his only offerings in future being his own breath. He gives away all worldly goods, changes his name to a religiously significant one, gives up his former identity and is now regarded as a different person. This ritual death is regarded as equivalent to civil death, so that according to some legal authorities his "widow" can remarry. Some renouncers go homeless, wandering constantly except for the rainy monsoon season; others live communally in monasteries. (*See also* Caste; Four Stages of Life; Mokṣa; Saṃnyāsin.)

⌘ SAṂNYĀSIN ⌘

Person who has adopted the Saṃnyāsa way of life. (*See also* Parivrājaka; Saṃnyāsa.)

⌘ SAṂSĀRA ⌘

Wandering around; the cycle (of life). The term is used for the cycle of life, death, and rebirth, and is contrasted with its opposite, liberation from rebirth (Mokṣa), which constitutes an end to Saṃsāra. The concept is first articulated in the Upaniṣads, where various versions of rebirth according to one's Karma are found. The usual conception of Saṃsāra is as an infinite series of rebirths, in which rebirth as a human being is only one of many possibilities, all other forms of life also being regarded as in Saṃsāra. Even the gods are often regarded as merely exalted beings who have, through good Karma, ascended to their current status, from which they will be reborn when enough of their good Karma is exhausted. Theistic traditions will identify with the eternal and unchanging Brahman the god to whom they are devoted, so that the object of their devotion is not part of Saṃsāra but its creator and ruler. (*See also* Death; Jīvan-mukti; Mokṣa; Preta; Rebirth.)

⌘ SAṂSKĀRA ⌘

Consecration. The term is used especially to refer to a purificatory ceremony that is a rite of passage to a new status. Twelve such rites are specified in the Dharma Śāstra literature as incumbent upon the three Twice-Born classes, the Brahmin, Kṣatriya, and Vaiśya: (1) Garbhādhāna, the impregnation rite, performed after menstruation has begun to insure conception; (2) Puṃsavana, production of a male, a rite performed in the third month of pregnancy so that the child conceived will be male; (3) Sīmantonnayana, the parting of the hair, observed by women while pregnant; (4) Jātakarman, birth ceremony, which includes touching the newborn's tongue three times with clarified butter (ghee) after reciting prayers; (5) Nāmakarman, the name-giving ceremony; (6) Niṣkramaṇa, going out, the rite of taking the child out of the house for the first time, at age four months, to see the sun; (7) Annaprāśana, eating food, the rite in which a child first has rice put into its mouth; (8) Cūḍākarman, forming the crest, the rite of tonsure or head-shaving, performed on the child in the first or third year of life; (9) Upanayana, leading toward, the rite of initiation in which the Guru confers upon a boy the sacred thread, thereby making him one of the Twice-Born (Dvija), and qualifying him to study the Veda, ideally to take place for a Brahmin at age eight, for a Kṣatriya at eleven, and for a Vaiśya at twelve; (10) Keśānta, cutting the hair, a rite performed on a young Brahmin at age sixteen, on a Kṣatriya at twenty-two, and on a Vaiśya at twenty-four; (11) Samāvartana, the returning home of a Brahmacārin or young Brahmin student of the Veda after completion of his studies at the residence of his Guru; and (12) Vivāha, leading away of the bride from her father's house in marriage. These rites are described in *Mānava Dharma Śāstra* 2.26–40, except for rite (10) at 2.65, rite (11) at 2.108, and the final rite of marriage at 3.20–44 and 9.71–100. (*See also* Dharma; *Mānava Dharma Śāstra*; Marriage; Sacred Thread; Twice-Born; Upanayana.)

⌘ SANDALWOOD ⌘

From the Sanskrit Candana; the tree *Santalum album* or any of several closely related trees. The heartwood of the tree has aromatic yellowish wood, and yields an oil used in perfume and incense manufacturing. It grows particularly in southern India.

⌘ ŚAṄKARA (or ŚAṂKARA) ⌘

South Indian Brahmin philosopher and exponent of Advaita Vedānta. Traditionally his dates are given as 788–820 C.E., but this may represent the period of his career as a Saṃnyāsin. Born in Kerala to a family of Nambūtiri Brahmins, he was raised by his mother after the early death of his father. He was schooled in the Vedānta, and after his renunciation lived in Vārāṇasī (Banaras), but also travelled widely in India. Śaṅkara composed commentaries on the major Upaniṣads, the *Bhagavad Gītā*, and *Brahma Sūtra*, as well as authoring the *Upadeśasāhasrī* (The Thousand

Teachings). In these works he consistently and brilliantly maintained that the self (Ātman) is identical with the Absolute (Brahman), a monistic doctrine in which the gods are regarded as part of the rebirth cycle (Saṃsāra) and devotion or ritual offerings to them may lead to a better rebirth but not liberation from rebirth (Mokṣa). In other words, the Absolute is Nirguṇa Brahman, without any attributes or qualities that can be specified or that limit it, while Saguṇa Brahman is regarded as any partial and lesser form of Brahman, including the gods to whom one might offer devotion. Liberation is to be attained only through knowledge of the self, which is also knowledge of Brahman. Śaṅkara's writings established Advaita Vedānta as the dominant Hindu philosophical tradition, and it continues to be very influential to the present day. He founded a monastic order, the Daśanāmi, with a monastery in each of the four corners of India: Puri in the east, Badrīnāth in the north, Dvārakā in the west, and Śṛṅgerī in the south which is the headquarters of the order. The abbots of these monasteries carry the title Śaṅkara-Ācārya, and are four of the most influential religious leaders of Hinduism. (*See also* Advaita Vedānta; *Brahma Sūtra*; Daśanāmi Order; Nambūtiri Brahmins; Nirguṇa Brahman; Śṛṅgerī.)

⌘ SANSKRIT ⌘

The classical language of ancient India. Most of the sacred texts of Hinduism are in Sanskrit. The name is derived from the term Saṃskṛta (perfected, refined), which can be contrasted with the vernacular dialects called Prakrit, derived from the term Prākṛta (natural, unrefined). The language is syllabic, written left to right with an alphabet of forty-nine letters. Pāṇini's brilliant linguistic analysis about 400 B.C.E. codified the Sanskrit language, and later grammarians largely followed his lead, though authors were still able to exercise their creativity to a considerable extent. The language of the Vedic texts, with its system of three tones, had changed somewhat by Pāṇini's era, the tones no longer being used. A millenium after Pāṇini, authors tended to use long compounds, thereby avoiding many of the complexities (and much of the clarity) of Sanskrit grammar. There is a vast literature in Sanskrit produced during the last four millenia. Discovery of Sanskrit by European scholars began in earnest with the work of Sir

William Jones, who stated in his 1786 address to the Asiatic Society of Bengal, "Sanskrit language, whatever be its antiquity, is of a wonderful structure; more perfect than the Greek, more copious than the Latin, and more exquisitely refined than either." The realization that Greek and Latin were closely related to Sanskrit stimulated scholarship on comparative linguistics and led to the conclusion that all three are descended from a common parent language, called Indo-European by linguists. Translation of Sanskrit texts has been a major preoccupation of Indology throughout the nineteenth and twentieth centuries, and there are still untranslated texts awaiting scholarly treatment. Sanskrit literature in translation has had a significant impact on Western literature and culture. For example, J. W. von Goethe found the opening scene of Kālidāsa's drama *Abhijñānaśākuntala*, in which the theme and setting are introduced informally by the stage director and actress, so fascinating that he borrowed that device for his own drama on Faust. European Romanticism in the nineteenth century derived considerable strength from the examples of mystery and mysticism found in abundance in Sanskrit literature. Though no longer a living, spoken language in the sense that one learns it by hearing it in the home from birth, it remains a language widely studied in the Indian public educational system, and it is used in religious ceremonies. Moreover, it is possible to read a Sanskrit newspaper or hear a daily summary of the news in Sanskrit on All India Radio. Sanskrit is the parent language of all the modern Indo-European languages native to India, including Hindi, Bengali, Marathi, and their numerous dialects. New words are still created in these languages by the use of Sanskrit, for example, television is called Dūradarśana (Doordarshan), in both cases meaning seeing from afar. (*See also* Dravidian; Gonda, Jan; Indo-European; Indology; Jones, Sir William; Kālidāsa; Pāṇini; Patañjali; Prakrit; Script; Smṛti; Śruti; Tamil.)

⌘ SANT ⌘

Holy person; saint. The term is applied to a group of religious leaders in north India, beginning in the fifteenth century, who promoted devotion (Bhakti). Rāmānanda is often cited as the first Sant, other prominent ones including Ravidās, Kabīr, and Nānak (the latter three of whom have poems included in the Sikh scripture, *Guru Granth Sahīb*). They were influenced by, and in turn exercised influence on, Vaiṣṇavism, Nāth Yoga traditions, and Sufi Islam. They expressed, in vernacular dialect, opposition to caste restrictions and hierarchy, ritualism, and institutionalized religion generally. (*See also* Bhakti; Kabīr; Nānak; Rāmānanda; Ravidās; Tukārām; Vaiṣṇavism.)

⌘ ŚĀNTI ⌘

Peace. Many of the Upaniṣads end with this word, repeated three times as a benediction.

⌘ SANTOSHI (SAṂTOṢĪ) MĀ ⌘

A popular goddess (The Mother Who Satisfies) in modern India. Devotion to her first manifested in western India in the 1970s in short, anonymously written brochures in modern, colloquial Hindi. She is linked to the Brahmanical tradition in some accounts, where Śiva and Parvatī, for the good of the world, tell Gaṇeśa to create a goddess who relieves suffering; she is thus Gaṇeśa's "daughter." In 1975 a popular film, *Jai Santoshi Mā*, was released that recounts her mythology. It centers on the devotion of a young woman, Satyavatī, and how her life was improved through devotion. The youngest woman in her husband's household, she was forced to do menial tasks until he deserted her and their son. She happened on a group of women doing rituals for Santoshi Mā and joined them. The goddess appeared to her husband in a dream and told him to return to his devoted wife, and he did, with great wealth. Through various trials, Satyavatī remained constant in her devotion and her sisters-in-law became devotees too, providing a happy ending for the film. Women have been attracted to the worship of this goddess. Every Friday devotees perform a rite called Vrata until their wishes are fulfilled: fasting and presenting offerings of sugar and chickpeas (staples in every Indian kitchen) before an image of the goddess, a simple ritual requiring no priest. When one's wishes are fulfilled, the ceremony of thanks (udyapana) is performed: serving a meal with no sour or bitter foods, accompanied by recitation of the goddess's story. The cult has benefitted from the use of new technologies of printing and film and has spread quickly. Santoshi Mā is depicted as young, benign looking, and beautiful, but holding weapons that suggest power and fierceness, a duality one sees in a goddess such as Durgā also. Santoshi Mā, like Gaṇeśa her "father," is not worshipped for release from rebirth, but for help and well-being in this life. (*See also* Durgā; Gaṇeśa; Goddess.)

⌘ SARASVATĪ ⌘

Vedic goddess of learning and eloquence. Celebrated in many poems of the *Ṛg Veda*, she is the major deity of only three: 6.61, 7.95, and 7.96. She is celebrated as both a river and a deity, bounteous and gracious in her bestowal of good fortune to humanity. She is at times identified with Vāc, the deified sacred speech. (*See also* Vāc.)

⌘ SARASVATĪ, DAYĀNAND ⌘

See Dayānand Sarasvatī.

⌘ ŚĀSTRA ⌘

Teaching. The name of a class of Sanskrit texts that give a systematic exposition of a body of knowledge. (*See also Artha Śāstra; Mānava Dharma Śāstra.*)

⌘ SATHYA SAI BABA ⌘

See Satya Sai Baba.

⌘ SATĪ ⌘

Virtuous woman. The term is applied to the woman who, widowed by the death of her husband, accompanies him into death by ritual suicide by fire on his funeral pyre. It may well be an ancient custom with Indo-European heritage, but in India was typically confined to the Kṣatriya (Warrior) class. As a practice, it seems to have increased in frequency with Muslim military activity in India as an alternative to captivity and enslavement. Muslim rulers in India made occasional efforts to discourage the tradition, and under British colonial rule in 1829 it was made illegal, a law independent India also seeks to enforce, though there are periodic instances of the practice. Rām Mohun Roy and the Brahmo Samāj in Bengal opposed the practice of Satī, and their vigorous efforts to discourage the practice were instrumental in the British decision to outlaw Satī. Since a widow is a burden to the family of her deceased husband, and a constant reminder of his absence, the family may pressure or even coerce the widow to join her husband in death. The term has come into English as "suttee," and with somewhat different meaning, referring to the act of burning rather than to the woman herself. Satī as a concept receives scriptural support in the Purāṇas in the form of a daughter of Dakṣa named Satī who chose Śiva as her husband and, when her father opposed the marriage, burned herself in protest, later being reborn and marrying Śiva. Mādrī, one of the two wives of Pāṇḍu in the *Mahābhārata*, became a Satī by immolating herself on his funeral pyre. Such scriptural examples became paradigms for Hindu women of certain eras. (*See also* Brahmo Samāj; British East India Company; Calcutta; Rāj; Roy, Rām Mohun.)

⌘ SATYA SAI BABA ⌘

Religious leader widely regarded as a saint (1926–). After a religious experience at age fourteen, he proclaimed himself a reincarnation of Sai Baba of Shirdi, a renowned holy man. He promotes Bhakti devotion and a lifestyle of discipline and self-control, including vegetarianism, abstinence from alcohol and drugs, and scriptural study. He is particularly famous for miracles such as manifesting lotuses in his hands. Unlike many Hindu Gurus of recent decades, he has never come to the West to attract followers. His primary Āśrama is at Puttaparthi in Andhra Pradesh, but he spends most of March through July at the Whitefields Āśrama near Bangalore.

⌘ SATYĀGRAHA ⌘

Holding Onto Truth. The term was used by Mahātmā Gāndhī to refer to the method of passive resistance in opposition to laws deemed unjust. Knowing that one is on the side of truth and that truth will ultimately prevail, one could rely upon this strength that comes from truth, love, and nonviolence. The term seems first to have been used by Gāndhī in 1908 in South Africa in response to a law requiring the registration and finger-printing of all Indians residing there. Breaking the law, and encouraging Indians to burn their registration papers, led to the imprisonment of Gāndhī and others. Gāndhī returned to India in 1914 and used the same approach there. His approach can be contrasted with other, more radical and violent approaches such as advocated by the Ghadr movement and Bal Gangadhar Tilak. The technique of civil disobedience to call attention to unjust laws was a powerful and effective means of protest against the British colonial authorities in India, and was instrumental in the successful campaign for independence. Gāndhī's use of the religiously significant ideal of nonviolence (Ahiṃsā), combined with his penchant for fasting and his simple lifestyle that was reminiscent of that of the renounced ascetic (Saṃnyāsin), were major factors in the success of his leadership. (*See also* Ahiṃsā; Gāndhī, Mohandās K., Ghadr Movement; Tilak, Bal Gangadhar.)

⌘ SAVARKAR, GANESH DAMODHAR ("VEER") ⌘

Hindu nationalist, revolutionary, and author (1883–1966). Residing in Britain from 1906 to 1910, he was arrested as a revolutionary and sentenced to fifty years' imprisonment in the Andaman Islands. While in prison, Savarkar wrote poems, essays, and the book entitled *Hindutvā*, which was first published anonymously in 1923. He was released from confinement in 1937 and became a leader of the nationalist movement, opposing Mahātmā Gāndhī's pacifist approach to political change. His expansive definition of a Hindu as one who regards the land of India (Bhārata) from the Indus River to the seas as his fatherland and his holy land was accepted by the Hindu Mahāsabhā as articulating their political position, in the hope of rallying Indians to oppose British colonial rule. The Rāṣṭrīya Svayamsevak Saṅgh views Savarkar as a great inspiration and patriot. (*See also* Ārya Samāj; Bhāratīya Janatā Party; Dayal, Har; Hindu Mahāsabhā; Rāj; Rāṣṭrīya Svayamsevak Saṅgh.)

⌘ SAVITṚ ⌘

The Vivifier; one of the twelve Āditya deities. Sometimes identified with, sometimes distinguished from Sūrya, the sun god, Savitṛ apparently represents the enlivening power of the sun. According to Sāyaṇa, Savitṛ is the name for the sun before it rises, while Sūrya is the name for the sun when manifest. Eleven poems in the *Ṛg Veda* are dedicated to Savitṛ exclusively (including 2.38, and 4.53), and he is invoked with other deities in several poems as well. The most famous verse in the whole Vedic literature, *Ṛg*

Veda 3.62.10, known as the Gāyatrī or Sāvitrī Mantra, is addressed to this deity, and may be translated as follows: "Let us receive that excellent, radiant light of the God Savitṛ that he may inspire our minds." The verse is recited by many Brahmins to the present day, particularly when they offer water to the sun at dawn. (*See also* Āditya; Gāyātrī; Sāvitrī; Sūrya.)

⌘ SĀVITRĪ ⌘

A verse addressed to Savitṛ, especially the verse of *Ṛg Veda* 3.62.10, known also as the Gāyatrī Mantra (see the translation above). The term is also used for initiation into one of the three twice-born classes by recitation of this Mantra and donning the sacred thread (Yajñopavīta) in a ceremony known as the Upanayana. Sāvitrī is also the name of a goddess who is the daughter of Savitṛ and wife of Brahmā, and the personification of the verse above; hence also the mystical "mother" of the three twice-born classes. Sāvitrī is also the name of a princess, daughter of King Aśvapati and wife of Prince Satyavat, born as a result of the king's worship of the goddess Sāvitrī; she saves her husband's life by her loyalty and cleverness in a story recounted in the *Mahābhārata* (3.277–283). (*See also* Gāyatrī; Sacred Thread; Saṃskāra; Savitṛ; Twice-Born; Upanayana.)

⌘ SCRIPT ⌘

Writing was used in India at least as early as the seventh century B.C.E. in the form of a script called Brāhmī, perhaps based on Semitic scripts. The inscriptions of Aśoka in the third century B.C.E. were in Brāhmī. About the fifth or fourth century B.C.E., another script came into use called Kharoṣṭhī. Evolving from these by the fourth century C.E. was the script known as Devanāgarī which, by the tenth or eleventh century, had developed into the form still used today in the writing of Sanskrit, Hindi, and Marathi. (*See also* Sanskrit.)

⌘ SCRIPTURES ⌘

In Hinduism, the greatest scriptural authority lies with Śruti (What Was Heard; Revelation), that is, the Vedic literature, including the Saṃhitā, Brāhmaṇa, Āraṇyaka, and Upaniṣad texts. All other literature is Smṛti (What Was Remembered; Tradition), and is regarded as having scriptural authority only to the extent that it does not conflict with Śruti. However, for Vaiṣṇavas, the *Bhagavad Gītā* is widely regarded as having authority comparable to Śruti, and in particular sects certain Purāṇa or Āgama texts or devotional poetry may be seen as authoritative. (*See also* Smṛti; Śruti; Veda.)

⌘ SELF ⌘

See Ātman. *See also* Jīva; Puruṣa.

⌘ SELF-REALIZATION FELLOWSHIP ⌘

Organization founded by Paramahaṃsa Yogānanda in 1935. He arrived in the United States in 1920 from India to attend the International Congress of Religious Liberals, and lectured widely throughout the United States. Yogānanda's Guru, Swāmī Śrī Yukteśwar, had been trained in Kriyā Yoga, the Discipline of Action, in which one attains direct knowledge of the Absolute through meditation. His Guru urged Yogānanda to establish the Yogoda Sat-Sanga in 1917 in India, and on his arrival in America he established a branch in Boston. He taught a variety of Yoga philosophically based on Advaita Vedānta, but including Tantric practices as well. Among the purposes of the Self-Realization Fellowship is teaching the unity of science and religion, the unity of humanity based on their communion with God, and the systematic methods of attaining God-consciousness. A monastic order including both monks and nuns provides leadership. After Yogānanda's death in 1952, leadership passed to Swāmī Rājasi Janakānanda (James Lynn), and in 1955 to Śrī Daya Mātā. The organization is headquartered in Los Angeles, and by the 1990s maintained eight Āśramas or meditation halls, and over a hundred smaller centers or meditation groups throughout the United States. (*See also* Yogānanda, Paramahaṃsa.)

⌘ SIDDHA ⌘

Perfected person; liberated person. The term may be used of any accomplished meditator, but has been applied particularly to Tantric masters regarded as possessing extraordinary powers and perfected, immortal bodies. (*See also* Nāth; Tantra.)

⌘ SIDDHA YOGA ⌘

One modern lineage of Kaula Tantric Kashmir Śaivism, unique for its success in the West. Founded by Swāmī Nityānanda in India, it was brought to the West by his disciple Swāmī Muktānanda in 1970. He was a charismatic and effective spokesman for the movement, with the result that he and his followers established several hundred meditation centers throughout the world. The movement's headquarters of Āśrama in the Catskill Mountains near South Fallsburg, New York, has several hundred residents. Muktānanda's death in 1982 left the movement's leadership to two Indian followers, Nityānanda and Cidvilāsānandā, a brother and sister. Three years later Nityānanda removed himself from involvement with the organization, leaving leadership to his sister. Born about 1956, she is called Gurumayī by followers. (*See also* Gaṇeśapurī Āśrama; Muktānanda, Swāmī.)

⌘ SĪTĀ ⌘

Furrow. In the *Ṛg Veda* (4.57) Sītā is addressed and given reverence so that an abundant harvest will occur. She is the heroine of the *Rāmāyaṇa* and wife of Rāma, where as an incarnation of Śrī (Lakṣmī) she represents prosperity, the earth, and the Goddess. When Rāma is exiled from the palace instead of enthroned, she insists on accompanying him into the forest. There she is abducted by the demon Rāvaṇa and held captive while he attempts to persuade her to forget Rāma and marry him. Sītā is finally rescued and restored to Rāma, but the question whether she has been faithful to Rāma in her captivity arises and requires the intervention of the gods to prevent her suicide. They return to their city of Ayodhyā, where he reigns as king, but again the question of fidelity arises among the populace and Rāma sends her away, because he cannot rule with such dissension occurring. Sītā asked the earth to swallow her, and she disappeared into a furrow, merging back into the Goddess who was her source. (*See also Rāmāyaṇa*; Śrī.)

⌘ ŚIVA ⌘

One of the major gods of Hinduism. He is often regarded as the god of Yoga, and sometimes as the Destroyer in the Trinity

(Trimūrti) with Brahmā the Creator and Viṣṇu the Preserver. Many scholars believe that there may be multiple streams of tradition in the worship of Śiva, including the Vedic god Rudra and perhaps one or more other gods of Indus Valley Civilization, Dravidian, or tribal origin. The striking figure on several seals from the Indus Valley Civilization that is seated cross-legged, surrounded by wild animals, is often regarded as a representation of a deity with Śiva-like qualities. Until there is agreement on the decipherment of the Indus Valley writing system, one can only speculate about the meaning of this figure to that civilization. In the *Ṛg Veda* (as in 1.114, and 2.33), Rudra is worshipped with an attitude of awe and fear, as the god of wild places and as one who can dispense healing medicines but whose wrath is fierce. He was excluded from the Vedic sacrifice and offerings were made to him outside the sacrificial compound so that he would stay away. The myth of the destruction of Dakṣa's sacrifice, told often in the *Mahābhārata* and Purāṇas, tells how he came to receive those offerings. Later Vedic literature begins to use the name Śiva (Auspicious), an epithet used euphemistically or hopefully, in conjunction with Rudra and other names. In the *Śvetāśvatara Upaniṣad*, Śiva is depicted as Brahman embodied, the Absolute, a Yogī who is the divine model of human practitioners of Yoga, and as the Lord whom one should worship with devotion (Bhakti), perhaps the earliest textual use of that important term. In the later Hindu tradition Śiva is worshiped for his grace in liberating beings from the cycle of rebirth. The Nāyanār poets of south India gave expression to their devotion to Śiva in songs that are still sung today, some twelve centuries after their composition. Śiva embodies the tension between the life of the householder and the life of the ascetic. He alternates between the two extremes, at one time being married to Pārvatī, or being a passionate lover, at another time being a celibate ascetic. Śiva is represented in two ways: (1) As a male ascetic with long matted hair, carrying a trident, often with four arms, sometimes with a third eye on his forehead symbolic of his mystical insight. A variant of this is his form as The Lord Who Is Half Female (Ardhanarīśvara), the right side male and left side female, showing the unity of Śiva and Śakti, transcending duality. (2) In a symbolic representation as the Liṅga, a phallic form that signifies power and creative force held in restraint. However represented, to his worshippers Śiva is God, the creator, preserver, and destroyer of the world, through whose grace the possibility of liberation exists. Among the many names used for Śiva are the following: Hara (Destroyer), Paśupati (Lord of Creatures), Śaṅkara (Beneficent), Mahādeva (The Great God), Īśāna (Ruler), and Īśa or Īśvara (Lord). The main festival of Śiva is Mahāśivarātri. (*See also* Liṅga; Mahāśivarātri; Nāṭarāja; Nāyanār; Pārvatī; Rudra; Śaivism; Third Eye; Trinity; Yoga.)

⌘ ŚIVĀJĪ ⌘

Marāṭha military leader (1627–1680). The son of Shāhjī Bhonsle, a minister of the small state of Bījapur near Pune in western India, Śivājī began his career as a bandit but by 1660 was attacking Mughal strongholds throughout the region. The Mughal emperor Aurangzeb forced Śivājī to surrender some of the forts he had seized in exchange for appointment as a Mughal vassal and commander of 5,000 troops. In an effort to win Śivājī's allegiance and pacify a troublesome region, Aurangzeb named him a Rāja in 1667, but Śivājī began to exact tribute from local Mughal officers. In 1674 he proclaimed himself an independent ruler in a great ceremony marked by enormous donations to the assembled Brahmins, and embarked on a campaign to the south that brought much-needed booty and large sections of Tamilnadu under his control. In effect, he had raised his caste status from Śūdra to Kṣatriya. Śivājī's devoutly religious mother had a powerful impact on him, and he became a patron and disciple of the two most prominent Hindu religious leaders of the region, Rāmdās and Tukārām. He was seen as the chief defender of Hinduism in opposition to the Muslim Mughals, and roused the Marāṭha people to a sense of nationalism that made them for a century the most dangerous opponents of the Mughal Empire. (*See also* Marāṭhas; Pune; Tukārām.)

⌘ ŚIVARĀTRI ⌘

See Mahāśivarātri.

⌘ SKANDA ⌘

God of War, also known as Kārttikeya, Guha, or Kumāra, and in south India, Murugan, Subrahmaṇya or Aiyanār. Skanda is regarded as the son of Śiva, though the connection between them is somewhat indirect. Myths of the origin of Skanda begin with the need of the gods for a general to lead their army in their combats with the demons. Agni's seed is collected and deposited among reeds in a pot in the mountains, from which is born the six-headed Skanda. His power is so great that the gods take refuge in him, Indra offers him command of the army, and Rudra-Śiva informs the gods that Skanda is a form of himself. Other myths recount that the gods had asked Śiva to desist from copulating with his wife Pārvatī, who in anger cursed the gods to be childless. The seed from which Skanda originated was Śiva's, conveyed by Agni to Gaṅgā and from her to a forest of reeds in the mountains where the six Kṛttikā women (wives of Ṛṣis) nurse him as his mothers (accounting for the name Kārttikeya). Skanda heroically delivers the gods from affliction by the demon embodying Pārvatī's curse. His origin in the mountains and the name Kumāra (young man) suggest the ascetic practice of celibacy, while the reed-forest (śara-vana) suggests arrows (śara), so that Skanda has the character of an ascetic and a warrior simultaneously, reminiscent of Rudra-Śiva. Śiva's adoption of him as his son parallels his adoption of Gaṇeśa, likewise produced in a miraculous fashion. Skanda can be regarded as possessing the same ambiguous nature as Rudra-Śiva, and as having the awesome power of the renounced ascetic and the fierce warrior. (*See also* God; Gupta; Kālidāsa; Rudra; Śiva.)

⌘ SMĀRTA ⌘

From the Smṛti, the term applied to a tradition of worship that sees itself as nonsectarian Hinduism based on the Vedic heritage. Those in the Smārta tradition emphasize the role of the householder within the context of caste hierarchy and the Four Stages of Life (Varṇāśrama-Dharma). Fulfillment of the social and religious obligations (Dharma) appropriate to one's particular caste status and stage of life is seen as the height of Brahmanical orthodoxy. Worship in this tradition is based on offerings made to a collection of five deities (Pañcāyatana-Pūjā): Viṣṇu, Śiva, Durgā, Gaṇeśa, and Sūrya. The first two are the main gods of the major sects, and Durgā represents the Goddess, either in association with Śiva as his Śakti or as independent of Śiva. Gaṇeśa is the widely popular god who removes obstacles to success, often worshipped first so that later offerings will be received, while Sūrya is the sun god of the Vedic tradition, to whom Smārta Brahmins offer water each morning with the Gāyatrī Mantra in an ancient ritual. One of the five deities is placed in the center, the other four arranged around the chosen deity (Iṣṭa-devatā) as subsidiary deities. Worship in this fashion is regarded as a duty, fulfillment of which brings good Karma, but not as a path to liberation from rebirth. Worship is conducted with Brahmanical Vedic, not Tantric, Mantras and texts. Worship is guided by the Mīmāṃsā philosophical tradition, in which proper performance of the duties enjoined by the Veda is the means to fulfillment and good Karma. Complementing this worship is the Advaita Vedānta philosophy of Śaṅkara, in which the gods are regarded as forms of Brahman, but only knowledge of Brahman brings liberation. (*See also* Advaita Vedānta; Dharma; Four Stages of Life; Iṣṭadevatā; Smṛti; Śrīvidyā Tantra.)

⌘ SMṚTI ⌘

That Which Is Remembered, the term used to refer to scriptures and other texts that are not the divinely revealed Vedic literature (Śruti). While Śruti is often regarded as eternal truth revealed to humanity by inspired Ṛṣis in the ancient past, Smṛti is regarded as authored by human beings, and therefore subject to error. Smṛti is usually regarded as authoritative to the extent that it is not in conflict with Śruti, the ultimate source of authority and meaning. Certain texts that fall into the Śmṛti category, however, are viewed by some Hindus as having the authority and importance of Vedic literature, for example, the *Bhagavad Gītā* for all Vaiṣṇavas, or the poems of the Nāyanār saints for south Indian Śiva devotees. In fact, since these later texts are much more accessible and relevant to the religious concerns of devotees, they may be much more significant than the theoretically authoritative, but actually ignored, Śruti texts. (*See also Mānava Dharma Śāstra*; Scripture; Smārta; Śruti.)

⌘ SOMA ⌘

A drink made by the early Āryans that is celebrated by them in Vedic poems for its inspirational qualities. Soma was apparently made by crushing mushrooms (probably *Amanita muscaria*, or fly agaric) in milk and water, then straining the liquid, which was consumed. The psychotropic or hallucinogenic properties of the drink were interpreted as visions of the gods. Brahmin priests drank Soma, then composed poems and communed with the gods; warriors drank Soma before battle and were made to feel invincible. *Ṛg Veda* 10.119, with its refrain, "Have I not drunk Soma?", is the joyous exclamation of one who has ingested the drink. The Soma sacrifice, in which Soma was offered to the gods, became a ritual of tremendous importance to the early Āryans, and the entire ninth book of the *Ṛg Veda* consists of poems to be used in the Soma sacrifice. Indra is particularly dedicated to drinking Soma, and is often depicted as drinking Soma before his combats, such as in *Ṛg Veda* 1.32, where repeatedly Indra is said to have drunk Soma before fighting Vṛtra. Soma is celebrated in the Veda as both the drink and a god, and in many references it is impossible to distinguish the two. It may also be compared with Amṛta, the Elixir of Immortality over which gods and demons fight in mythology. (*See also* Amṛta; Indra; Yajña.)

⌘ SOMNĀTH (SOMANĀTHA) ⌘

Lord of the Moon, a name of Śiva. It is also the name of a very large and wealthy temple in Gujarāt. Its ancient history is obscure; legendary accounts say that it was built by Somarāja of gold, then rebuilt by Rāvaṇa in silver, by Kṛṣṇa in wood, and by Bhīmadeva in stone. The Muslim scholar and traveller al-Bīrūnī was so impressed with the temple that he described its wonders at length. It was said to have employed some 1,000 priests, 500 Devadāsī dancing girls, 300 musicians, and 300 barbers to shave the heads of pilgrims to the shrine. This description of its wealth brought Mahmud of Ghazni on a raid in 1026 C.E. He plundered the temple, then destroyed it, carrying off the shattered remnant of the seven-foot polished stone Liṅga image to his capital, where he installed it in the threshold of a mosque, to be stepped on by devout Muslims. Hindus rebuilt the temple, which was destroyed again in 1297 and 1394, both times rebuilt, and then decisively destroyed in 1706 by Aurangzeb the Mughal emperor. The temple was not rebuilt until 1950, this time at the urging of S. V. Patel and with governmental aid. Somnāth stands for some Hindus as a symbol of the defeats and religiously motivated insults inflicted on Hindus by Muslims, and for that reason was chosen as the starting point for the Ratha Yātra (Chariot Procession) to Ayodhyā, a politically inspired event led by the Bhāratīya Janatā Party and Vishva Hindu Parishad in 1990. (*See also* Devadāsī; Pilgrimage; Temple.)

⌘ ŚRĀDDHA ⌘

Faithful; the name of a ritual performed for deceased ancestors. Rituals include the daily offering of water in memory of the deceased, as well as periodic offerings of balls of grain (Piṇḍa). Offerings are made to the father, grandfather, and great-grandfather on both the paternal and maternal sides of the family. Śrāddha rites are distinct from the actual funeral ritual (Antyeṣṭi) itself, which is regarded as having provided a spiritual body for the deceased. Śrāddha rites place the deceased among the Pitṛs (Fathers, or Ancestors) who enjoy an afterlife in the celestial realm of Pitṛ Loka. Offerings of water and food provide needed sustenance for the deceased in the afterlife, without which the deceased would be a wandering, hungry ghost (Preta) who could haunt the living. Śrāddha is a ritual that was current in the Vedic era (1500 to 700 B.C.E.), and has persisted to the present despite almost universal acceptance of the idea of rebirth according to one's Karma. (*See also* Ancestral Rites; Death; Funeral; Gayā; Pitṛ; Preta; Rebirth.)

⌘ ŚRAUTA SŪTRAS ⌘

Ritual texts concerning the Vedic sacrifice (Yajña). Composed in Sanskrit, perhaps between 400 B.C.E. and 400 C.E., these texts give systematic descriptions of the ritual procedures for conducting a Yajña, the solemn, public sacrificial offerings. (*See also* Gṛhya Sūtras; Yajña.)

⌘ ŚRĪ ⌘

Prosperity; auspiciousness. The word is used to refer to prosperity and to a Goddess who embodies prosperity. The name occurs once in the *Ṛg Veda* (8.2.19), and often in the *Atharva Veda* and Brāhmaṇa literature. *Śatapatha Brāhmaṇa* (9.4.3) recounts the myth of origins of Śrī, who emerged from Prajāpati embodying all good things that people desire. The gods appropriated from Śrī qualities they desired (Varuṇa her sovereignty, Indra her power, etc.). In a later passage of the text (13.2.6) concerning the Horse Sacrifice, Śrī is linked with kingship, so that she is depicted as married to the king and as embodying his success. In the mythology of the Brāhmaṇas, Śrī is often the object of contention between the gods and demons, sovereignty and success going to the side possessing Śrī. She comes to be linked with Lakṣmī, another goddess embodying prosperity and success, who emerged from the churning of the ocean, the two names becoming interchangeable. Śrī-Lakṣmī is the wife of Viṣṇu, and as such is central to the devotional tradition of Śrīvaiṣṇavism. (*See also* Dīpāvali; Draupadī; Goddess; Gupta; Rāmānuja; Śrīraṅgam; Śrīvaiṣṇavism; Śrīvidyā Tantra; Vaiṣṇavism; Viṣṇu.)

⌘ ŚRĪRAṄGAM ⌘

The center of the Śrīvaiṣṇava tradition, a massive temple complex on an island in the Kauverī River near Tiruchirapalli (Trichy), central Tamilnadu. The complex is surrounded by seven concentric walls with twenty-one Gopuram gateways, perhaps the largest such complex in India. The tallest Gopuram stands seventy-three meters high, and was completed only in 1987, but most of the complex was built during the fourteenth through seventeenth centuries C.E. Viṣṇu is the main deity of this temple. In January each year there is a processional festival in which a Viṣṇu image is pulled through the streets on a large cart that is decorated to look like both a chariot and a temple. The nearby Śrī Jambukeśvara Temple with five concentric walls and seven Gopurams is dedicated to Śiva, its central image being a Liṅga immersed in water that flows from a spring in the Garbhagṛha (central shrine room). (*See also* Śrīvaiṣṇavism; Temple; Vaiṣṇavism; Viṣṇu.)

⌘ ŚRĪVAIṢṆAVISM ⌘

Major sect of south India, dedicated to the worship of Viṣṇu. It traces its foundation to the devotional poetry of the Āḻvārs, particularly Nammāḻvār (probably eighth century C.E.), whose poems are collected as the text *Tiruvāymoḻi*. The learned Brahmin Nāthamuni (tenth century) codified the collection and transposed the Tamil style of recitation in accord with Vedic techniques of recitation, introducing the tradition of using the poems in temple rituals. The resulting textual collection is known as the *Prabandham*, or *Nālāyira Divya Prabandham*. Nāthamuni's grandson Yāmuna Ācārya translated into Sanskrit some of these Tamil poems in his text *Stotraratna*, and established the theological framework of the tradition. Some of his disciples were teachers of Rāmānuja, whose charismatic leadership and learned commentary on the *Brahma Sūtra* established Śrīvaiṣṇavism as an orthodox Vedānta tradition. Shortly after the death of Rāmānuja, the movement divided into two schools known as Vaṭakalai (Northern) under the leadership of Vedāntadeśika, and Tenkalai (Southern) led by Lokācārya Piḷḷai. Their differences were over both languages and doctrines. The Northern school preferred Sanskrit texts, while the Southern school preferred Tamil texts. The Northern school viewed liberation from rebirth as including human effort in the form of ethical behavior, comparable to the baby monkey who must cling to its mother for transport, while the Southern school viewed liberation as due entirely to divine grace, comparable to the kitten being transported by its mother's firm hold on the back of its neck without any effort by the kitten. The goddess Śrī, consort of Viṣṇu and regarded as inseparable from him, is prominent in the tradition, providing a divine feminine principle for worship. The center of the Śrīvaiṣṇava tradition is Śrīraṅgam, the massive temple complex on an island in the Kauverī River near Tiruchirapalli. (*See also* Āḻvārs; Bhakti; Rāmānuja; Śrī; Śrīraṅgam; Vaiṣṇavism; Viṣṇu; Yāmuna.)

⌘ ŚRĪVIDYĀ TANTRA ⌘

A pan-Indian tradition of devotion to the Mother Goddess (Devī, or Śakti). The name may be translated as Auspicious (Śrī) Wisdom (Vidyā). The Goddess is manifested in three hierarchically arrayed forms: (1) the iconic and anthropomorphic image of the goddess Lalitā Tripurasundarī, wife of Śiva; (2) the Goddess's subtle form as the Śrīvidyā Mantra; and (3) the transcendent manifestation in the form of the Śrī-Yantra or Śrī-Cakra, a geometrical diagram at the center of which are nine interlocking triangles representative of the creative power of the Goddess. The tradition was created and developed by Smārta Brahmins who were learned in the Sanskrit, Brahmanical, Vedic tradition, and who have asserted that they are upholding both the Vedic and Tantric traditions, with separate initiations for each. Śrīvidyā can be traced back to the sixth century C.E., and has preserved and elaborated upon texts and traditions of Kaula "Left-Hand" Tantrism. (*See also* Bhāskararāya Makhin; Brahmanism; Kaula Tantrism; Śakti; Śiva; Smārta; Tantra; Yantra.)

⌘ ŚṚṄGERĪ ⌘

Center of the Daśanāmi monastic order and Advaita Vedānta tradition founded by Śaṅkara in the ninth century. The Śaṅkara-Ācārya who heads the order is here, and is the abbot of the Vidyāśaṅkara Temple, established by Śaṅkara as one of four monasteries of the tradition, Puri, Badrīnāth, and Dvārakā being the other sites. (*See also* Advaita Vedānta; Daśanāmi Order; Śaṅkara.)

⌘ ŚRUTI ⌘

What Was Heard; Revelation. The term is applied to the Vedic literature, including Saṃhitā, Brāhmaṇa, Āraṇyaka, and Upaniṣad texts. All other literature is Smṛti (What Is Remembered; Tradition), and is regarded as having scriptural authority only to the extent that it does not conflict with Śruti. The Vedic literature is regarded as revealed truth because it is eternal truth perceived by the ancient seers (Ṛṣis) and then transmitted to humanity. Hindus have generally regarded the Śruti as not of human origin, either as uncreated and eternal, or created by a god (such as Brahmā) or the gods at the creation. (*See also* Āraṇyaka; Brāhmaṇa; Ṛṣi; Saṃhitā; Sanskrit; Scripture; Smṛti; Upaniṣad; Veda.)

⌘ ŚŪDRA ⌘

Serf; servant. Śūdra is the name of the social class ranked fourth and lowest in the caste system. Śūdras were and are regarded as non-Āryan in heritage, in contrast to the three higher-ranked caste groups (Brahmin, Kṣatriya, and Vaiśya) which are of Āryan heritage, at least theoretically. While these three groups receive an initiation that is regarded as a second birth, which causes them to be regarded as the Twice-Born (Dvija) classes and entitles them to wear the Sacred Thread and perform Vedic rites,

Śūdras receive no such initiation and are not to wear the Sacred Thread, nor to hear the Veda recited nor witness a Vedic sacrifice. The exclusion of Śūdras from Vedic and Brahmanical religious activities required that they develop their own patterns of religious expression, Pūjā perhaps being such a development. *Ṛg Veda* 10.90, the Puruṣa Hymn, describes the caste system as originating from the sacrifice and dismemberment of the primordial man, Brahmins being produced from his head, Kṣatriyas from his arms, Vaiśyas from his thighs, and Śūdras from his feet. This divinely ordained social order places the Śūdra at the bottom of the hierarchically arranged system, and the Dharma literature makes clear that the social and religious duties of the Śūdra are simply to serve the other classes. Śūdras are not Outcastes; they have a Dharma and are part of the caste system. While probably more numerous than the three upper castes combined, their status within traditional Indian society was low and their rights were very limited. The *Mānava Dharma Śāstra* states that the Śūdra is not to own property (8.416), and that a Twice-Born person who kills a Śūdra commits only a minor offense (11.67). A Twice-Born person, through commission of certain offenses, could fall to the status of a Śūdra, but there was no provision for elevation of a Śūdra to higher status. Bhakti devotional traditions generally are open to the participation of all, and many of the saints of such traditions, including the Nāyanār, Āḻvār, and Sant traditions, have been Śūdras. The Constitution of the Republic of India, adopted in 1950, states that it is illegal to discriminate against anyone based on their caste status, and the government of India has reserved a percentage of seats in colleges and universities and in government service for members of the Backward Classes (Outcastes and Śūdras) in an effort to improve their social status. (*See also* Caste; Dāsa; Dharma; *Mānava Dharma Śāstra*; Outcaste; Puruṣa; Twice-Born.)

⌘ ŚUKA ⌘

Name of the son of Vyāsa. The story of Śuka in the *Mahābhārata* (12.310–320) is as follows. Vyāsa had pleased Śiva with his ascetic practices (Tapas) and his devotion (Bhakti), so that Śiva granted him the boon of a son. Later, at the sight of a celestial nymph, Vyāsa shed his seed and from it was immediately born Śuka.

After instruction from Vyāsa and other teachers, Śuka decided to renounce and become an ascetic (Saṃnyāsin) to pursue liberation from rebirth (Mokṣa) single-mindedly. Diligent practice of Tapas and Yoga led to Śuka attaining Mokṣa; he is described as vanishing through the Sun. But Vyāsa had become very attached to his son and was grief stricken at his absence. Śiva consoled Vyāsa and give him the boon of having a shadow-image of his son for company. The story highlights the contrast between the pursuit of Mokṣa (as typified by the ascetic Śuka) and the fulfillment of the obligations of Dharma (as typified by the priest and Guru Vyāsa). (*See also* Mokṣa; Saṃnyāsa; Vyāsa.)

⌘ SUKTHANKAR, V. S. ⌘

Indologist (1887–1943). Educated at St. Xavier's College in Bombay, he attended Cambridge University, studying mathematics. He went to Berlin and studied Sanskrit under Heinrich Lüders. On his return to India, he worked for the Archaeological Survery of India. From 1925 until his death, he was general editor for the Bhandarkar Oriental Research Institute's critical edition of the *Mahābhārata*. (*See also* Indology.)

⌘ SUMANTU ⌘

According to the *Mahābhārata* (1.57.74–75, and 12.314–315), Vyāsa divided the one Veda into four texts, and transmitted them along with the *Mahābhārata* as the fifth Veda through his five Brahmin disciples, without indicating clearly whether all five learned all the material or divided it between them. Purāṇas specify a division of labor among the disciples so that Sumantu learned the *Atharva Veda*. (*See also Atharva Veda*; *Mahābhārata*; Purāṇa; Vyāsa.)

⌘ SUN ⌘

See Savitṛ; Sūrya.

⌘ SŪRYA ⌘

One of the major Vedic deities, the Sun God, celebrated in poems of the *Ṛg Veda* such as 1.50 and 1.115. There he seems to be identified with Savitṛ (the Illuminator) who brings insight, inspiration, and enlightenment. According to Sāyaṇa, Savitṛ is the name for the sun before it rises, while Sūrya is the name for the sun when manifest. Sūrya as the sun is a celestial deity of great power, the source of light, warmth, and life itself, without whom crops would not grow and human life would not be possible. Sūrya is worshipped as one of the five deities, of which one is the chosen deity of that individual worshipper, in the Smārta Brahmin tradition. The existence of a Purāṇa dedicated to Sūrya, and the large temple dedicated to Sūrya at Konarak in Orissa in the form of the Sun God's chariot, are indications of devotion to Sūrya in post-Vedic India. (*See also* Konārak; Savitṛ; Smārta.)

⌘ SŪTA ⌘

Name of a Jāti or class of court poets and bards who also functioned as chariot drivers for warriors. Thus, they were present at battles and were later able to recount the heroic deeds of warriors in their assemblies. The *Mahābhārata* depicts itself as recited by Ugraśravas (Mighty Voice) Sauti, the son and pupil of a Sūta named Lomaharṣaṇa (Hair-Raiser) who had been one of Vyāsa's pupils and had heard the composition recited. Texts on Dharma usually describe the Sūta as the offspring of a mixed union between a Brahmin and a Kṣatriya warrior, indicative of the view that they have qualities of each. (*See also* Jāti; Lomaharṣaṇa Sūta; Vyāsa.)

⌘ SUTTEE ⌘

See Satī.

⌘ SWAMI (SVĀMĪ, SVĀMIN) ⌘

Master. The term is used particularly for one's spiritual master, or Guru, and is a term of great respect. (*See also* Guru.)

⌘ SWĀMĪ NĀRĀYAṆ MOVEMENT ⌘

A revivalist movement founded in the nineteenth century by Śrī Sahajānand Swāmī (1781–1830), or Swāmī Nārāyaṇ. He travelled extensively in India promoting a religious path based on ethical living, nonviolence (Ahiṃsā), and a version of the Qualified Nondualist (Viśiṣṭha-Advaita) Vedānta of Rāmānuja. Swāmī Nārāyaṇ is himself an object of worship in this sect, widely regarded as a manifestation of Kṛṣṇa. The movement became popular throughout India but especially in Gujarāt, western India, from which it has been taken by immigrants to Hindu communities overseas where they endeavor to maintain traditional Hindu values and practices, and their membership in this sect is an important aspect of their identity.

⌘ SWASTIKA (SVASTIKA) ⌘

Auspicious symbol. From the Sanskrit words (su + asti + ka), meaning marker of goodness. The Swastika is a cross with each of its four arms turned at a right angle, either clockwise or counterclockwise. It may have solar associations, and is a dynamic representation suggestive of motion or rotation. Variations on the symbol have been found in various cultures, but it is most often seen in Hindu and Buddhist iconography. Its appropriation by the Nazi Party in Germany for almost two decades has done little to reduce its appeal to Hindus as a traditional symbol of religious significance.

— T —

⌘ TAGORE, RABINDRANĀTH ⌘

Author, and the first Asian to win the Nobel Prize for Literature (1861–1941). Born into an aristocratic, wealthy Bengali family as the son of Debendranāth Tagore, Rabindranāth studied law in England briefly (1878–1880), but was educated mostly in India. Already as a teenager he was publishing poetry, and throughout his life wrote poems, plays, essays, novels, and songs. His book of poems entitled *Gītāñjali*, published in Bengali in 1910 and in his English translation in 1912, won the Nobel Prize for Literature in 1913. Knighted by Britain in 1915, he disavowed the honor in 1919 in protest over the Amritsar Massacre. In 1901 Tagore founded Śāntiniketan as an effort to blend Western and traditional Indian educational methods; this evolved into Viśva-Bhārati University where his philosophy was articulated through the curriculum. He emphasized creativity, the importance of the natural world, and that the curriculum had to be relevant to a student's culture and interests.

⌘ TAMIL ⌘

The most widely spoken of the Dravidian languages of south India. Some fifty million people speak Tamil, an ancient, classical language with a long literary history. It is written in a syllabic script based on the old Brāhmī script, with thirty letters, written left to right. About 1900 it seemed as if the Brahmin dialect as spoken in Madras would become the standard dialect of Tamil, but a reaction against it, known as Pure Tamil, has become dominant recently. The Pure Tamil movement is based on a non-Brahmin dialect as spoken in central Tamilnadu, and is an effort to free the Dravidian language of its vocabulary borrowed from Sanskrit, seen as foreign to Tamil. The Pure Tamil linguistic movement coincides with the rise of political parties promoting Dravidian, as opposed to north Indian, cultural values, again because the latter are regarded as foreign. (*See also* Dravidian; Indo-European; Sanskrit.)

⌘ TANJORE ⌘

See Thañjavūr.

⌘ TANTRA ⌘

Extension; System. Texts calling themselves Tantras began to appear in India, as written Sanskrit texts, about the ninth century C.E. They present systems of ritual practice (Sādhana) or spiritual discipline leading to liberating knowledge, but the practices and texts are esoteric due to the language being encoded so that only those who have received initiation (Dīkṣā) can understand it. Tantric practices are not confined to a few sects, but are found throughout all major branches of Hinduism, including Vaiṣṇava, Śaiva, and Śākta groups; Buddhism and Jainism also have developed Tantric traditions. Defining Tantra or Tantrism is best accomplished with a polythetic approach, that is, to the extent that the following features appear, a text or tradition may be regarded as Tantric. Though some may want to be seen as an "extension" of the Vedic heritage, Tantric texts and traditions are extra-Vedic and esoteric. They teach spiritual disciplines and Yoga practices such as Haṭha and Kuṇḍalinī, and employ Mantra recitation, visualization of Yantra or Maṇḍala meditation diagrams, and the use of prohibited substances (such as meat or alcohol), or antinomian practices (such as sex outside of marriage) as aids in attaining liberation. In such practices, the guidance of an adept practitioner as one's Guru is essential, for the Guru reveals the secret techniques and meanings to those whom the Guru deems qualified, and the initiation is not based on conventional criteria such as caste or clan or gender. Tantrism combines theism and monism, so that God is conceived as Brahman, the impersonal Absolute, yet at the same time is manifest in forms both as deities outside oneself and as divine powers within one's own body. Tantrics often employ bipolar imagery based on gender, so that the Absolute is embodied both as Goddess and God and as female and male human beings who can realize their identity with the Absolute. Tantric influence has been strong within Hinduism since about the eleventh century C.E. Vaiṣṇava traditions of Tantra center on Kṛṣṇa and Rādhā. Śaiva Tantric traditions emphasize Śiva and his consort Pārvatī or Devī. Śākta Tantric traditions place the Goddess Śakti as foremost, and, when paired with her consort Śiva, he is depicted as inert and dependent on her energizing power to rouse him to activity. The study of Hindu Tantra has only recently begun to emerge as a subdiscipline within Indology, overcoming major obstacles in the form of decades of misunderstanding and condemnation of Tantric traditions on moral grounds, its own esotericism making study of Tantrism a particularly difficult undertaking. (*See also* Abhinavagupta; Bāul; Cakra; Five M's; Kāpālika; Kashmir Śaivism; Kaula Tantrism; Kuṇḍalinī; Left-Hand Tantra; Right-Hand Tantra; Sādhana; Sahajīya; Śrīvidyā Tantra.)

⌘ TAPAS ⌘

Heat; power of asceticism. In the *Ṛg Veda* (for example, 10.129, and 10.190), Tapas is a creative force, by means of which chaos becomes cosmos. Particularly in interaction with another form of heat, Kāma (desire), Tapas causes the world to come into being in Vedic creation myths. Vedic deities such as Agni and Sūrya have Tapas as one of their qualities, while Indra generates Tapas in the heat of battle. In the sacrificial ritual (Yajña), the sacrificer must undergo an initiatory isolation in which he sits before a fire and builds up Tapas, and priests engaged in the ritual activity also build up Tapas. The myths and rituals both attribute to Tapas the power to create a new reality. Asceticism soon came to be the primary means by which Tapas was produced. The celibate Brahmacārin (as in *Atharva Veda* 11.5) is seen as generating Tapas by his ascetic practice; see also *Atharva Veda* 17.1.24; *Śatapatha Brāhmaṇa* 10.5.3.1, and 11.5.8.1. In the Upaniṣads and later literature the term "Tapas" comes to include an array of ascetic practices: celibacy, fasting, silence, breath control, difficult postures, mortification such as exposure to cold and heat (sitting amidst the five fires of the noon sun and four bonfires), and various forms of meditation are all regarded as producing Tapas. These practices were so widely regarded as powerful that one of the frequent mythic themes in literature is the threat to the world's order and to the gods from power accumulated by an ascetic, as a result of which the gods try to distract the ascetic from his Tapas-producing actions, usually by sending a celestial nymph (Apsaras) to seduce him. The power of asceticism has been incorporated in Hindu tradition by an attempt to limit it, as a lifestyle, to very late in life, the third and fourth of the four stages of life, but many ascetics have adopted that way of life at a young age. Routinization of Tapas and its power can be seen in devotional practices such as the vow (Vrata) or fast, whereby one may subject oneself to an ascetic regimen for a specified time period. The term Tapas is used both for the ascetic practices and the power generated by those practices, and continues to be a very important concept in most Hindu religious traditions. (*See also* Brahmacarya; Creation; Kāma; Yajña; Yoga.)

⌘ TEJAS ⌘

Splendor; brilliance; energy. Tejas is a quality that gods have in abundance, but also that healthy human beings have. Durgā was created from the fiery energy of the Tejas of all the gods so that she could defeat the demon Mahiṣa.

⌘ TEMPLE ⌘

The Hindu temple has for centuries been the center of public worship. Temple building in permanent materials, initially brick and soon thereafter stone, seems to have begun about the fifth century C.E. in north India. Prior to this, temples may have been built of wood as royal palaces were. Two basic architectual styles have evolved, the northern and southern, though Bengal in the north and Kerala in the south provide exceptions to the general patterns. The northern style involves construction of a tower (śikhara) that comes to a single point over the main shrine. The southern style temples have placed the main towers (Gopuram) above the gates in walls that encircle the sanctuaries; towers are topped by barrel-vaulted finials. While temples of all types can accommodate groups of devotees in the temple compounds, only the largest temples allow the assembly of a substantial number of devotees inside the building. The central shrine of a Hindu temple typically contains one or more icons (Mūrti) of the deity or deities, but is not designed for congregational worship. Many temples have occasional or even regular processional rituals in which the icons are taken out of the shrine and the public is allowed to have an auspicious viewing (Darśana) of the image of the deity. Priests conduct rituals of offering (Pūjā) to the god or gods of the temple on behalf of devotees, who may also bring to the temple donations in the form of money, food, flowers, and other goods. Temple servants perform a variety of tasks to aid the expression of devotion, including making flower garlands, preparing food, and, in the case of Kerala temples, performing Kūṭiyāṭṭam dramas for the deity and devotees. (*See also* Aihole; Ayodhyā; Bādāmī; Belur; Bhuvaneśvara; Cidambaram; Darśana; Devadāsī; Elephanta; Guruvayūr; Halebid; Jagannātha; Kāñcīpuram; Khajurāho; Konārak; Kūṭiyāṭṭam; Madurai; Māmallapuram; Mūrti; Paṭṭadakal; Pūjā; Puri; Somnāth; Śrīraṅgam; Śṛṅgerī; Thañjavūr; Thrissur; Tirupathi; Ujjain; Vārāṇasī; Vṛndāvana.)

⌘ THAÑJAVŪR (TANJORE) ⌘

Ancient capital of the Coḻa Empire, ninth to thirteenth century C.E. It is the site of the Bṛhadīśvara Temple, a structure with a tower sixty-three meters high. The temple is dedicated to Śiva, and includes some 250 Liṅgas in niches along the outer walls. One of India's largest sculptures of Śiva's bull vehicle Nandi (six meters long and three meters high) is to be found guarding the inner courtyard. (*See also* Coḻa.)

⌘ THEOSOPHICAL SOCIETY ⌘

Name of an organization founded in New York City in 1875 by Helena P. Blavatsky and Col. Henry S. Olcott. Among its purposes were investigation of and experimentation with mysticism and meditational techniques, and promoting universal brotherhood. In 1879 it relocated to India and established its headquarters at Adyār, then outside of Madras, now a suburb of the city. In its eclectic teachings are many concepts borrowed from Hindu religious traditions, notably the idea of rebirth according to Karma and the possibility of liberation from rebirth. Additionally, however, the purely Western idea of progress or evolution toward a higher state, both of the individual spiritual seeker and of humanity as a whole, is an important idea in Theosophical teachings. The Society was instrumental in encouraging urban and Westernized Hindus to value their own religious traditions and spiritual heritage, and led efforts to resist Christian missionary activity in India. It also was supportive of India's independence movement, Annie Besant even serving as, and being jailed for being, head of the Indian National Congress during World War I. Her effort to train and promote Jiddu Krishnamurti as the next great World Teacher, and his subsequent rejection of any association with the Theosophical Society in that role, damaged the credibility of the organization and probably contributed to its decline. The Theosophical Society remains an international organization dedicated to promoting understanding of Hindu thought, and its *Adyār Library Bulletin* is a valuable publisher of scholarly studies. (*See also* Besant, Annie; Blavatsky, Helena Petrovna; Krishnamurti, Jiddu; Olcott, Henry Steele.)

⌘ THIRD EYE ⌘

Meditational traditions often depict the meditator as having a third eye in the middle of the forehead, between and above the eyebrows. Such an eye represents the special faculty of insight that is developed with Yoga meditation. Frequently it is through such a third eye that insight is said to be granted by Īśvara or Śiva. Śiva himself is often depicted as having a third eye. (*See also* Śiva; Yoga.)

⌘ THIRUVANANTHAPURAM (TRIVANDRUM) ⌘

Capital of Kerala, and site of the Śrī Padmanābhaswāmy temple. Built in 1733 by the Mahārāja of Travancore (southern

Kerala), this Viṣṇu temple is in the Dravidian or southern style and the walls enclose a tank for ritual bathing. (*See also* Padmanābhi.)

⌘ THRISSUR (TRICHUR) ⌘

Central Kerala city, and site of the Vaḍakkunāthan temple. This large Śiva temple dominates the center of the city and is one of the most active centers for performances of Kūṭiyāṭṭam, the classical Sanskrit theatre tradition that has survived in Kerala's major temples for centuries. The nearby temple in Guruvayūr features a unique annual dramatic performance of the life of Kṛṣṇa on its temple theatre stage. Thrissur's annual Pooram festival is one of south India's largest celebrations, and features processions of spectacularly decorated temple elephants. (*See also* Guruvayūr; Kūṭiyāṭṭam.)

⌘ THUGS or ṬHAGS ⌘

A sect devoted to Bhavānī Kālī, members of which conducted human sacrifices to the goddess. Their methods for procuring their offerings included kidnapping and posing as merchants to join caravans which they would attack in the night, killing their male victims by strangulation. They were especially numerous in the area of Uttar Pradesh, where their main sacred site was an ancient Kālī temple at Mirzāpur. The earliest known reference to them dates from the seventh century C.E. The British colonial authorities first took note of them in 1799, and came to regard them as a threat to public order, vigorously stamping out the sect during the 1830s. The last known Thug was hanged in 1882. The word Ṭhag in Hindi is probably derived from the Sanskrit sthagaḥ, meaning one who is concealed, a cheat, and has come into English as "thug," with the meaning of cutthroat or hoodlum. (*See also* Kālī.)

⌘ TILAK, BAL GANGADHAR ⌘

Nationalist political leader and religious leader (1857–1920). Tilak, known by the title Lokmānya (Honored by All), worked as a journalist in western India and came to be a leader in the independence movement. Tilak sought to rally Hindus to fight for their freedom against British colonial power, and wrote a commentary on the *Bhagavad Gītā* in which he presented his view that the text called for action in support of what is right. For Tilak, the *Gītā* was the theoretical and theological basis for political activism, and he rejected all efforts at compromise or gradual reform, arguing that violence was justified if the cause was righteous, and he felt that independence was such a cause. Tilak encouraged the development in Mahārāṣṭra of the Gaṇeśa festival as a celebration of Hindu culture, and saw it as an opportunity to rally Hindus to the cause of national liberation. (*See also* Gāndhī, Mohandās K.; Gaṇeśa; Ghadr Movement; Rāj.)

⌘ TĪRTHA ⌘

Crossing-point, or ford. The term is used for places where one could cross a river, but more significantly and broadly for sacred places where one can cross over to the farther shore of the afterlife, securing for oneself a rebirth in a heavenly realm, or liberation from rebirth. Particular spots at riverbanks or beside lakes, and, by extension, other places of pilgrimage such as mountains, cities such as Ayodhyā, or regions such as Vraja, came to be seen as sacred because of their association with the mythic deeds of gods and heroes and because of their power to absolve one of bad Karma or produce good Karma. (*See also* Kumbha Melā; Pilgrimage; Puṣkara; Tirumāla; Vārāṇasī.)

⌘ TIRUPATHI ⌘

Temple site in southern Andhra Pradesh also called Tirumāla. It is one of the major pilgrimage destinations in India, averaging some 30,000 pilgrims per day. The temple is dedicated to Veṅkaṭeśvara, regarded as a form of Viṣṇu. This temple is unusual in allowing non-Hindus into the sanctuary to have auspicious sight (Darśana) of the image. Interestingly, the image itself has its eyes covered because its direct gaze is regarded as too powerful to be endured. The large number of pilgrims is due to the widespread belief that any request made before the image will be granted. The temple staff of over 5,000 supervises the crowd of pilgrims and moves them through the sanctuary rapidly. The temple is perhaps the richest in India, with an annual income of some five billion Rupees, which is used to support a wide range of charitable causes, including schools, orphanages, housing for pilgrims, and medical care for the poor. (*See also* Veṅkaṭeśvara; Viṣṇu.)

⌘ *TIRUVĀYMOḺI* ⌘

The major text attributed to Nammāḻvār (eighth or ninth century C.E.). Composed in Tamil, a vernacular language of southern India, these poems are the first vernacular works regarded as comparable to the Veda in authority and sanctity. They are highly emotional poems treating devotion to Viṣṇu, often from the perspective of a young woman longing for her lover, and became very popular throughout Tamilnadu. They form part of the *Prabandham*, or *Nālāyira Divya Prabandham*, recited since the tenth century in temple rituals and in the homes of Śrīvaiṣṇava devotees. (*See also* Āḻvārs; Bhakti; Nammāḻvār; Śrīvaiṣṇavism; Vaiṣṇavism.)

⌘ TRANSCENDENTAL MEDITATION ⌘

Tradition of meditation begun by Maharishi Mahesh Yogi (born in 1911). The practice is also known as the Science of Creative Intelligence, and often simply as TM. It is based on classical Yoga teachings, and emphasizes calming the body and mind, and utilizes a Mantra, a word or phrase imparted from the Guru secretly and recited repeatedly in silence by the meditator as an aid to concentration. The technique is taught to anyone without regard to lifestyle, and without the requirement of celibacy that is traditional in classical Yoga practice. TM promises to make one better at whatever one does due to clarity of mind. TM has been presented as the solution to a vast array of social problems, and the assertion has been made that if one per cent of the world's population were to practice TM, a new age would begin. Later, the Maharishi claimed that if only the square root of one per cent, some 7,000 people, were to practice the TM Sidhi program in the same place at the same time, peace would reign and an Age of Enlightenment would dawn. One of the major centers of the TM movement is Maharishi International University in Fairfield, Iowa, where the organization offers advanced meditation courses and academic degrees. The movement gained attention on a worldwide scale when the Beatles went to India to meet the Maharishi in the 1960s. During the 1990s the organization has focussed on trying to persuade governments to support financially its plans for achieving peace through meditation, and on preparing to open a theme park called Vedaland outside Orlando, Florida, near Disney World, at which Hindu culture and meditation would be featured attractions. (*See also* Maharishi Mahesh Yogi; Yoga.)

⌘ TRAYĪ VIDYĀ ⌘

Triple knowledge, a phrase used to describe the three Vedas (*Ṛg*, *Yajur*, and *Sāma*) as a group, particularly prior to the acceptance of the *Atharva Veda* as the fourth Veda. (*See also* Nambūṭiri Brahmins; Veda; Vyāsa.)

⌘ TRINITY (TRIMŪRTI) ⌘

The "three forms" of the divine: Brahmā the Creator, Viṣṇu the Preserver, Śiva the Destroyer. While this would seem to constitute a clear division of labor among the major gods, so that they could be seen as cooperating to achieve a common purpose, one rarely finds such a view expressed in religious texts. Parts of the *Mahābhārata* may have the best articulation of the idea, with Viṣṇu dominant in the story but yielding to Śiva periodically for his destructive activity. In fact, most Purāṇas appear to have been subjected to sectarian influences, so that those making explicit reference to this idea do so usually in the context of either Viṣṇu or Śiva being depicted as supreme, aspects of the deity fulfilling each role. (*See also* Brahmā; Mūrti; Śiva; Viṣṇu.)

⌘ TUKĀRĀM ⌘

Saint in western India (1568–1650). Born in a Śūdra family, he became a devotee of Viṣṇu in the form of Viṭhobā, a form popular in his native Mahārāṣṭra. He was a member of the Vārkarī Panth, a Bhakti sect in which devotion was expressed through singing the praises of the Lord and through meditative concentration on the Lord. He used the vernacular Marathi language to communicate directly with the common people. (*See also* Bhakti; Marāṭhas; Sant; Śivāji; Viṣṇu.)

⌘ TULSĪDĀS ⌘

North Indian poet and saint (1532–1623). Born an impoverished Brahmin in Vārāṇasī (Banaras), he became one of the most famous authors of Indian literary history, so that some have regarded him as a reincarnation of Vālmīki, the first poet (Ādi Kavi) and the *Rāmāyaṇa*'s reputed composer. He was nonsectarian in his approach, using the name Rām to refer to God as had many saints before him. Tulsīdās composed the *Rām Carit Mānas*, a poetic retelling of the *Rāmāyaṇa* in the vernacular language of Hindi, as well as other works. Though little is known of his life, apparently his decision to transmit the teachings of the *Rāmāyaṇa* in the language of common people, thereby undercutting the authority of Brahmins and their control over access to such religious instruction, was opposed by some Brahmins in Vārāṇasī and was a contentious issue between them. (*See also Rāmāyaṇa; Rām Carit Mānas;* Rāmlīlā.)

⌘ TURĪYA ⌘

See Consciousness, States of.

⌘ TVAṢṬṚ ⌘

One of the twelve Ādityas, the divine carpenter, artisan, and maker of implements in Vedic literature. He is praised in the *Ṛg Veda* as presiding over good births and long lifespans (as in 10.18.6), as the creator of humans and animals (1.188), and as the fashioner of Indra's thunderbolt weapon (as in 1.32.2). (*See also* Āditya; Dhātṛ.)

⌘ TWICE-BORN ⌘

Translation of the Sanskrit term "Dvija," used in reference to the three upper social classes in the caste system: the Brahmins (Brāhmaṇa), warriors (Kṣatriya), and commoners (Vaiśya). They are "Twice-Born" because, in addition to their actual, natural birth, they receive a second birth at their initiation into Āryan society, at which they receive the sacred thread (Yajñopavīta) and recite the Gāyatrī or Sāvitrī Mantra, very often receiving a new name as well. Noninitiated persons are referred to as "onceborn" and would be Śūdras or Outcastes. (*See also* Brāhmaṇa; Brahmin; Caste; Gāyatrī; Kṣatriya; Sacred Thread; Saṃskāra; Sāvitrī; Upanayana; Vaiśya.)

— U —

⌘ UDAIGIRI ⌘

Site in central Madhya Pradesh of caves and temples dating from the Gupta period. Five kilometers northwest of Vidiśā are twenty cave shrines in a hillside. Two are Jain caves, the rest Hindu. Candra Gupta II is commemorated in inscriptions such as the one at the monumental sculpture of the Varāha (Boar) Avatāra of Viṣṇu, in which the Boar's act of saving earth from a flood is compared with the emperor's act of saving the earth from a flood of barbarian Śaka invaders. The ruins of a sixth-century C.E. temple are at the top of the hill. (*See also* Gupta.)

⌘ UDGĀTṚ ⌘

Priest who sings the Sāma Veda at sacrificial rituals. (*See also* Sāma Veda; Yajña.)

⌘ UDIPI ⌘

Site of the life of Madhva, a Vaiṣṇava theologian and Vedānta philosopher. The Kṛṣṇa temple here is large and active.

⌘ UJJAIN (UJJAYINĪ) ⌘

Site of the Kumbha Melā festival every twelve years; the last one was in 1992, the next one is to be in 2004. On the banks of the Śiprā River, it was once known as Avantī and was an important city and trading center in the third century B.C.E. Candra Gupta II made it his capital about 400 C.E., and the city is well described in Kālidāsa's poem *Meghadūta*. The most important temple in Ujjain is the Mahākāleśvara, dedicated to Śiva, which contains one of twelve Liṅgas thought to have inherent Śakti, a Jyotir-Liṅga (Liṅga of Light). The name refers to the myth of Śiva's manifestation as a towering Liṅga of fire or light that showed his superiority to Brahmā and Viṣṇu. (*See also* Kālidāsa; Kumbha Melā; Śiva; Vikramāditya.)

⌘ UMĀ ⌘

See Pārvatī.

⌘ UPANAYANA ⌘

"Leading toward," a term used in reference to the ceremony of receiving the sacred thread emblematic of membership in one of the twice-born classes of Āryan society. The Guru would lead the initiate, typically a young male, in the ritual. The Brahmin ideally would be initiated in the seventh or eighth year, the warrior in the eleventh, and the commoner in the twelfth. This is one of the twelve Saṃskāra, or life-cycle rituals specified in the literature on Dharma. (*See also* Caste; Guru; Sacred Thread; Saṃskāra; Twice-Born.)

⌘ UPANIṢADS ⌘

Late Vedic Sanskrit texts composed and transmitted orally by anonymous sages. The word itself means "sitting down around," which indicates that these teachings were transmitted by teachers whose selected pupils sat down around them in forest retreats. The Upaniṣads were traditionally regarded as "the end of the Veda" (Vedānta), meaning that they form the closing chapters of the Vedic collection. They also constitute the end of the Veda in the sense that they purport to present the hidden meaning or the "real message" of the Veda's words. About 250 texts call themselves Upaniṣads. The thirteen earliest and most important ones, the Vedic Upaniṣads, each attached to one of the Saṃhitās as a commentary, probably were composed from the seventh to fourth centuries B.C.E. in north India, and have been the most influential. There are also some short Upaniṣads about asceticism and the practice of Yoga, and some lesser known sectarian texts using the name Upaniṣad that were composed as late as the sixteenth century. The Vedic Upaniṣads generally present the monistic view that Brahman is the only reality, and that the individual self or soul (Ātman) is no different from Brahman. While the performance of appropriate ritual actions and good deeds are conducive to good karma and a good rebirth, or a temporary heavenly reward, only knowledge of Brahman leads to immortality and an end to rebirth. Experiencing Brahman in this life is transformative and causes one to transcend desire for worldly things. Ignorance leads to rebirth, while knowledge of Brahman leads to escape from rebirth. The Upaniṣads have the earliest expressions of the concept of rebirth according to the law of Karma. Later Upaniṣads present the practice of Yoga as the means whereby one can know Brahman. Some Upaniṣads present a conception of Ultimate Reality that is theistic, as in the *Śvetāśvatara Upaniṣad* where Rudra (Śiva) is identified as Brahman with form and personality, a personal Lord to whom one is to be devoted; such devotion leads to liberation from rebirth. (*See also* Ātman; Brahman; *Bṛhadāraṇyaka Upaniṣad*; *Chāndogya Upaniṣad*; Rebirth; Saṃhitā; Vedānta; Yoga.)

⌘ URVAŚĪ ⌘

Name of a celestial nymph (Apsaras). She figures in a tale first told in *Ṛg Veda* 10.95, elaborated upon variously in later literature including *Śatapatha Brāhmaṇa*, *Mahābhārata*, Purāṇas, and most fully and inventively in Kālidāsa's brilliant drama *Vikramorvaśī*. According to the story Urvaśī was banished from heaven to earth, where the human king Purūravas fell in love with her. She consented to live with him on the conditions that he agree to care for her two rams and that she never see him naked. For several years they lived together, until the Gandharvas (heavenly musicians) conspired to bring her back to heaven. They abducted one of Urvaśī's rams one night, and when Purūravas jumped out of bed, the Gandharvas caused a flash of lightning to illuminate him so that Urvaśī saw him naked. The violation of her conditions caused Urvaśī to vanish, and Purūravas wandered around searching for her (a motif on which Kālidāsa has elaborated extensively). His distressed pleading eventually caused Urvaśī to return to Purūravas and they had a son to continue the king's lineage. (*See also* Kālidāsa; Purūravas.)

⌘ UṢAS ⌘

The Dawn, celebrated as a beautiful goddess in the *Ṛg Veda* (1.48, 1.49, and 1.92, for example). In the latter poem, the ever-new sunrise is thought of also as ancient, and compared with the wasting away of the lives of individual human beings while the human race persists. The most famous poem to Dawn in the *Ṛg Veda* is certainly 1.113, frequently cited as a remarkable achievement of poetic use of language. Here the Daughter of Heaven is celebrated for awakening all creatures to carry out their varied activities, and for making a path for the sun to follow.

⌘ UTTARA MĪMĀṂSĀ ⌘

See Vedānta.

— V —

⌘ VĀC ⌘

Speech personified as a goddess. She symbolically represents the power of sacred utterance (Mantra). Since every ritual action in the Vedic sacrifice was accompanied by, and made effective by, the recitation of specified sounds, Vāc was regarded as possessing great power. She is depicted in *Ṛg Veda* 10.125 as praising herself as the preserver of the world and the gods, and as having the power to make a sage and a possessor of Brahman of whomever she loves. In post-Vedic Hinduism Vāc is often identified with Sarasvatī. (*See also* Brahman; Goddess; Mantra; Sarasvatī; Veda; Yajña.)

⌘ VĀCASPATI MIŚRA ⌘

A Brahmin of Mithila who lived in the ninth century C.E. He wrote commentaries on each of the six systems of philosophy regarded as orthodox in Hinduism, and a commentary on the *Yoga Sūtra* of Patañjali. (*See also* Philosophical Schools.)

⌘ VAIKHĀNASA ⌘

Name of a community of Brahmins in Tamilnadu and Andhra Pradesh states. Traditionally, they have served as temple priests for Vaiṣṇava temple rituals in this region.

⌘ VAIKUṆṬHA ⌘

Irresistible; a name used for Indra in the *Ṛg Veda* (10.47 to 10.50 feature Indra Vaikuṇṭha as both Ṛṣi and Deva). The name is taken over later by Viṣṇu as one of his epithets, and becomes the name of his celestial realm in which devotees can be reborn after death. (*See also* Goloka; Indra; Vaiṣṇavism; Viṣṇu; Vṛndāvana.)

⌘ VAIŚAṂPĀYANA ⌘

According to the *Mahābhārata* (1.57.74–75, and 12.314–315), Vyāsa divided the one Veda into four texts, and transmitted them along with the *Mahābhārata* as the fifth Veda through his five Brahmin disciples, without indicating clearly whether all five learned all the material or divided it between them. Purāṇas specify a division of labor among the disciples so that Vaiśaṃpāyana learned the *Yajur Veda*. He also is depicted as the reciter of the *Mahābhārata* throughout the text, having recited Vyāsa's composition to king Janamejaya (great-grandson of Arjuna) at the Snake Sacrifice at the request of his Guru. (*See also Mahābhārata*; Purāṇa; Vyāsa.)

⌘ VAIŚEṢIKA ⌘

Distinctionism, one of the six philosophical traditions regarded as orthodox in Hinduism. This tradition is said to have first been taught by Kaṇāda, perhaps about the fifth century B.C.E. Later authors in the tradition introduce the idea of an Īśvara (Lord) whose will affects the harmonious interaction of the world's eternal atoms, but Kaṇāda posits no such deity. The material world is composed of eternal particles, so small as to be invisible, that combine to make the many substances we see. Each person's Ātman (self, soul) is similarly eternal and uncreated. Liberation from rebirth is held to occur when the individual has attained knowledge of ultimate truth through good conduct, asceticism, and Yoga. This system of thought is paired with Nyāya (Logical Analysis) as its most closely related school of thought. (*See also* Nyāya; Philosophical Schools.)

⌘ VAIṢṆAVISM ⌘

The worship of Viṣṇu. Already in the *Ṛg Veda* there are indications of the importance of Viṣṇu, despite the relatively small number of poems dedicated to him. For example, in *Ṛg Veda* 1.154, Viṣṇu's heroic deed of measuring out the earth by taking three strides (Trivikrama) is celebrated. In so doing, he encompasses the entire cosmos and makes human life possible. With his highest step, in heaven, he creates a place of refuge where those who love the gods rejoice, and to which ancient Āryans wanted to go at death. Viṣṇu thus seems to be a god of transcendence and totality much more so than most of the other gods of the Vedic pantheon. This emerges more clearly in the Brāhmaṇas, where attention is directed toward analyzing the nature of ritual sacrifice, and Viṣṇu is said to be the sacrifice (for example, *Śatapatha Brāhmaṇa* 3.2.1.38, and 4.2.3.10). Several streams of tradition seem to have come together to make up the figure of Viṣṇu in addition to the Vedic god already mentioned. The Brāhmaṇas refer repeatedly to Nārāyaṇa, an ascetic deity who comes to be identified with Viṣṇu. In addition, tribal and Dravidian contributions may be evident in the figures of some of the Avatāras (incarnations), notably Kṛṣṇa, who is also known by such names as Bhagavan and Vāsudeva and almost certainly is himself a composite figure. The Bhāgavata cult, members of which worshipped Bhagavan Kṛṣṇa with devotion, is perhaps the earliest Bhakti movement. Members accepted the authority of the Vedic and Brahmanical scriptures, and added their own special text, the *Bhagavad Gītā* (perhaps second century B.C.E.), which they regarded as a revelation from God. Bhagavan Kṛṣṇa came to be identified with the Brahmanical deity Viṣṇu. Worship of Viṣṇu in the form of one or more of his Avatāras, of which ten are commonly listed, though sometimes more, is the most popular and widespread way of being religious in India. Rāma, the prince of Ayodhyā, and Kṛṣṇa, the divine child, adventurous youth and heroic prince, are the two most popular forms in which reverence is paid to Viṣṇu. In south India, the tendency is to see Viṣṇu as the Absolute, and Kṛṣṇa or Rāma as forms he takes. In north India, the tendency is to see Kṛṣṇa as the Absolute, and Viṣṇu as a form he takes. Vaiṣṇavism exists in a variety of regional and national traditions. Primarily south Indian traditions include Śrīvaiṣṇavism, and Madhva's Dvaita Vedānta; primarily north Indian traditions include the Nimbārka, Vallabha, and Caitanya lineages devoted to Kṛṣṇa, as well as traditions devoted to Rāma. (*See also* Avatāra; *Bhagavad Gītā*; Bhagavan; Bhāgavata; *Bhāgavata Purāṇa*; Caitanya; Gopī; Gosvāmins; Hare Krishna Movement; *Harivaṃśa*; Kṛṣṇa; Madhva; Nārāyaṇa; Nimbārka; Padmanābhi; Pañcarātra; Rāma; Śrī; Śrīvaiṣṇavism; Trinity; Vaikuṇṭha; Vallabha; Veṅkaṭeśvara; Viṣṇu; Vṛndāvana.)

⌘ VAIŚYA ⌘

Commoner, the third-ranking group in social status within the caste system. The Puruṣa Hymn (*Ṛg Veda* 10.90), in which the system of social organization we call the caste system is depicted as divinely created through the sacrificial dismemberment of the Cosmic Person Puruṣa, describes the Vaiśya as produced from the thighs of Puruṣa. This indicates a close relationship with the powers of fertility and procreation, and the Vaiśya are in fact responsible for the raising of cattle and other animals, production of grain and other foods, and the manufacture of products. The Vaiśya were among the "Twice-Born," meaning that they traditionally received initiation into Āryan society and were allowed to hear the recitation of the Veda and to study and memorize portions of the Vedic collection. They were expected to offer domestic sacrifices on their own behalf, and to attend and perhaps contribute to the large-scale public sacrifices (Yajña) at which the patrons would be the clan chieftains and rulers. The Dharma of the Vaiśya could be characterized as a responsibility to be productive members of society, to donate to those who were deserving, and to study the Veda. (*See also* Caste; Dharma; Puruṣa.)

⌘ VĀJAPEYA ⌘

Drink of Strength, the name of an important royal ritual. It is a one-day Soma sacrifice to be celebrated by a ruler who aspires to victory in battle or imperial status. The ritual is described in the *Śatapatha Brāhmaṇa* (5.1.1), and features a race by seventeen chariots, as well as the consumption of Soma and Surā (grain liquor). An unusual aspect of the rite occurs when the sacrificer and his wife are to climb a pole as a symbolic ascent to heaven. (*See also* Horse Sacrifice; Rājasūya; Yajña.)

⌘ VĀK ⌘

See Vāc.

⌘ VALLABHA ⌘

Vaiṣṇava teacher (1479–1531 C.E.) who founded a devotional tradition (Saṃpradāya) that bears his name. The Vallabha Saṃpradāya is also known as the Puṣṭi Mārg (Path of Prosperity), emphasizing both the reliance on God's grace that leads to welfare, and the largely merchant class following of this movement. Vallabha was a Brahmin from south India who moved north to Gujarāt and made pilgrimages to Vṛndāvana, the site of Kṛṣṇa's earthly youth and loveplay, and Vallabha is regarded by his followers as an incarnation (Avatāra) of Kṛṣṇa. Direct male descendants of the founder are known by the title Mahārāja (Great Ruler), and have authority within the organization as temple priests and spiritual preceptors (Gurus). He accepted as authoritative scriptures the Veda, *Brahma Sūtra, Bhagavad Gītā*, and *Bhāgavata Purāṇa*, seeing in them a progressively clearer revelation of the divine as Kṛṣṇa. Vallabha combined Advaita Vedānta and theism, so that all souls are in reality identical with Kṛṣṇa, which one can discover through devotion and the grace of Kṛṣṇa. Devotees worship Kṛṣṇa in the form of the infant and youth who lived among cowherds, and seek to have with him one of the four relationships as either his (1) servant, (2) friend, (3) parent, or (4) lover. Erotic aspects of Kṛṣṇa's love for the Gopī milkmaids, said to have been ritually imitated by those within the organization, have involved the movement in controversy, particularly during the British colonial era. There are probably about five million devotees in this tradition in northwestern India, Mathurā and Vṛndāvana being important centers of the sect. (*See also* Advaita Vedānta; Avatāra; Divine Light Mission; Gopī; Kṛṣṇa; Vaiṣṇavism; Vṛndāvana.)

⌘ VĀLMĪKI ⌘

Brahmin sage to whom composition of the *Rāmāyaṇa* is attributed. He is credited with creation of the śloka verse form, in which most of the *Rāmāyaṇa, Mahābhārata*, Purāṇas, and other works are composed. As the *Rāmāyaṇa* is regarded as the first example of the poetic genre (Kāvya), he is the first poet (Ādi-Kavi) in the literary history of India. The Hindi poet Tulsīdās has been regarded as the reincarnation of Vālmīki for rendering the story of Rāma into the vernacular in so poetic a fashion. (*See also Rāmāyaṇa*; Tulsīdās.)

⌘ VĀMADEVA ⌘

The major seer (Ṛṣi) of Book 4 of the *Ṛg Veda* and patriarch of one of the Brahmin families credited with preservation and transmission of the *Ṛg Veda*. (*See also Ṛg Veda*; Ṛṣi.)

⌘ VĀMANA ⌘

The Dwarf Avatāra of Viṣṇu, the fifth in lists of ten incarnations. Bali, grandson of Prahlāda, became a great ruler of the Asuras (demons) and oppressed the earth. In the form of a dwarf, Viṣṇu approached Bali and asked to be granted the land he could cover in three paces. In his arrogance, Bali agreed, and the dwarf immediately grew to enormous proportions, covering the three worlds in his three strides. Variant versions of the myth recount how his strides covered earth, the atmosphere, and heaven, or earth, heaven, and the nether regions. Some versions have Bali presenting his head as the place for the third step of Viṣṇu, who presses him down into the nether realm. The myth has a long history, and can be traced back to the *Ṛg Veda*, where Viṣṇu Trivikrama (three strides) is celebrated for measuring out the three worlds with his strides. (*See also* Avatāra; Narasiṃha; Viṣṇu.)

⌘ VĀNAPRASTHA ⌘

Forest Dweller. The term is used to refer to the third of the Four Stages of Life, in which one retires from active pursuit of one's career and familial concerns to a life of simple, quiet contemplation and religious ritual, perhaps accompanied by one's spouse. (*See also* Four Stages of Life.)

⌘ VARĀHA ⌘

The Boar Avatāra of Viṣṇu, the third in lists of ten incarnations. Once when a demon was troubling the ocean, beating it with his cudgel, Viṣṇu took the form of a giant boar to counteract the demon's actions. When the demon saw the boar, he took hold of the earth and dived to the bottom of the ocean with her. The boar dived after them, killed the demon, and rescued earth, bringing her back to the surface on his tusk. (*See also* Avatāra; Darbha; Viṣṇu.)

⌘ VĀRĀṆASĪ (BANARAS, KĀŚĪ) ⌘

The most sacred city to Hindus and a place of pilgrimage. The name Vārāṇasī is said to be derived from two rivers, the Varaṇā and Asī. The name Kāśī means shining, or splendid, and is often translated as City of Light. Vārāṇasī is particularly sacred to Śiva, but temples dedicated to all the gods abound here. Situated on the northern bank (actually western at this location) of the Ganges River, Vārāṇasī is one of the most ancient cities in the world that is still inhabited. It was already a major metropolis twenty-five centuries ago when the Buddha gave his first sermon on the edge of town at Sārnāth after his enlightenment. Unlike most other Indian cities, where the cremation ground is located outside the city to the south and regarded as ritually polluting, cremation takes place within Vārāṇasī along the Ganges on Ghāṭs, sets of stairs leading down to the river. There are about 100 Ghāṭs in the city, Maṇikarṇika and Hariścandra being the burning Ghāṭs where bodies are cremated. To die in Vārāṇasī is regarded as highly auspicious, even assuring the attainment of liberation from rebirth (Mokṣa). Hindus come to the city on pilgrimage from all over India, and indeed the world, to visit its temples and to immerse themselves, especially just after sunrise, in the waters of the Ganges, regarded as purifying and as eliminating bad Karma. Bathing on the same day at five Ghāṭs (Asī, Daśāśvamedha, Barṇasaṅgam, Pañcagaṅgā, and Maṇikarṇika) is a ritual many pilgrims perform. The most important temple is the Viśvanātha or Golden temple, so named for its gold-sheathed dome; built in 1776, it is across the street from a Muslim mosque built by Aurangzeb on its original site. The Durgā temple (commonly called the Monkey Temple because of the large number of resident monkeys) is a very traditional temple, while its neighbor, the Tulsī Mānas temple, is unusual and modern. Built in 1964, its walls are engraved with verses from the *Rām Carit Mānas* by Tulsīdās, and scenes from Rāma's story, and it has a motorized Hanuman statue that opens its chest to reveal Rāma in Hanuman's heart! Another modern temple is the new Viśvanātha temple near Benaras Hindu University, built by the Birla family of industrialists and open to all without regard to caste or religion. Long a major center of traditional scholarship, Vārāṇasī is also the site of one of India's main Sanskrit universities and of Benaras Hindu University. (*See also* Pilgrimage.)

⌘ VARṆA ⌘

See Caste.

⌘ VARṆĀŚRAMA-DHARMA ⌘

See Four Goals of Humanity; Four Stages of Life.

⌘ VARUṆA ⌘

One of the major Vedic gods. He is a celestial god who is the guardian of cosmic order (Ṛta), though not its creator. He judges human conduct, and punishes sinners. In the *Ṛg Veda* (as in 7.86.4) he is often depicted as stern and awe-inspiring, and is asked that he forgive the misdeeds of those who praise him: "O Varuṇa, what was the terrible crime for which you want to destroy your friend who praises you? Proclaim it to me so that I may quickly humble myself before you and be free of sin, for you cannot be deceived and you exercise dominion." He is at times credited with creating or ordering the world, as in *Ṛg Veda* 5.85.1, where he is said to have "spread out the earth, as a butcher does a hide, as a carpet for the sun." Varuṇa is the chief one of the Vedic gods (Deva) who is also called an Asura in the Veda. The term Asura later was used exclusively for the demons who are the enemies of the gods, and there are indications that Varuṇa changed sides and joined the gods. He is also, however, counted as one of the twelve Ādityas among the Devas, emphasizing the complexity of this figure in Vedic mythology. With the decline of the Vedic sacrifice, Varuṇa was no longer worshipped and was relegated to the role of World Guardian (Lokapāla), presiding over the western quarter. His role as Lord of the Ocean is a faint remembrance of his association with the Asuras and the chaos that preceded the establishment of order by the gods. The name Varuṇa is widely regarded as cognate with the name of the Greek god Ouranos, with whom he has mythological affinities. (*See also* Āditya; Asura; Deva; Ṛta; World Guardians.)

⌘ VASIṢṬHA ⌘

Brahmin sage and the major seer (Ṛṣi) of Book 7 of the *Ṛg Veda* and patriarch of one of the Brahmin families credited with preservation and transmission of the *Ṛg Veda*. His name is the superlative of vasu (good, excellent), so means "most excellent, best," appropriate for one who owns the cow Nandinī that grants all wishes. Indian literature often depicts him as in conflict with Viśvāmitra, a sage who was born a warrior but transformed himself into a Brahmin. Several of Vasiṣṭha's poems depict him as the priest of Sudās, ruler of the Tṛtsu clan (for example, *Ṛg Veda* 7.18, and 7.33). The *Mahābhārata* depicts him as priest of the solar dynasty of Ikṣvāku, and as the father of Śakti and grandfather of Parāśara, thus Vyāsa's grandfather. The *Rāmāyaṇa* depicts him as the priest of Rāma's family. (*See also Ṛg Veda*; Ṛṣi; Viśvāmitra; Vyāsa.)

⌘ VĀSUDEVA ⌘

A name of Kṛṣṇa, usually regarded as a patronymic based on the name of his father Vasudeva (the ā signifying that he is Vasudeva's son). (*See also* Kṛṣṇa; Pañcarātra.)

⌘ VĀTSYĀYANA ⌘

Author of the *Kāma Sūtra*, a Brahmin who probably lived in Pāṭaliputra about 400 C.E., at a time when it was the capital of the Gupta Empire. (*See also Kāma Sūtra*.)

⌘ VĀYU ⌘

The God of Wind in the Veda. He is often celebrated for his power and strength, and invited to drink Soma at the sacrifice (as in *Ṛg Veda* 1.134–135, and 4.46 to 4.48). In such contexts, he is often paired with Indra, with whom he has in common both the love for Soma and great strength. In later literature, Vāyu is the father of the heroes Hanuman in the *Rāmāyaṇa* and Bhīma in the *Mahābhārata*, to whom he imparts his exceptional strength. Vāyu is regarded as the World Guardian of the northwest direction. (*See also* Hanuman; World Guardians.)

⌘ VEDA ⌘

Knowledge. The term is applied to the entire corpus of literature including the Saṃhitā, Brāhmaṇa, Āraṇyaka, and Upaniṣad collections as a whole. Each of the four Saṃhitā collections (*Ṛg*, *Yajur*, *Sāma*, and *Atharva*) is known as a Veda. Certain texts refer to themselves as "the fifth Veda," including the *Mahābhārata* and the *Nāṭya Śāstra*, indicative of their composers' aspiration that the text be seen as authoritative and as part of the Vedic heritage. The *Chāndogya Upaniṣad* (7.1, 7.2, and 7.7) also indicates that the Itihāsa and Purāṇa collections constitute the fifth Veda. The *Artha Śāstra* (1.3.1–2) similarly refers to Itihāsa-Veda as constituting the fifth Veda. The term is also applied by extension to various other collections of knowledge, including medical knowledge (Āyurveda) and knowledge of archery (Dhanurveda). (*See also* Āraṇyaka; Brāhmaṇa; Saṃhitā; Scripture; Śruti; Trayī Vidyā; Upaniṣad.)

⌘ VEDĀNTA ⌘

The End of the Veda, a term used to refer to the Upaniṣads as the concluding portion of the Vedic literature. As such, the Vedānta is the final segment of the Śruti, the revealed truth. The term Vedānta is also applied to the philosophical school based on the Upaniṣads, one of the six philosophical schools recognized by Hindus as orthodox; it is sometimes called Uttara (Later) Mīmāṃsā, and is paired with Pūrva (Prior) Mīmāṃsā, which is an enquiry into the meaning of the Veda. Three main interpretations of Vedānta exist: (1) Advaita (Nondualistic) Vedānta, as articulated by Śaṅkara, in which the individual self or soul is identical with Brahman, the Absolute; (2) Viśiṣṭha-Advaita (Qualified Nondualistic) Vedānta, articulated by Rāmānuja, in which the soul is united, but not identical, with the Absolute; and (3) Dvaita (Dualistic) Vedānta, as articulated by Madhva, in which the individual soul is distinct from the Absolute. Vedānta has been the most influential of the philosophical schools over the last thousand years. (*See also* Advaita Vedānta; Dvaita Vedānta; Madhva; Philosophical Schools; Rāmānuja; Śaṅkara; Upaniṣads; Vedānta Society; Viśiṣṭha-Advaita Vedānta.)

⌘ VEDĀNTA SOCIETY ⌘

Name of an organization founded by Vivekānanda shortly after his appearance at the World Parliament of Religions in Chicago in 1893. The Ramakrishna Maṭh and the Ramakrishna Mission direct the activities of the Vedānta Society, which has a well-organized presence in major cities in North America. The tolerant and universalist views of Ramakrishna, in which all religions were regarded as valid means of achieving transformation of the self, are reflected in the publications and activities of the Vedānta Society. It promotes in North America a nonsectarian and nondenominational variety of Hinduism that is largely in accord with the Advaita Vedānta philosophical tradition. (*See also* Rāmakrishna; Vedānta; Vivekānanda.)

⌘ *VEDĀNTA SŪTRA* ⌘

See Brahma Sūtra.

⌘ VEDA-VYĀSA ⌘

See Vyāsa.

⌘ VEDI (later VEDĪ) ⌘

The shallow mound or pit at the center of the sacrificial compound at a Vedic sacrifice. It was to be four-sided, with concave sides. The Vedi, covered with cut Kuśa grass, held sacrificial implements such as ladles and spoons when they were not being used, and was also the spot at which the gods were invited to sit during the sacrifice. (*See also* Kuśa; Yajña.)

⌘ VEṄKAṬEŚVARA ⌘

Deity worshipped in south India as a form of Viṣṇu. The most revered temple dedicated to Veṅkaṭeśvara is on the sacred hill of Tirumāla, near Tirupathi in southern Andhra Pradesh. The image in the temple has its eyes covered, because the direct gaze of the deity is regarded as overpowering. Because of a belief that a request made before the image of Veṅkaṭeśvara will be granted, this image is enormously popular, the temple has an income of some five billion Rupees per year from pilgrims, and the temple has a staff of over 5,000 employees. This temple is very unusual in allowing non-Hindus to view the image in the Garbhagṛha (shrine room). (*See also* Darśana; Temple; Tirumāla; Viṣṇu.)

⌘ V.H.P ⌘

See Vishva Hindu Parishad.

⌘ VIJAYANAGAR ⌘

City of Victory, the name of the city founded in 1336 by a confederacy of south Indian rulers as a bulwark against advancing Muslim forces. It controlled the southern part of the subcontinent, growing wealthy from the spice trade and cotton industry. Within seven concentric walls, the city is said to have had a population of half a million, and covered thirty-three square miles. Imperial support was granted to the worship of Viṣṇu, Śiva, and the Goddess, as well as to Jainism. The disastrous battle of Talikota in 1565 brought an end to its power and the city was sacked by Muslim soldiers. The ruins are beside Hampi, Karnataka.

⌘ VIKRAMĀDITYA ⌘

Sun of Heroism, the name of a celebrated king who is reputed to have ruled much of north India from Ujjain (Ujjayinī). Numerous legends have been associated with this great king, including that he presided over a court at which nine accomplished authors and scholars were in attendance, Kālidāsa among them, and that he defeated the barbarian Śakas in western India. Also associated with the name is the Vikrama era, a frequently used calendrical system in north India in which the Vikrama year 1 correlates with 58–57 B.C.E. No doubt, several prominent kings have used the title Vikramāditya and there may well be conflation of their histories and legends. Much of what is said of Vikramāditya corresponds well with what is known of Candra Gupta II (who ruled from 375 to 415 C.E.) of the Gupta dynasty. Not only did he apparently have Ujjayinī as his capital and Kālidāsa at his court, but he also defeated invading barbarian Śaka warriors, a feat commemorated by the monumental Varāha (Boar Incarnation of Viṣṇu) relief sculpture at Udaigiri, with its inscription dated 401–402 C.E. Vikramāditya was one of the titles used by Candra Gupta II. (*See also* Gupta; Kālidāsa; Ujjain.)

⌘ VĪRAŚAIVA ⌘

See Liṅgāyat.

⌘ VISHVA HINDU PARISHAD (VIŚVA HINDŪ PARIṢAD) ⌘

The All-Hindu Council, the name of an organization founded in 1964. It is a religious and cultural group that has many members in common with the Rāṣṭrīya Svayamsevak Saṅgh. One of its main purposes has been to articulate a set of ideas, and specify a set of ritual practices, to which all Hindus could assent, thereby forging greater unity among Hindus of various sects and traditions. (*See also* Bhāratīya Janatā Party; Hindu Mahāsabhā; Rāṣṭrīya Svayamsevak Saṅgh.)

⌘ VIŚIṢṬHA-ADVAITA VEDĀNTA ⌘

Qualified Nondualistic Vedānta, the name of Rāmānuja's interpretation of the Upaniṣads and Vaiṣṇava theology. According to Rāmānuja, Brahman, the impersonal Absolute, is also Viṣṇu, the personal God and Supreme Lord. God created the world due to his Līlā, his unmotivated play, not because he needs human devotion. The individual human souls are regarded as attributes of God, separated from God only due to ignorance. Through devotion (Bhakti) to God, and with God's grace (Prasāda), the devotee can attain union with God, yet retain individuality and self-consciousness. Rāmānuja's articulation of Vedānta thought became the theological basis of many devotional movements and sects, particularly the Śrīvaiṣṇava tradition of south India. (*See also* Rāmānuja; Śrīvaiṣṇavism; Vedānta.)

⌘ VIṢṆU ⌘

An important Vedic god and, in his forms of Rāma and Kṛṣṇa, the most popular god of Hinduism in recent centuries. In the *Ṛg Veda*, Viṣṇu appears as the performer of heroic deeds, including as an assistant to Indra, for which he is sometimes called Upendra (little Indra), the two frequently paired. But Viṣṇu also is credited with being one who "measured out the earth, who propped up the upper dwelling-place . . ." (*Ṛg Veda* 1.154.1), that is, he created space in which humanity could live on earth. This same poem, and others, praise him for taking three strides which established earth, atmosphere, and heaven, with his own realm Vaikuṇṭha in highest heaven where those devoted to him could go at death. He is said to support all beings, and may well have been much more important to Āryans of the Vedic period than the small number of poems dedicated to him in the *Ṛg Veda* would seem to indicate. His importance emerges clearly in literature such as the *Rāmāyaṇa* and *Mahābhārata*, where he is depicted sending a portion of himself to earth to take human form (as Rāma and Kṛṣṇa, respectively) to restore Dharma and defeat the forces of disorder. This idea developed into the Avatāra doctrine, the cornerstone of all theologies centered on Viṣṇu. Ten Avatāra forms, or manifestations of Viṣṇu, are described in the Purāṇas and their mythic deeds are recounted. Among them, the main ones that have inspired devotion and active cultic worship are Rāma and Kṛṣṇa. In most such traditions, Viṣṇu is understood to be the form of Ultimate Reality, and he periodically sends manifestations of himself to aid humanity. Hence he is regarded by many Hindus as having responsibility for maintaining the world, Brahmā acting as creator and Śiva as destroyer. Those particularly devoted to him, however, would tend to attribute all these roles to Viṣṇu. One of the major themes in theologies focussed on Viṣṇu is his unmotivated playful activity (Līlā), in accord with which he creates and sustains the world. He does so not due to any need of his own, but for enjoyment. Though not mentioned in the earliest literature, Viṣṇu is later strongly identified with his consort Lakṣmī or Śrī, Prosperity embodied, and while he has no children by her, he has many in his various incarnations. Viṣṇu is also paired at times with Earth (Bhū, or Bhūdevī), and with the goddess Durgā, she being either his wife or his sister who marries Śiva. Iconographic representations of Viṣṇu on shrines in homes and temples often depict him as dark blue with four arms, holding a discus and a conch shell. At times, Viṣṇu is regarded as the Preserver of the World, acting in concert with Brahmā as Creator and Śiva as Destroyer, the three together known as the Trimūrti (Trinity). Perhaps as many as half of all Hindus today are primarily devoted to Viṣṇu. (*See also* Avatāra; Kṛṣṇa; Līlā; Rāma; Śrī; Trinity; Vaikuṇṭha; Vaiṣṇavism; Veṅkaṭeśvara.)

⌘ VIṢṆUPUR (BISHNUPUR) ⌘

City in West Bengal noted for its artisans. It was the capital of the Malla dynasty, local rulers in the sixteenth to nineteenth centuries. The brick temples they built are covered with terracotta tiles depicting scenes from the *Rāmāyaṇa* and *Mahābhārata*. It is also the setting for three films on Hinduism made by Harvard University and Ákos Östör, entitled *Loving Krishna*, *Sons of Shiva*, and *Serpent Mother*, featuring festivals devoted to Kṛṣṇa, Śiva, and Manasā.

⌘ VIŚVĀMITRA ⌘

The major seer (Ṛṣi) of Book 3 of the *Ṛg Veda* and patriarch of one of the Brahmin families credited with preservation and transmission of the *Ṛg Veda*. He is unique among prominent Brahmins in the Veda for having been born a Kṣatriya (descended from Purūravas) and having transformed himself into a Brahmin. He is frequently depicted in literature as in conflict with Vasiṣṭha, with whom he once served as priests of the ruler Sudās. When Sudās made known his preference for Vasiṣṭha, Viśvāmitra went over to the opposing camp, the Bharata family, to serve as their priest. As indicated in *Ṛg Veda* 3.33, he aided the Bharata family in their unsuccessful fight against Sudās, compelling two rivers to allow the escaping Bharata warriors to cross them safely. The *Mahābhārata* and *Rāmāyaṇa* recount how Viśvāmitra, frustrated in his desire to obtain Vasiṣṭha's cow, the cow of plenty that granted all wishes, determined that he would, through the practice of austerities, transform himself into a Brahmin. While engaged in that effort, the gods endeavored to divert him from his course by having the celestial nymph Menakā seduce him; from their union was born Śakuntalā. Eventually he succeeded in being recognized as a Brahmin and Ṛṣi. His competition with Vasiṣṭha may be seen as a symbolic representation of the conflict between Kṣatriyas and Brahmins. (*See also* *Ṛg Veda*; Ṛṣi; Vasiṣṭha.)

⌘ VIŚVEDEVAS ⌘

All gods. In the *Ṛg Veda*, it is often difficult to tell whether this term is applied to the whole of the Vedic pantheon (as is apparently the case in *Ṛg Veda* 8.27 to 8.30) or is being used as the name of a particular troop of gods.

⌘ VIVASVAT ⌘

One of the twelve Ādityas, the Sun. He is the father of the Aśvin twins and Vaivasvata Manu (from whom the solar dynasty arose) and the twins Yama and Yamī. (*See also* Āditya; Manu; Yama.)

⌘ VIVEKĀNANDA ⌘

Religious name of the Bengali reformer and social activist (1863–1902). Born as Narendranāth Datta in a Kṣatriya family, he was educated at the Mission College in Calcutta. In 1881 he met the saint Rāmakrishna and took him as his Guru. Rāmakrishna guided him to a religious experience of Kālī, and named him his successor. For the next several years, Vivekānanda wandered in India, developing his perspective that combined the monism of Advaita Vedānta with the devotionalism of Rāmakrishna. Vivekānanda meditated on an island at Kanyākumārī in 1892 to prepare himself for his mission to the West. He was patronized by a Rāja who supported his travel to the United States, where he represented Hinduism at the World Parliament of Religions in Chicago in 1893. He was a dynamic and persuasive speaker who presented Hinduism as embodying universal truth, and was in demand as a lecturer for the next several years. He founded the Vedānta Society in New York City in 1895 as a way of carrying on his teachings and those of Rāmakrishna. On his return to India he founded and, for the last five years of his life, led the Rāmakrishna Mission, a social service organization, and the Rāmakrishna Order, a monastic order. He is certainly one of the individuals who, in the past century, has had the greatest impact on the self-understanding of Hindus and on the effort to bring Hindus together into a single religious movement. Vivekānanda's formulation of the essential Hindu worldview, a perspective often described as neo-Hinduism, is not only what most Westerners believe Hinduism to be, but is also what many urban, educated Hindus of the twentieth century would say Hinduism is. (*See also* Ramakrishna; Vedānta Society.)

⌘ VRAJA ⌘

The name of the region surrounding the pilgrimage site of Vṛndāvana. Though used in recent centuries as the proper name of the area, there is some question whether in ancient times the term may have applied to the portable encampment of cowherds. (*See also* Vṛndāvana.)

⌘ VRĀTYA ⌘

One subject to a vow. The term is used for what were apparently early Āryan, but perhaps non-Vedic or unorthodox, fraternities of warrior-ascetics. They may well have been in the first wave of Āryan migration into South Asia, and the area they are particularly associated with is Māgadha (modern Bihār), far to the east of the Brahmanical heartland. The *Atharva Veda*'s fifteenth chapter (Vrātya Khāṇḍa) concerns the Vrātyas, and in that section of the text breath control, celibacy, and a ritual of sexual fertility known as the Great Vow (Mahāvrata) are attributed to them. This suggests that Vrātyas may have been developing methods of Yogic and Tantric meditation, and may have been instrumental in introducing these practices into Brahmanical society. In the *Mānava Dharma Śāstra*, Vrātyas were understood to be Āryans who had not taken Vedic initiation at the proper time or had stopped reciting the Gāyatrī or Sāvitrī Mantra; a ritual of purification was developed for them. It is also possible that they were raiding bands of Āryans who were in need of purificatory rites to allow reintegration into Brahmanical society.

⌘ VṚNDĀVANA ⌘

A town in central India regarded as sacred for its association with Kṛṣṇa. Hindus who worship Kṛṣṇa make pilgrimages to this site to have the religious experience of seeing where Kṛṣṇa walked and met his beloved consort Rādhā. Classical Sanskrit texts, such as the tenth-century *Bhāgavata Purāṇa* and twelfth-century *Gītagovinda*, describe the natural beauty of the entire forested region of Vraja surrounding the town, its loveliness cited as evidence that this location was blessed with a divine presence. For worshippers of Kṛṣṇa, Vṛndāvana's groves and lush pastures are the very image of paradise; indeed, they regard the earthly town as no different from Kṛṣṇa's heavenly realm and use the same name for both. As a religious practice to deepen their devotion they visualize themselves in Vṛndāvana with Kṛṣṇa in the sylvan scenes described in the classical texts. Their religious goal is, through devotion to Kṛṣṇa on earth, to attain eternal life in Kṛṣṇa's paradise, there to serve Kṛṣṇa devotedly forever. Because of deforestation, the area has been the focus of a tree-planting program sponsored by the World Wide Fund for Nature in an effort to restore its natural beauty. There are about 4,000 temples in Vṛndāvana. Among the most important is the Govinda Deva temple, built in 1590 by Rāja Mān Singh of Jaipur; originally seven stories, it lost its top four stories when Aurangzeb dismantled them, but its vaulted ceiling is an architectural marvel. The Hare Krishna (International Society for Krishna Consciousness) temple, called Krishna Balarām, is an impressively large structure of white marble. The entire region is regarded as sacred by devotees of Kṛṣṇa, who will make pilgrimage in circular fashion to have auspicious sight (Darśana) of the places mentioned in scriptures, including Mount Govardhana, Mathurā, and the Yamunā River. (*See also Bhāgavata Purāṇa; Gītagovinda;* Gosvāmins; Govardhana, Mount; Kṛṣṇa; Pilgrimage; Rādhā; Vaikuṇṭha; Vraja.)

⌘ VṚTRA ⌘

Obstructor; Restrainer. This is the name of a demon who is the enemy of Indra in the *Ṛg Veda*, associated with restraining the waters or cattle, preventing their free circulation. Vṛtra is depicted in the Vedic literature as a powerful enemy causing drought and darkness, son of Dānu (thus, a Dānava). In poems such as *Ṛg Veda*

1.32 and 1.33, Indra kills Vṛtra, releasing the waters or cows, making life possible for Indra's worshippers. Vṛtra is also likened to or identified with a serpentine monster Ahi, and other demonic forces whom the gods defeat such as Namuci, Śuṣṇa, and Śaṃbara. Interpretations of the meaning of the figure Vṛtra have ranged from the clouds split by Indra's thunderbolt to release rain as the monsoon, to human enemies, perhaps the remnants of the Indus Valley Civilization with their elaborate irrigation systems and walled cities. (*See also* Indra; Namuci; *Ṛg Veda*.)

⌘ VYĀSA ⌘

Title of the Brahmin sage Kṛṣṇa Dvaipāyana. The *Mahābhārata* (1.54; 1.57; and 1.99) recounts how he was born to Satyavatī, daughter of a king of fishermen, when visited by the Vedic seer (Ṛṣi) Parāśara. She operated a ferryboat crossing the Yamunā River when the seer asked to be rowed across. In mid-river he proposed a tryst to her; she consented, fearful of his curse, and was granted the boon of restored virginity by him. Her child was born immediately on an island in the river, and she named him Kṛṣṇa (black or dark) for his color, and Dvaipāyana (island-born) for the location. He announced his intention to go to the forest to practice asceticism, and never lived with either of his parents, but told his mother that he would appear if needed when she thought of him. His mother, who had married a Bhārata ruler, called upon him to father a son for the Bhārata dynasty and he fathered the warriors Dhṛtarāṣṭra and Pāṇḍu who ruled successively and whose sons fought for sovereignty in the *Mahābhārata*. He is also said to have had an ascetic son named Śuka who attained liberation from rebirth. The title of Vyāsa (derived from the verbal prefix and root vi + ās) came from his literary feat of dividing the Veda into four smaller texts. He is credited by the *Mahābhārata* (1.57.70–73) with realizing that the declining capacities of human beings in the degenerate era of Kali yuga made difficult their memorization of the entire Veda, so he divided it into four collections so as to benefit both Brahman and Brahmins. He later composed the *Mahābhārata* and the Purāṇa collection as historical works of religious significance. Four pupils (Paila, Sumantu, Jaimini, and Vaiśaṃpāyana) memorized and transmitted one Veda each, while Lomaharṣaṇa Sūta memorized the Purāṇa collection.

Vyāsa thus stands for the process of composition and transmission of the sacred literature of the Brahmanical and Hindu traditions, symbolically representing all the anonymous authors who contributed to India's literary history. The *Mahābhārata* makes reference twice to Vyāsa being an incarnation of Nārāyaṇa Viṣṇu (12.334.9, and 12.337), but he clearly has greater affinity with Brahmā. Purāṇas often list Vyāsa as an Avatāra of Viṣṇu in lists of incarnations longer than ten. (*See also* Avatāra; Jaimini; Lomaharṣaṇa Sūta; *Mahābhārata*; Paila; Purāṇa; Śuka; Sumantu; Vaiśaṃpāyana; Veda.)

⌘ VYŪHA ⌘

Manifestation. The term is used particularly to refer to a doctrine of the Pañcarātra sect that is comparable to the Avatāra idea. The doctrine, unique to the Pañcarātra tradition, states that Viṣṇu manifested himself in the world with his full nature and attributes, appearing as Vāsudeva, Saṃkarṣaṇa, Pradyumna, and Aniruddha. From the Pañcarātra perspective, an Avatāra is a lesser, only partial, manifestation of God. The Vyūha doctrine came to be integrated, with some difficulty, into Vaiṣṇava theology. (*See also* Avatāra; Balarāma; Pañcarātra; Vaiṣṇavism; Vāsudeva; Viṣṇu.)

— W —

⌘ WAKING CONSCIOUSNESS ⌘

See Consciousness, States of.

⌘ WARRIOR ⌘

See Kṣatriya.

⌘ WIDOW IMMOLATION ⌘

See Satī.

⌘ WILSON, HORACE HAYMAN ⌘

British Indologist and scholar of Sanskrit literature (1786–1860). He lived in India from 1808 to 1832, and in 1833 was appointed the first Boden Professor of Sanskrit, endowed by Joseph Boden in 1811 at Oxford University. A prolific translator, Wilson published works on Indian law, numismatics, drama, history, and a translation of the *Ṛg Veda*. (*See also* Indology; Sanskrit.)

⌘ WIND ⌘

See Prāṇa; Vāyu.

⌘ WORK ⌘

See Karma.

⌘ WORLD AGES ⌘

Hindus almost universally accept a view of time as cyclical, an idea first clearly articulated in the Upaniṣads and elaborated upon subsequently. While various different ways of counting the years in the World Ages can be found, a popular enumeration of them is the following. There are four eons (Yuga) in each Mahāyuga, or cycle: Kṛta or Satya Yuga (lasting 4,000 divine years), Tretā Yuga (3,000), Dvāpara (2,000), and Kali (1,000). Each Yuga is worse than the one before it. Preceding each such Yuga is a period of unmanifest potentiality or latency, lasting respectively 800 divine years, 600, 400, and 200. Thus each Mahāyuga lasts 12,000 divine years, equivalent to 1,555,200,000 human years. A thousand such Mahāyugas equals a Kalpa, or a day in the life of Brahmā, the creator God who presides over the world. Then follows a night of Brahmā, in which the world is unmanifest. After 100 years of such days and nights, the lifespan of this Brahmā is exhausted and all is absorbed back into its divine source, from which a new creation begins. This cyclic and infinite view of time is typical of Hindu and other Indic religious traditions, including the Jain and Buddhist traditions. (*See also* Brahmā; Creation; Kali Yuga; Kalkin; Mārkaṇḍeya.)

⌘ WORLD GUARDIANS ⌘

A set of eight gods regarded as guardian deities, presiding over the four cardinal and four intermediate directions. As given in most texts, they are as follows: Indra in the East, Agni (Fire) in the Southeast, Yama in the South, Sūrya (Sun) in the Southwest,

Varuṇa in the West, Vāyu (Wind) in the Northwest, Kubera in the North, Soma or Candra (Moon) in the Northeast. Other sources may include additional Guardians, or substitute a different Guardian for one of the intermediate directions. (*See also* Loka.)

— X —

There are no entries for X.

— Y —

⌘ YAJÑA ⌘

The Vedic sacrifice. The typical Yajña included the participation of Āryan Brahmins, warriors and commoners, and explicitly excluded non-Āryan people. One prominent male of the community, usually a clan chieftain or powerful warrior, served as the patron of the ritual and was accompanied by his wife. Prior to the ritual itself, the patron was to be consecrated and prepared for the Yajña by a period of ascetic isolation and contemplation. On a flat piece of ground, a shallow pit or mound (Vedi) would be created and lined with Kuśa grass, where the gods would be invited to sit and where ritual implements not in use would be placed. Three altars would be built (Āhavanīya, Dakṣiṇa, and Gārhapatya) either of local stone or mud-brick, and fires kindled in each altar. One or more animals would be killed by strangulation, then cut up, pieces of them cooked and eaten by those present, other parts offered to the gods by burning them in the fire. The cow was the animal most commonly offered in sacrifice, but the goat and horse were also offered depending on the ritual and the god(s) being celebrated. The entire ritual event was accompanied by recitation of poems from the Veda in praise of the god(s) who were being celebrated and whose blessings were being requested. Offerings were also made to the ancestors (Pitṛ) to sustain them in the afterlife. Specific requests for worldly benefits might be made, such as for victory in battle, sovereignty, prosperity, long life, or offspring. In addition, the patron was regarded as transformed by the rite and was thought to attain immortality among the ancestors and the gods in heaven. The sacrificial ritual was regarded as the means by which human beings had access to

Brahman, the sacred cosmic force underlying all reality, and which was manifest in the form of words in the Veda. Sacrifice was also conceived as having the effect of renewing and sustaining the cosmos by replicating the original act of creation whereby the world was created. (*See also* Āhavanīya; Brahman; Brahmán; Cow, Sacred; Dakṣiṇa; Gārhapatya; Kuśa; Pitṛ; Pūjā; Saṃhitā; Veda; Vedi.)

⌘ YĀJÑAVALKYA ⌘

The name of a famous teacher, depicted in the *Bṛhadāraṇyaka Upaniṣad* (4.4.5 to 4.4.7, for example) as articulating the idea of rebirth according to the law of Karma. He teaches that after death, the Ātman (soul or self) of a person who still has desire is born again into a situation appropriate to the nature of that person's actions before death. One who is without worldly desire is not reborn: being Brahman, he goes to Brahman after death, becoming immortal. Various works composed in later centuries bear the name of this famous sage, including a Dharma Śāstra, and it is unknown whether the authors are attributing their work to him or are named after him. (*See also* Ātman; Brahman; *Bṛhadāraṇyaka Upaniṣad*; Karma.)

⌘ *YAJUR VEDA* ⌘

One of the three original Vedas; a text composed largely of selections from the *Ṛg Veda*, with instructions for the manual activities of priests in the sacrifice. It was the special function of the Adhvaryu priest to mutter verses from the Yajur Veda while engaged in the actions of slaughtering sacrificial animals to be offered to the Gods. The *Mahābhārata* credits Vyāsa with dividing what had been one Veda into four texts (*Ṛg*, *Yajur*, *Sāma*, and *Atharva*) and teaching his disciples his edited version; Purāṇas credit each pupil with learning one of the Vedas, Vaiśaṃpāyana transmitting the *Yajur Veda*. (*See also* Adhvaryu; Trayī Vidyā; Vaiśaṃpāyana; Veda; Vyāsa; Yajña.)

⌘ YAMA ⌘

God of the underworld and the dead. Yama and his twin sister Yamī are, in *Ṛg Veda* 10.10, the first human pair, from whom all others are descended. As the first human being to die, Yama was made the overlord of the realm of the dead, and judge of human behavior. He is depicted in the *Mahābhārata* (3.295–298) as Dharma embodied, testing Yudhiṣṭhira with riddles about the social and religious obligations (Dharma) humans face, and rewarding Yudhiṣṭhira, his own son, with knowledge of his own future. Both Yama and Yudhiṣṭhira are called Dharma-Rājā (King of Dharma). (*See also* Dharma.)

⌘ YĀMUNA ⌘

Theologian and author (tenth-eleventh century C.E.), known also as Yāmuna Ācārya, who was instrumental in the establishment of the Śrīvaiṣṇava tradition. He was powerfully affected by the devotional poetry of the Āḻvārs, composed in Tamil. He wrote works in Sanskrit, both original works and translations from Tamil. In so doing, he brought together the Brahmanical and non-Brahmanical traditions of devotion. His main contribution was that his works and the community he had formed attracted Rāmānuja, who became the principal theologian and organizer of the Śrīvaiṣṇava tradition. (*See also* Rāmānuja; Śrīvaiṣṇavism.)

⌘ YAMUNĀ RIVER ⌘

A river widely regarded as sacred. It emerges from the Himālayas, flows past Delhi, Vṛndāvana, and Mathurā and joins the Ganges at Prayāga. (*See also* Ganges River.)

⌘ YANTRA ⌘

A diagram, usually symmetrical, used in ritual activity and worship. A Yantra symbolically represents the self or body and the cosmos, these seen as microcosm and macrocosm. Typically, a Yantra will include forms of the square, concentric circles, and/or interlocking or overlapping triangles, focussing on a central point. The use of Yantras is particularly prevalent in Tantric and goddess-related worship. (*See also* Goddess; Maṇḍala; Śrīvidyā Tantra; Tantra.)

⌘ YOGA ⌘

A mental and physical discipline practiced for religious purposes. Yoga is one of the six philosophical schools regarded as orthodox by Hindus, and paired with Sāṃkhya as the tradition with which it is most similar. As defined in the *Yoga Sūtra* (1.2) of Patañjali, the classic text on the subject, Yoga is the suppression of mental fluctuations. The discipline is designed to produce an improved ability to focus the mind on a single object, and through meditation to attain knowledge of Brahman. Yoga has eight limbs or components, as follows. (1) Restraints: preliminary practices of a moral nature, prohibiting violence, lying, stealing, greed, and sex. (2) Disciplines: beneficial actions to be performed, including the cultivation of cleanliness, serenity, the study of yoga philosophy, ascetic lifestyle, and making the Lord (Īśvara) the motive of all one's actions. (3) Postures: especially the distinctive lotus posture (Padma-āsana) to allow a long period of sitting with minimal physical effort and discomfort. (4) Rhythmic breathing: the most important element of the practice. Regularizing inhalation and exhalation calms body and mind. Control of breath (prāṇāyāma) includes the practice of making the four moments of breathing (inhaling, holding the breath, exhaling, holding the breath) all the same duration. (5) Freeing the mind from sense objects: turning the senses inward. This makes the mind independent of its environment, instead of being dominated by the processing of incoming sensory information. (6) Concentration: fixing the mind on a single point. Sometimes a meditation diagram (Maṇḍala) is used. Chanting a Mantra repeatedly can also serve to concentrate the mind. (7) Meditation: prolonged concentration on a religiously significant object or idea. The purpose is to attain union with the object of meditation, to know it directly. (8) Samādhi: the goal of Yoga practice, a state of equilibrium and isolation (Kaivalya). Brahman is known, or experienced. All one's karma is destroyed, so no rebirth will occur after death. Instead, the successful practitioner of Yoga attains union with Brahman. It is important to note that other varieties of Yoga also exist, but are not treated in Patañjali's work, including Haṭha Yoga and Kuṇḍalinī Yoga, in which energy is to be aroused in the body. (*See also* Brahman; Haṭha Yoga; Īśvara; Kaivalya; Kuṇḍalinī; Lotus Posture; Maṇḍala; Mantra; Mokṣa; Patañjali; Path of Knowledge; Prāṇa; Samādhi; Yantra; *Yoga Sūtra*.)

⌘ *YOGA SŪTRA* ⌘

The classic text on the discipline of Yoga. Attributed to Patañjali, it is very difficult to date. The text presents material that the author states is not his own creation, but only a summary of the tradition as transmitted from ancient times. It may have been composed between the second century B.C.E. and second century C.E. Here (1.2) Yoga is defined as the suppression of mental fluctuations, and the text describes the types of distractions and hindrances the practitioner may encounter, particularly in its chapter 1. Chapter 2 details the eight limbs of Yoga practice, a path to systematic development of one's mental control. Chapter 3 presents information on the higher stages of the practice, and the powers (Siddhi, Vibhūti) that can accompany practice of Yoga, but are not its purpose. Chapter 4 presents philosophical perspectives on Yoga and describes the end of practice, Kaivalya or liberation. (*See also* Patañjali; Yoga.)

⌘ YOGĀNANDA, PARAMAHAṂSA (also PARAMAHANSA) ⌘

Guru (1893–1952 C.E.) who taught Yoga in the West. He founded the Self-Realization Fellowship, and saw it become a worldwide organization in his lifetime. He taught what he called Kriyā Yoga (Yoga of Action) and said that it was the classical Yoga system as expounded by Patañjali (for example, in *Yoga Sūtra* 2.1 and following verses). In fact, though, some of Yogānanda's teachings show Tantric influences such as Kuṇḍalinī Yoga practices. His *Autobiography of a Yogi*, first published in 1946, reprinted and translated many times, did much to spread his teachings. (*See also* Self-Realization Fellowship.)

⌘ *YOGA-VĀSIṢṬHA-RĀMĀYAṆA* ⌘

A Sanskrit poem of some 30,000 verses teaching a monistic doctrine. It is traditionally attributed to Vālmīki, composer of the *Rāmāyaṇa*, but probably dates from the tenth to twelfth centuries C.E. The text is a dialogue between Rāma and his guru Vasiṣṭha, in which the Advaita Vedānta perspective is promulgated. All that exists is a single divine Consciousness, and the myriad objects of the conventional world are like images in the mind of an artist. Due to ignorance, we tend to perceive the world as external to and separate from ourselves, but in reality only the Absolute exists. The mind creates its own bondage and its own liberation, and experiencing the reality of the one divine Consciousness terminates bondage. (*See also* Advaita Vedānta; *Rāmāyaṇa*; Vasiṣṭha.)

⌘ YOGĪ ⌘

Male practitioner of Yoga. Another form of this word is Yogin. (*See also* Yoga.)

⌘ YOGINĪ ⌘

Female practitioner of Yoga. The term is also sometimes used to describe females endowed with magical or demonic powers. (*See also* Yoga.)

⌘ YUGA ⌘

See World Ages.

— Z —

⌘ ZAEHNER, ROBERT CHARLES ⌘

Scholar of comparative religions (1913–1974). He served in Iran during World War II, and developed an interest in Zoroastrianism. Zaehner held the Spalding Chair in Eastern Religions and Ethics at Oxford University from 1953 to 1974, and published several studies on Hinduism, including a popular introduction to Hinduism. (*See also* Indology.)

About the Author

Bruce M. Sullivan (B.A., Trinity University; M.A., Trinity University; Ph.D., The University of Chicago) is professor of religious studies and Asian studies at Northern Arizona University. His previous books include *Kṛṣṇa Dvaipāyana Vyāsa and the* Mahābhārata: *A New Interpretation* (2nd edition: *Seer of the Fifth Veda*) and *The Sun God's Daughter and King Saṃvaraṇa:* Tapatī-Saṃvaraṇa *and the Kūṭiyāṭṭam Drama Tradition* (coauthored with N. P. Unni). He has published professional articles in the *Journal of the American Academy of Religion, Asian Theatre Journal, Literature and Theology, International Journal of Hindu Studies, Annals of the Bhandarkar Oriental Research Institute,* and the *Journal of Vaiṣṇava Studies.* In addition, he has published chapters in *Purifying the Earthly Body of God: Religion and Ecology in Hindu India,* and *This Sacred Earth: Religion, Nature, Environment,* and *Modern Evaluation of the* Mahābhārata. He has served in various capacities in the American Academy of Religion, and has been active in the Association for Asian Studies and the American Oriental Society.